Evaluation

as

Feedback and Guide

Prepared by the ASCD 1967 Yearbook Committee

Fred T. Wilhelms, Chairman and Editor

Association for Supervision and Curriculum Development, NEA
1201 Sixteenth Street, N.W.
Washington, D.C. 20036

NEA Stock Number: 610-17700

Reprinted August 1970

Library of Congress Catalog Card Number: 44-6213

Contents

67112

Foreword

THIS is a timely book. With all of American education struggling to redefine itself in the light of new expectations and the ferment of social change, our beliefs and practices about evaluation play a crucial role. As the authors point out, the feedback we get from evaluation *controls our next steps*. It is essential, therefore, that the information we get from evaluation be as accurate and as congruent with our best objectives as we can make it. At the moment that is not true. We have outgrown ourselves. Instead of speeding progress, our concepts and practices of evaluation often mislead us or waste our energies in endless numbering of things that do not matter. The Association, therefore, is deeply grateful for the contribution this Yearbook Committee has made in updating our thinking by reexamining objectives, broadening perspectives and pointing the way to promising alternatives.

In 1965 the Executive Committee of the Association for Supervision and Curriculum Development published a set of "Guidelines for National Assessment of Educational Outcomes." In the preamble to those guidelines the Executive Committee stated:

Accurate assessment of educational outcomes is essential for sound planning and effective stimulation of growth in our educational structure. Assessment has always been an integral aspect of curriculum development and is a major responsibility of curriculum workers. This responsibility is especially critical in a time of awakened public concern, massive federal commitment and widespread professional reappraisal of our educational endeavors. It is, therefore, necessary that curriculum workers everywhere develop new procedures for assessment far beyond present levels to meet properly the changing needs of our times.

Whatever goals or procedures for assessment are applied to education have inevitable effects upon the nature and functions of the curriculum. This inescapable relationship must be clearly understood by curriculum and assessment workers alike, for the consequences of blindness are intolerable. We cannot afford to destroy with one hand what is built at great cost with the other.

We believe this yearbook is a fitting expression of the broader concepts called for in those guidelines. The questions it raises and the solutions it suggests should provide us fuel for dialogue and debate for some time. That is the function of a yearbook. We are pleased indeed to offer

Evaluation as Feedback and Guide as our ASCD 1967 Yearbook contribution to the profession.

Special acknowledgment is made to the chairman, the members of the Committee and the contributors responsible for this ASCD 1967 Yearbook, whose names are listed on pages 278-79. In addition to these persons responsible for the content of the yearbook, others assisted in its production. Robert R. Leeper, Editor and Associate Secretary of the Association, was in charge of final editing and publication. Mary Ann Lurch, Ruth P. Ely and Teola T. Jones guided the technical production of the volume. The cover design is the work of Brooke Todd, of Brooke Todd & Associates, Washington, D.C.

December 1966   ARTHUR W. COMBS, *President*
                                   Association for Supervision
                                   and Curriculum Development

Preface

IT WOULD probably be an interesting game to trace out the intellectual history of any yearbook committee. In the long hours of discussion some ideas that, at one stage, are advocated with passionate conviction later fade and disappear from view; others emerge quietly and slowly gain a firm hold. Time and time again, after periods of frustration, everything suddenly "comes clear"—only to dissolve once more into confusion as some unresolved issue comes back into prominence. Yet, little by little, the dominant themes emerge. And, even if disagreement persists on specifics, the committee stands solid on a basic position.

In this report nothing has been done to cover up or "edit out" such differences as did persist. The authors of the several chapters have been encouraged to write firm statements of their views, as those views stood after long group discussion. Therefore, inevitably, there are some inconsistencies within the book.

But, in a more fundamental way, the committee stands solidly unified. It shares a deep conviction that the purpose of evaluation is to provide feedback and guidance to the whole educational process at every level. It believes that the going system of evaluation, which has largely drifted into the service of marking and grading and crediting, must be replaced by a system dedicated to the fundamental needs of the learner and teacher as well as those of the curriculum designer and policy maker.

Believing this, the committee has seen no option but to call for radical change. Still, it is one thing to advocate discarding the evaluation system we have—that argument is easy enough to establish—but it is quite another thing to build something better in its place. At least half of this volume is devoted to description of the system that can be achieved if schools are willing to make a bold new start. The committee hopes that this description will be viewed as a set of preliminary working sketches rather than as a finished blueprint. The question is not whether every detail is immediately right; at this stage of development no one is in position to say how everything should go. The question is, rather, whether the proposed structure is basically sound; if it is, then it can be refined and improved as experience comes in.

This committee has confidence in that basic structure. It believes that schools have already put up far too long with a system of evaluation known to be inadequate and distortive. It hopes that its work will start a revolution.

As chairman, I wish to express my profound appreciation of the work of all the members of this committee. They have been an exhilarating crew to work with, and they have contributed hundreds of hours of hard work. Not all of them are represented by chapters in this final draft; but all of them were active in thinking it through, developing preliminary papers on which later work could be based, and constantly reshaping the report as we moved toward clarity. Finally, I know that all of them would wish me to express our gratitude to Robert R. Leeper and his staff who have labored so hard to turn our collection of papers into a presentable document.

December 1966   FRED T. WILHELMS
Chairman and Editor
ASCD 1967 Yearbook Committee

Part One

The Problems and the Possibilities

BACK *in the Middle West, of a Sunday afternoon, a lot of farmers used to walk around with their hands in their pockets and do an hour or two of what they called "Sunday farming." They didn't work very hard at it—you weren't supposed to work on Sunday. They just looked over the way things were going and sized up the problems and the jobs they had on their hands. But it was also their time to dream a little about the way things might be and to cherish their hopes for the future. Over time, out of some combination of tough-minded size-up and optimistic vision, they shaped up a plan of action.*

Maybe the function of this first Part is not too different from that. If we in education are going to shape up plans for the evaluation system we need, we have to be pretty toughly aware of the way things have been going. But, at least equally, we need to see how things could be.

The function of this yearbook is not to provide one more technical manual on how to evaluate. The question before us is how to use evaluation as a positive force toward better teaching, better learning, and a better balanced curriculum. To answer that large question we must—like those Sunday farmers—shake off our workday preoccupations and stand off to one side for a long, thoughtful look: What is evaluation, really? What does it have to contribute to the fundamental tasks of education? Then we can look at the evaluation we now have: What does it accomplish? Where does it fall short? And then we will be ready to start planning how to get from where we are to where we want to be.

1

1

Evaluation as Feedback

Fred T. Wilhelms

THE GREAT breakthrough in technology—the one commonly called "automation" and, even more, the one called "cybernation"—is the offspring of feedback. The scientists and engineers learned how to build right into a machine the capacity to gather data from what the machine had just done and what had happened as a result, and feed those data back into a decision system controlling what the machine should do next.

That basic invention opened up a whole new world of technology. At the peak of that technology stands the computer. It can be programmed to "keep in mind" a complex set of purposes, criteria, rules and policies—the background factors that must lie behind any specific action. Then a constant stream of data, arising out of the ongoing process, is fed back into its calculations. "Considering" these data in terms of the background factors, the computer constantly "decides" what needs to be done next. It keeps making whatever adjustments are necessary to keep the whole process moving forward toward its goal.

But human beings—all organisms, for that matter—had anticipated technology by thousands of years. In some ways even the brain of a pigeon is "better" than the most complex computer yet developed. People have always operated on feedback. Sometimes they do it deliberately. Then they reflect upon their basic purposes and the values they hold dear; they ponder over how a situation has worked out to this point and the problems they have to solve to achieve their goal; finally, either slowly or in a flash, they make up their minds as to what is the best thing to do next. They could not do this well if they lacked a basic sense of direction, of purposes and values and criteria to judge by; but neither could they do it with growing precision if they did not have a constant stream of information feeding back into their minds out of what was going on and how it was working.

More often—all the time, in fact—people are gathering data without even knowing it and taking the next step that just seems to come naturally. The background factors are taken for granted—one knows he intends to drive to the office—and the sensory data come in unnoticed, to keep him on his course. But always feedback is coming in, and the quality of the next step depends on how well that feedback is blended with basic purposes and converted into decisions.

For as long as there have been social organizations, they, too, have used feedback. On occasion they do it thoughtfully and wisely, reflecting upon their long-term objectives and analyzing their current data; more often they do it crudely and half-intuitively. But, at least in some vague, inchoate way, every community, family, or school system is forever sizing up how things are going and making up its mind what to do next.

Schools organize a special variety of feedback. They call it *evaluation*. Most of it goes on informally, half-intuitively; the most visible—but not necessarily the most important—part of it goes on through a complex of quizzing and testing and examining and comes out in a system of grades and marks and credits.

Yet regardless of whether the evaluation is formal or informal— and equally regardless of whether it is "good" or "sensitive" or "adequate"—it has one thing in common with every other system of feedback: When it has been blended into the background system of purposes and values and policies, *it controls the next step*. This is simply a fact of life; all our decisions are conditioned by perceptions of how we are doing in terms of what we hope to do. The purpose of this yearbook is to explore ways of developing systems of evaluation which will feed back to every level the kinds of data needed to improve these perceptions and, consequently, to improve all our educational decisions.

Feedback Has Many Consumers

Much of the real evaluation, too often unnoticed, goes on within the individual pupil, as he is constantly "aware-ing" himself and the situation around him, sizing up the value of what the school offers him, and making his decisions—conscious or unconscious, but in either case *plenary*—about his next investments of energy. A first criterion of evaluation must be how well it is converted into genuine feedback to the pupil, whether it leads him steadily toward sharper, more valid perceptions, and therefore toward wiser decisions and actions.

Much of evaluation is centered in the teacher. He is constantly using his personal sensitivity plus whatever diagnostic aids he can devise to calibrate his next choice of subject matter and method. This is the sector of evaluation most commonly noticed and worked at. As the teacher proceeds with his work, he is expected to listen and watch and test—to search in every way for the data that arise out of the process. The question still remains whether his total system of searching yields him the feedback he needs to guide him to the wisest adaptations.

Important parts of evaluation are lodged in the school's bigger organizational centers—among the supervisors and curriculum workers, in the principals' offices, in the headquarters of the superintendent, or at the level of the county, the state, or the federal authorities—as well as in the general public. These parts lead to large, sweeping decisions about what to emphasize in the curriculum, about facilities to build, about schemes of organization to adopt, and about the allocation of financial support. Here, again, as in the case of the individual pupil, the use of evaluation is too often unnoticed. Judgments *are* made and profoundly important decisions are based upon them—but they are far too often the judgments of hunch and impression and rumor and even prejudice, because an organized flow of significant feedback has been neglected.

The essential, unremitting fact is that at every level it is *evaluative feedback*—and, again, regardless of whether it is "good" or "sensitive" or "adequate"—whether it is based on the reasoned analysis of sound data or only on some vague impression—that conditions what happens next. It conditions what pupils do, what teachers do, what school officials do, and what the supporting public does.

Evaluation Must Meet Multiple Criteria

Of course, the feedback system which exerts all this force involves an enormous complex—far too much to be treated in this book. At one end of the scale, much of it lies within the private world of each child or teacher; at the other end of the scale much of it is hidden in the subtle interaction of public opinion. In a very real way it is all relevant to the evaluation which schools carry on, but it is not all accessible to an organized program—and it would be too bulky to handle, anyway. This book will confine itself to a much narrower scope.

Yet, no matter where one draws the line, the test of an evaluation system is simply this: *Does it deliver the feedback that is needed, when it is needed, to the persons or groups who need it?*

If any system of evaluation is to meet this test, it must satisfy several basic criteria:

1. *Evaluation must facilitate self-evaluation.* The most fundamentally important outcome of evaluation is what happens within the learner himself. In the narrower terms of subject matter he needs to understand with some precision what is to be learned and "what it is all about" (i.e.,

why it is important, how it relates to other subject matter and to himself). To whatever extent he has succeeded, he needs to know about it, for a sense of success contributes energy for the next task; to whatever extent he has not yet achieved mastery, he needs to know what the gaps are, so that he can figure out what to do about them. In some degree he has to be equipped to be his own diagnostician, because in the final analysis he will be his own diagnostician anyway—he is the person who is in control of his learning energies—and it is better that he do the job well.

In the broader terms of the learner's development as a person, it is essential that evaluation help him steadily toward a valid and healthy image of himself. It is especially important for him to learn about his strengths and resources, in a way that genuinely leads him to incorporate these into his self-concept. It is also essential that evaluation should enrich his conception of the life-space he has to operate in, by expanding his vision of the opportunities and the choices that can be open to him and by enriching his background perceptions of purposes and values to judge by. Of course, it is also important to help him appraise realistically his residual weaknesses and the limitations of his resources, if this can be done in such a way as to create a genuine challenge. But most evaluation probably rushes in too soon and concentrates too much on the catching of "failures." Youngsters who accumulate a sense of strength and resource and opportunity gain the psychological freedom to look with clear eyes at their remaining problems. Those who are overwhelmed by a hopeless sense of failure are forced, for their own self-preservation, to distort the evidence, and never become good diagnosticians.

Taken altogether, the kind of feedback which a young person receives from a system of evaluation is crucial in his learning and development. It can lead him forward to precisely calibrated learning efforts on an ever-broadening front as well as to an enriched conception of himself and of his purposes and values and ultimate goals. Or it can strain and distort him, narrow his vision and purpose, and bring him little but a sense of defeat.

2. *Evaluation must encompass every objective valued by the school.* We are talking here of the *total* evaluation system, which includes much that depends on personal sensitivity and intuition, not merely of the testing-and-marking system, which may have to be more limited. Nevertheless, we cannot shake off the fact that it is the feedback generated by evaluation which conditions what everybody does next. And there cannot be thoughtful improvement on lines where there is no feedback.

If a history teacher says he is aiming for big generalizations but organizes his evaluative feedback in terms of the memorization of facts, his students will soon attend to the facts—and so, eventually, will he. Nothing will true up their learning and his teaching better than a widening of his evaluation. One fact is that he cannot improve his procedures unless he knows the results of what he has already been doing. Another fact is that unless there is something to deepen his awareness of a line of effort, he will slack off in the effort itself, shifting his energies toward those outcomes of which he *is* aware.

If the goals of a school include—along with the mastery of subject matter—such important "side effects" as a spirit of inquiry, sensitivity to beauty, and a moral commitment to conscientious citizenship, then these must steadily be within the view of the school's evaluation, too. The obligation is virtually a moral one: Whenever an institution commits itself to any purpose, it takes on the obligation to keep finding out how well it is achieving that purpose. Otherwise it cannot improve its efforts. The obligation is also a pragmatic one: Unless the school keeps trying to find out how well it is succeeding with a purpose, the purpose itself is likely to atrophy. Any school which hopes to maintain a balance among its multiple objectives—to maintain this balance in the instruction teachers provide and in the learning students devote energy to—must strive first of all for breadth and balance in its evaluation of those objectives.

In fact, this perception has governed much of the conceptualization of this yearbook: The best guide to curriculum improvement is evaluation; and to be an adequate guide the system of evaluation has to be as "big" as the purposes of the curriculum development itself.

3. *Evaluation must facilitate learning and teaching.* Instructional diagnosis lies at the very heart of good teaching. After each bit of evaluative data comes in, the teacher should be a little surer of how to proceed next. The all-too-common confusion of evaluation with grading tends to produce an image of evaluation as a terminal thing. But its far more significant function is a constant probing for the best way to move forward.

It is not the teacher alone who needs the diagnosis. After each bit of evaluation, the student, too, should know better where he stands and how to move ahead. And this purpose of diagnosis should be so apparent in the evaluative devices used that the student will see diagnosis as an aid, not as a trap set to catch him in failure.

4. *Evaluation must produce records appropriate to the purposes for which records are essential.* We intend to raise serious questions about the present system of grades and marks and credits—questions so grave that *they force us to propose that the system be discarded.* But the proposal does not stem from our taking the record-generating function of evaluation lightly; quite the contrary, we consider it terribly important that the records be so good that whenever they are needed they can deliver exactly that information which is truly significant.

Obviously, classroom teachers need some kinds of records purely for their own private purposes, as an aid to their instruction. These can and should vary with the nature of the subject matter and situation, as well as with the teacher's personal style. There is no particular need for uniformity, and anything that "works" for a given teacher is fine.

In this book we shall often speak of *evaluation for the record*. To experienced educators the phrase immediately creates an image of the transcripts and other records we send to another school when a student transfers or to a college when he graduates; transcripts made up of grades and credits and test scores and the like. These records are enormously important at critical times in a student's life. Here, at least, the school is reporting to other professionals, who presumably know how to read the records. Even so, the question remains whether the reports we send are actually good stewards of the data we wish to convey—and also whether those data are, in fact, the most significant things we could pass on.

But schools also report to employers, whose need for information may be very different and whose ability to interpret the typical record may be questionable. Furthermore—and more fundamentally important —teachers and other staff members need to bring the learner himself into interaction with the evaluative process. The records which a teacher or counselor needs in order to communicate meaningfully to him may be very different again from a mere list of grades. And the record of the interaction itself may later be highly significant. Finally, there is great need to communicate clearly to parents—and, once more, the kinds of records that will help most may have their own peculiarities.

We are not trying to create an image of a vast volume of records. We are trying to say that records are used in a variety of ways, and that there probably needs to be a variety of kinds. In every case the essential thing is that the records be able *to say what really counts* and say it in a way that genuinely communicates.

5. *Evaluation must provide continuing feedback into the larger questions of curriculum development and educational policy.* It is one thing for a history teacher to organize a continuing feedback to guide him in teaching his class. It may take quite a different order of evaluation to tell whether his history teaching would be more effective if he injected more economic and anthropological content into it. It may require still something more to guide a school's relative investment in the social studies as against the sciences and the humanities.

It is one thing to measure results and establish that the audio-lingual way of teaching a foreign language produces better speakers of that language than does a grammatical approach. It is another thing to find out whether the audio-lingual system aids or hinders the students' understanding of the culture behind the language or their appreciation of its literature. The school is full of such situations, where even the most precise measurement along one line may leave untouched larger questions of ultimate total effect.

It is important to emphasize that evaluation must concern itself with all the important objectives of a school rather than only a narrow band out of the total spectrum. In a curious way, however, it is even necessary on occasion for evaluation to "get outside of" the established objectives and raise still larger questions. Why, after years of instruction in composition, do so many adults "freeze up" when they face even the simplest writing task? Does cultural relativism in the social studies lead students to an "anything goes" philosophy? The most important educational choices often involve whole blocks of curriculum, or programs differing in *kind* rather than in detail; if evaluation is to live up to its responsibilities, it must provide data for this order of choices, too.

Typically, decisions of this order are not made within the individual classroom, perhaps not even within the individual school. They are made by curriculum committees, administrators, and boards of education. This raises the problem of organizing data and channeling them so that they will be available to the persons or groups that actually make the choices. Since these are among the most important decisions made in any school, it is obviously crucial that they be based on genuinely evaluative feedback.

Time Out, To Dream a Little

In this imperfect world it is not likely that any school system will ever devise a program of evaluation that will meet all five of these criteria perfectly. But suppose it could. What would be the results?

Every teacher would soon be teaching with greater precision, because he would be getting data constantly on what was "working" and what was not, what was already mastered and what remained to be learned. The ideal of "diagnostic teaching" would be close to fulfillment. Meanwhile the student himself would be channeling his own efforts with greater precision for he, too, would have a clear sense of direction.

When a student is transferred to other teachers or another institution, the new institution or teachers could pick him up smoothly and move forward with him, for they would have ways of knowing the things that really matter about him. Parents could be helped to become superior counselors to their children, for the school could help them toward true insight. Employers could choose their employees with more discernment and give them assignments fitted to their capacities and interests.

But in the long run even these great gains might be overshadowed by still greater ones. The public and the profession would be in position to make wiser fundamental decisions about changes in the educational program as a whole—or large parts of it. Fresh, daring questions could be raised, and there would be at least some ways of getting at evidence with which to answer them creatively. Because a wide spread of educational purposes could be kept constantly in clear view, it would be difficult for partial and narrow-based efforts to be substituted for the whole.

Perhaps the greatest gains of all would occur within the young person himself. As he learned not only to see his academic progress with clear eyes, but also to appraise himself validly, he would be more and more in position to take charge of his own life space and guide his own learning energies. The whole spirit of a school constantly guided by thoughtful evaluation would be healthy and constructive. For, as everyone became more and more aware of purposes and progress, and as diagnosis came to be seen as an ally, the old lines of antagonisms and cross-purposes must surely be erased.

An idealistic picture? Yes, but only because educators cannot yet produce such perfect evaluation—not because it would not realistically have such effects if we could produce it. There is no more realistic fact in the realm of human life than that we are all governed by our perception of the feedback we receive—and the nearer we come to having the feedback we need, the more nearly we approach wisdom at the next step.

All this is another way of saying that there is a great deal more to evaluation than first meets the eye. All too commonly it has been seen as if it were only measurement—a way of getting at marks and grades and credits. But when we view *evaluation as feedback* we instantly see how it resonates back through every stage of the educational process. Good evaluation has a way of stimulating deliberate thought about basic purposes and values and goals. One cannot measure progress toward a goal without knowing what that goal is. And every thoughtful effort to measure such progress brings the goal itself into renewed visibility.

If the evaluation is of sufficient scope and if it is handled through an interactive process, it has this clarifying, renewing effect upon learners, teachers, higher educational officers, and public alike. It helps everybody who is involved to think more clearly about what he is after and how he is getting along. In the long run, then, a high-quality evaluation program is the surest guarantee a learner, a teacher, or a school system can have of the ability constantly to envision valid objectives, plan for their achievement, look successes and failures in the eye, and develop new plans as these are needed.

How Does Reality Compare with the Dream?

How does the system of evaluation we now have stand up in the light of such a description? Even to ask the question is to have a quick and woeful perception of how very far it falls short. Yet perhaps it is unfair and unprofitable to judge any human institution against an absolute ideal. Let us, instead, try to size up realistically how well the typical system of evaluation does the five essential jobs.

1. *Does the system we have facilitate self-evaluation?* Not very well, by and large. One has to be careful here, for it makes an enormous difference in what school or what classroom the youngster finds himself. (Having said that, let us add a more general acknowledgment: We recognize that in speaking of "the system we have," we are implying a uniformity which does not exist. We trust the reader to recognize this also and to bear in mind that we are talking about certain fairly general characteristics which tend to run through a variety of patterns.) If a pupil is working with warm, sensitive teachers in a school that is open and friendly, he will have many chances to catch glimpses of his true potential.

But, by and large, the system is simply not geared to making significant feedback available to the pupil. Particularly those portions which to the pupil are most prestigious and important (i.e., the quizzing, testing, grading and marking, which have such weight in his life) have serious flaws.

For one thing, these measures are largely confined to the intellectual mastery of subject matter, tending to make all else seem extraneous. Almost worse, they generally interpret such mastery in terms of a bare memorization of factual details, ignoring the more fundamentally important generalizations, appreciations, and creative ideas. If the results tell the student anything about himself it is a bare sort of message.

Furthermore, even within these limits, the climate of formal evaluation is often so threatening as virtually to close out honest self-appraisal. Especially to the less able student, the main thrust of the effort may seem to be to "catch him out," to reveal as many as possible of his weaknesses, errors and failures. Human beings are so constituted that they can look at themselves with clear eyes only when they are in a relaxed, supportive situation. When they feel themselves persistently threatened they distort the feedback offered them to make it match the self-concept they need.

Finally, in most formal evaluation situations, it was never the intention of the school to involve the student cooperatively and to develop his powers of self-diagnosis. The teacher does the diagnosing and returns a mark and a scatter of red ink. Even if the teacher's diagnosis is perfectly sound, the student is unlikely to understand it as the teacher does —and even less likely to learn the process of diagnosing himself.

All in all, the evaluation system most learners experience may lead about as often to self-distortion as to perceptive self-appraisal. This is probably less true—or at least it may be less damaging—in the case of bright, attractive youngsters who are constantly receiving good news both through the formal media of marks and grades and through the personal cues supplied by their interactions with their peers and teachers. It is terribly true in the case of the less able and less attractive.

No human being can be expected to continue to "take" the volume of negative information such youngsters receive through their grades and marks and the way others treat them. They are literally forced to distort the cues into some kind of congruence with a bearable self-image. It is no wonder at all if they withdraw into private despair or flare out in public rebellion. In the process they lose the opportunity to learn about their real strengths and resources. The evaluation we have has a great deal to answer for, in its destruction of potentially sound human beings. No school system with a commitment to mental health and self-actualization ought to tolerate the sheer immorality of such a process.

2. *Does the evaluation we have encompass every objective valued by the school?* Obviously not—at least not in any balanced way. Here and there some scattered attention may be given to the more remote objectives, such as the development of a personal system of values. But at the same time such overwhelming weight is placed on a narrow range of purposes that the others virtually disappear from view.

Of course, the egregious fact in this connection is the constant testing of what is easiest to measure: memory of factual detail and manipulation of mechanical skills. In the crisis points of his academic life—when his "success" or "failure" is at stake—the student is taught by the tests set before him that survival depends on such memorization and manipulation. Small wonder if he concentrates his attention there, if he neglects the larger ideas or falls away from active questioning and creative divergence!

And it is no trivial side effect that over time, in some subtle way, the teacher's own efforts will also follow where his own tests—and those external tests which he is asked to administer—lead him. If he tests for facts he will teach facts; if he were to test for creativity he might at least try to teach toward it.

This is no small thing. It leads to massive distortion of energy input by both students and teachers. In recent years valuable new programs of science and mathematics have been "sold" on their ability to get away from rote memorization and manipulation, to create a new spirit of inquiry and sense of discovery, to build a new level of divergent thought and creativity. Yet if the measures used to evaluate them do not themselves highlight these great values—if they regress to the old narrow emphases—then it is a cinch that the programs, too, will regress.

The disease is endemic. We have courses ostensibly dedicated to the building of good citizenship—and measured in terms of knowledge of governmental structure. We have courses devoted to the "appreciation" of literature—and evaluated by knowledge of authors' names and movements and literary types.

But if the evaluation focus is stultifyingly narrow even within the range of *academic* goals, it is doubly dangerous in its exclusion of more personal variables. It is bad enough when the paraphernalia of tests and grades diminish attention to insight and understanding in favor of bare knowledge. It is even worse if they foreclose attention to ideals and values and personal traits in favor of the coldly intellectual.

The net result, over time, is that not only pupils and teachers but also parents and the general public make judgments and decisions affecting the entirety of education on the basis of evidence from one skimpy sector.

3. *Does the evaluation we have facilitate learning and teaching?* Here, especially if we confine ourselves to the teaching and learning of a set body of academic subject matter, the answer is considerably more positive. Particularly from the teacher's point of view. Good teachers commonly combine an intuitive discernment with fairly sensitive measures to assess what is going on and to calibrate their next steps. If few of them achieve the high ideal implied by the phrase "diagnostic teaching," many do maintain a running evaluation that tells them much about what to do.

From the learner's point of view the answer probably can not be quite so positive. Even if his teacher has a pretty good running diagnosis, *he* may not be sharing in it. When the teacher painstakingly marks his English composition with red ink, the teacher may arrive at an excellent analysis of what is needed; when the discouraged student glances at his ink-splashed effort, he may only learn that he is a poor writer. Still, even this student does get a fairly good running account of his mistakes and sometimes of his successes. The evaluation we now have is probably at its best in shaping the internal decisions within each classroom.

But even this is true only if the curriculum is confined to the regularized learning of a set body of subject matter, with limited objectives. In the very process of guiding that reasonably well, the intra-classroom evaluation program may be damping down attention to larger, more fundamentally important goals. Thus, the English teacher who so conscientiously took time to edit the composition just mentioned probably spent nearly all that time to mark errors in an effort to teach *correctness of form.* He may have paid almost no attention to *what the student had to say.* In his zeal for one set of purposes, he passed up the opportunity to help the student consider his logic or his implied values or his adherence to the truth. Evaluation has been so tragically successful in concentrating attention and energy on the narrowest objectives that marks and grades based on those objectives become almost an obsession. And all that falls outside the marking-grading system suffers.

This last point needs further extension. We have developed a preoccupation with everlastingly grading everything in sight. (There is even a case on record of a teacher who graded the sympathetic letters her pupils wrote her while she was ill!) Many teachers almost automatically look at every pupil product in terms of the grade it deserves. And so, all too naturally, students have come to see their purpose as "working for a grade." The obsession virtually blots out their real purposes. Parents pick up the message and add their pressure. Because the mode is so prevalent, many adults, both lay and professional—and even many children—cannot really conceptualize a pupil's doing purposive work except under the compulsion of "getting a grade." There can be no question but that this side effect of the evaluation system we have now is a major deterrent to genuine teaching and learning.

4. *Does the evaluation we have produce records appropriate to the purposes for which records are essential?* That the system generates records in considerable volume is not to be questioned. Thus, when a student has come through to the twelfth grade, a well organized high school is in position to tell a prospective college a great many facts about him. It could supply a good many vital statistics such as age, height, weight, a health record, and a record of attendance, along with at least one score indicating general academic aptitude. It could furnish some indications of the student's record of "citizenship" and of his participation in student activities. What it could do best of all is to record how much time the student has spent in each subject, and what grades he has earned. On the basis of these grades it could compute his rank-in-class. In addition, it might offer a considerable number of scores on various standardized tests.

These records are not to be sneered at. In the hands of an expert counselor who adds interpretive comments, such a record can be highly revealing. It is significant that many colleges consider the record inadequate and ask for a record of performance on something like the College Entrance Examination Board's special tests; but then it is also significant that the student's grade-point average is usually considered a better predictor of his college performance than the examination scores are—though the two together are still better. It is significant, too, that when research is contemplated the grade records are rarely thought adequate; nearly always the researcher substitutes measures which he hopes will be more precise.

Undoubtedly, if we measure the records a school can ordinarily supply against the absolute ideal that it ought to have to be able to paint a highly revealing portrait of him—to tell whatever is truly significant—the records will seem mechanistic and unrevealing. Nevertheless, it may well be true that the records themselves are less to be criticized than the process of getting them. The fact is that the process of accumulating those records has constituted an enormous preoccupation among teachers and pupils alike. The most trivial papers have been treated as if they existed largely to create a record. The student has been marked and graded day after day until the getting of good marks has become a goal in itself, with intrinsic learning left a very bad second. There is evidence that on the average the best way to get those marks is to think convergently, to do the standard task in the expected way; the creative student who persists in thinking divergently often comes off second best.

Furthermore, as already pointed out, the records school people typically create are those which will be meaningful and useful to other professional educators. In the process they have largely ignored other kinds of records: the kinds needed by a teacher—or counselor—in planning for groups or individuals; the kinds that would be meaningful to the youngster himself, or to his parents; the kinds that would be really significant to employers.

5. *Does the evaluation we have provide continuing feedback into the larger questions of curriculum development and educational policy?* The answer is a resounding *no!* Oh, there cannot help being a certain intuitive formation of opinion out of experience, which is not entirely without validity. When experienced teachers grow discontented with one approach and choose to try another, their opinion certainly deserves weight even if they cannot mobilize hard data.

Yet there are dangers in this. The shifts that result from changing styles of opinion often rest on about as much rationality as the annual decrees from Paris on the length of women's skirts. A clever writer decides that phonics are the *open sesame* to all reading and the public puts on the heat; some college professors who have not been inside a school for a decade argue for a different choice of literature; a new administrator parlays a personal hunch into a new curricular organization. In case after case sweeping decisions are made because nobody can adduce any really cogent evidence. And when those who have created an innovation look back, they remind one of Genesis: "And God saw everything that He had made, and behold, it was very good."

The "new" programs in mathematics and science are not really so new any more. They were "sold" not merely on the claim that they represented more important content but equally on the argument that they would build a new spirit of inquiry and creativity, a new surge of genuinely scientific attitude. Who knows whether they are actually achieving these things—or whether some of them are doing it better than others? After all these years, how much is really known on the crucial question of what is sound preparation for vocational life? The cold fact is that the evaluation system we now have puts great energy into grading students and considerable energy into guiding day-to-day teacher-and-pupil conduct within a classroom and within a set course of study, but it yields little evidence on which to assess the longer-range choices of curriculum and policy.

Furthermore, even when evaluation does yield evidence that might be useful in such choices, there is rarely any systematic channeling of the information to the points where the decisions are made. The fact that data exist does not automatically convert them into feedback. That depends on their converging systematically and steadily to the decision points. It is an anomaly that educators work so hard to true up the relatively "little" intra-class decisions and rest content to play the big ones by ear. It will take great revision of our evaluative efforts to produce data that bear on the large choices; it may take even more work to build a system that will convert these data into functioning feedback.

This Analysis Leads to Radical Conclusions

Taken all in all, when it is measured—even rather tolerantly—against our five basic questions, the evaluation we now have comes off badly. On the first and last questions it comes off very badly indeed, for it is most grossly inadequate in providing valid feedback to the individual learner himself and to the larger units of the school system. But it is equally to be condemned for the narrowness of its focus, because in its gross exaggeration of the more mechanical, easier-to-measure features of education, it virtually blots the broader, more fundamental objectives out of sight. The end result is not simply bad evaluation; it is distorted teaching and learning.

We believe that much of the trouble goes back to the marking-grading system and the kinds of records which it produces. The records are themselves inadequate; even the narrative record and the parent conference at the elementary level tell far too little of what is most significant. But the process of getting those records—the eternal preoccupation with marking and grading now spreading even in elementary schools —is even worse. Here the problem is not mere inadequacy but real destructiveness and distortion.

Educators have caviled at the going system of readiness tests, marks, grades and Carnegie units for so long that such quibbling has become a cliché. But this Yearbook Committee is convinced that the time has come to *do something* about this situation. We do not pretend to be able to see all the way to the ultimate substitutes. Yet neither do we see the situation as being so hopelessly frozen upon us that we must sit helpless and not even take the first steps.

Therefore, in this book, we shall propose what amounts to two new systems, both of which can function for a while in a supplementary way alongside the old one while better replacements are being developed.

One of these, to be presented late in the volume, has to do primarily with getting data for the record. It will demand also a different way of keeping the records. And it carries with it school organization designed to facilitate the deliberate and continuing use of feedback to answer the larger questions of curriculum and policy. This system is not simply being announced *ex cathedra,* for some of our members have carried out a fairly extensive tryout. On the other hand, we have had time only for some preliminary development and can hardly pretend that the system is a finished product.

As will be made clear at that point, the proposed system has to do chiefly with material to be used in the formal records and in an organized feedback system. It is *not* meant to constitute the total system of evaluation. Our logic in attacking the whole problem at this apparently least important place is that we hope to get the grading and marking function "off the back" of the instructional program. We have already made it clear that we see the perpetual preoccupation with grading and marking and the making of records as a hazard to good teaching and learning. Our proposal is to set these necessary functions off to one side, accomplish them through a definite and planned series of evaluative activities —and clear the rest of the instructional program for what matters more.

If this can be done, it will leave teachers and learners free to develop and use evaluative feedback for far more important purposes. This brings us to our second set of proposals (which will actually be presented first). These have to do with the instructional diagnosis which the teacher needs in order to sharpen his teaching. At least equally, they have to do with the active involvement of the learner himself in the process, at this point going far beyond the usual preoccupations with knowledge and skills to a concern for the learner's total growth. We shall work for an atmosphere free of tension in which learners and teachers can use diagnosis in a mutually helpful, open way, and the youngsters can learn progressively to appraise themselves. All this will not happen by itself; there will still be much to be done before we arrive at the idea of "diagnostic teaching"—but at least the way will be open.

In the remainder of this book, Chapter 2 will continue with a critique of the present situation and the forces involved in it. Chapters 3, 4 and 5 will be concerned with self-evaluation and the instructional feedback system. Chapters 6 and 7 will describe the developing system which has been in tryout. Finally, in Chapter 8, we shall allow ourselves the luxury of looking ahead ten years or so and sketching what such a system may have proved capable of providing.

2

The Evaluation We Have

Clifford F. S. Bebell

E VALUATION might be called the "sick man" of education. As the preceding chapter reveals, evaluation consumes an over-large portion of the energies of teachers and students and does so to the detriment and even the distortion of learning. Countless educators (and parents and students!) have long believed this and have issued complaints, criticisms, and calls for change. But few steps have been taken.

There is a remarkable durability about existing evaluation structures—and strictures. With little change, our present system of marks and examinations has endured for generations. It is true that much has been added—standardized tests, observational check lists, sociometric devices, projective techniques, anecdotal records, to name a few—but little that existed previously has been subtracted, or even altered perceptibly. The marks assigned by teachers and the procedures they use in calculating them were once employed by the teachers' teachers, and remain familiar, often painfully familiar, to parents.

There must be some explanation for the persistence of a system which has been so long condemned. Many reasons have been advanced, few of them convincing.

Perhaps the most widely held belief is that grades are demanded by parents, and that schools provide them primarily because of this pressure, somewhat against their better judgment. This is a myth! Those who try to change the system usually find that teachers constitute the most intransigent group.

Those who have succeeded in inaugurating new methods of evaluation have often found parents to be enthusiastic supporters. Of course, many innovators have found the opposite, too, but their difficulties are usually traceable to insufficient planning rather than to the change itself. Parents cannot be blamed for the present system of evaluation, and certainly not parents alone.

Another explanation often advanced to justify the use of grades attributes the present procedure to the demands of colleges. This says that grades are necessary in the competition for college entrance, and schools challenging the system will jeopardize their graduates' chances for further education. Although there is doubtless some truth in this assertion, there is also room for considerable qualification. College admissions officers have increasingly turned to other data to supplement the information yielded by high school grades. They have also vigorously and insistently affirmed their willingness to cooperate with schools wishing to experiment. While many public school people perceive a Trojan horse in these proclamations, the experience of schools which *have* experimented tends to lend some credence to them. The evidence is not convincing that the colleges insist on grades. Instead, college spokesmen argue eloquently that the basic bloc of resistance is in the public schools themselves.

A third line of analysis points to school transfer as a major cause of inertia in the present situation. Everyone understands the system, it is reasoned, and therefore the system is invaluable in easing the problems occasioned by a student's changing schools. It is difficult to find merit in this argument. For one thing, studies have shown that course titles and grades do not communicate consistently or clearly reveal the meaning of those who created them. For another, schools are notorious for looking at transcripts only to get a most general idea of what a student has taken and how good he is. His future schedule is often based mostly upon what is usual in the school he enters, with such modification as is readily available to all students in the school. There seems to be little or nothing in the problem of school transfer that demands a continuance of present evaluation systems.

In brief, there seems to be little evidence anywhere of a need for continuing present evaluation procedures. Other arguments are less widely used or accepted than those just discussed, and none is compelling. Yet resistance to change is everywhere present. Understanding of the resistance is essential if change is to be effected. What *is* the explanation of such resistance?

The Emotionality of Evaluation

Probably the resistance to change lies in the feelings engendered by evaluation. And evaluation, beyond any doubt, does have a hot emotional charge. All of us have experienced this, and though most educators are among the "winners" in the present system, probably none has failed to feel the anxieties it produces. Who can question its power? Certainly not anyone who has turned, or has failed to turn, any of the tight corners of evaluation, either in school or out. Such experiences as final examinations, acceptance by a fraternity or sorority, admission to college, selective-service examinations, dismissal from a job are visceral as well as intellectual.

Education has traditionally focused upon the development of man's rationality. It is paradoxical that a nonrational force should have so much influence upon programs for the development of the intellect. And yet, it is only if the role of emotion in learning is first acknowledged and then understood that progress can be made toward using it defensibly and professionally. The first step must be recognition of the existence of emotionality in the schools.

Only with difficulty can many persons be persuaded as to the existence of the emotional nature of their resistance to change. To the extent that they acknowledge the presence of emotionality, they view it as an undesirable and extrinsic element which should be eliminated or at least controlled. Frequently they use such intemperate language in asserting the irrelevance of emotion to learning that they remind one of the stereotypic movie character who exclaims, "Excited! Who's excited?" The invective which has been leveled at the statement "the whole child comes to school" is an illustration of this. The statement is so obviously true that it has become a truism, yet in some circles it is anathema.

Evaluation is a finger probing at our anxieties, while yet prodding us to higher achievement. Especially is this so when we ourselves do the prodding. To be sure, evaluation can be satisfying as well as threatening. However we must learn to maximize the positive thrust and minimize the negative.

Perhaps the basic issue is not so much whether evaluation is nasty, but whether it does the job, whether it gets the data which are needed, and feeds these back in a form in which they can be used. Another way of saying the same thing is that there exists both a need to know and a need to use knowledge to improve the teaching-learning situation. If either seriously impedes the other, the result is educational disaster. We must not use evaluative procedures which "test to destruction," in a manner analogous to the manufacturer who determines the breaking point of a product by actually breaking it.

In Chapter 1 we made the point that evaluation controls the next step. Perhaps now we should add that this control may be emotional or unconscious as well as intellectual and intentional, or may involve other factors than those realized, and these latter factors may be the dominant ones. We must learn how feelings aid or block feedback. The impact of evaluation may be visceral, but its interpretation and use must be intellectual.

Yet the intensity of the evaluative experience is such that a possibility of self-delusion, of suppression and rationalization, is always present. Indeed, the arguments advanced by those who would preserve the status quo often smack of the mechanisms of defense and avoidance. It is difficult, and yet vital, to look clearly at this area, which is so filled with opportunities for self-deception. The whole child does indeed come to school, and we need to understand how his rational development is influenced by his nonrational nature.

Not only is it difficult for many persons to recognize the presence of emotionality in education, many even remain unconvinced of the essential role of evaluation. They view it more as a satellite activity— one which is supplementary rather than central in importance. They see it merely as a record rather than as a mainspring of learning. Typical of such individuals is the teacher who complains that students place too much emphasis on grades, while he himself does likewise at the nearby teacher education institution.

Others acknowledge the importance of evaluation, but give it lip service only. They make little effort to examine and use its power in effecting educational outcomes, and rarely see the relevance of evaluation to their own work.

We are not suggesting that all persons holding the views outlined are rationalizing or self-deceptive. We are seeking rather to call attention to the difficulty of clear analysis and to suggest an explanation for the obdurate quality of the system now current in schools. The importance of the problem demands thorough examination in spite of the difficulties. Perhaps both the importance and the difficulties result from the same emotional base.

In the following sections we shall look at two main areas, the marking-grading system and the use of tests and examinations. There are many other focal points of evaluation in the schools, but these two are both the most prominent and those which are most in need of action.

The Marking-Grading System

I've just *got* to keep a 'B+' average if I'm ever going to get to college.

If you get all 'A's' on your next report card, I'll get you a bicycle.

I don't see why you can't get as good marks as Mary does; you've got as good a mind as she has.

How could you give me a 'D'? I worked so hard this semester.

I don't care if you *were* second in the class; there's no reason why you can't be first.

Some members of this faculty are apparently reluctant to give 'F's'.

Why did you flunk me, Miss Jones? I thought you liked me.

How can I *do* this to them? The ones I have to fail are the ones I most want to help.

I get a pain in my belly every time I have to turn grades in.

Marking is the evaluation procedure that everyone knows and no one understands. Its caustic quality has been felt by all; we have received grades as students and most of us have assigned them as teachers. We know the system and we have felt its weight; but we do not agree on its role or results. Among both educators and lay citizens, especially parents, there is much conflict and confusion regarding the purposes for which marks are intended or the meaning which they bear.

What are the functions of marks? In 1947 Wrinkle discussed this question in a book destined to become a classic on the subject. He listed four functions that marks are intended to fulfill, and although other statements have appeared in the twenty years since then, no essential alteration in this listing has occurred. Perhaps, as the French say, "The more it changes, the more it is the same thing."

We shall base our analysis on Wrinkle's list:

1. *Administrative functions:* Marks indicate whether a student has passed or failed, whether he should be promoted or required to repeat the grade or course, and whether he should be graduated. They are used in transferring a student from one school to another and in judging candidates for admission to college. They may be used by employers in evaluating prospective employees.

2. *Guidance functions:* Marks are used in guidance and counseling in identifying areas of special ability and inability, in deciding on the advisability of enrolling the student in certain courses and keeping him out of others, and in determining the number of courses in which he may be enrolled.

3. *Information functions:* Marks are the chief means employed by the school in giving information to students and their parents regarding the student's achievement, progress, and success or failure in his schoolwork.

4. *Motivation and discipline functions:* Marks are used to stimulate students to make greater effort in their learning activities. They are used for the same purpose in determining eligibility to honors of many different kinds such as participation in school activities, eligibility to play on the team, membership in selected groups, the winning of scholarships, etc.[1]

---

[1] William L. Wrinkle. *Improving Marking and Reporting Practices in Elementary and Secondary Schools.* New York: Holt, Rinehart and Winston, Inc., 1947. p. 31-32. Copyright 1947 by William L. Wrinkle. Used by permission of Holt, Rinehart and Winston, Inc., publishers.

It is almost unbelievable, is it not, that simple numbers or letters can carry the burden of reporting students' achievement in entire courses, that so much information, usable for so many purposes, can be so readily compressed? Indeed it is unbelievable, and one reason for not believing it is that it is not so. *Grades simply do not do what they set out to do.*

Administrative Functions. Let us take the administrative functions first. Of course, students are often promoted, retained or graduated on a basis of their grade-point average. It is also true that colleges look at the high school records of applicants for admission, particularly as these records indicate the student's rank in class. Marks are used to a smaller extent in judging job applications or in considering students who transfer from one school to another.

However, to say that marks are used does not say that they succeed. The basic question is this: Do marks achieve such dependability or carry such rich meaning that an individual or institution using them for administrative purposes can do so with confidence that the results will be educationally sound? The answer must be an unequivocal *no!*

In part, this answer is predicated upon practices of schools and colleges themselves. Increasingly these institutions are relying upon a wide variety of data in considering a student. Colleges insist upon achievement and aptitude test scores and other pieces of information about applicants in addition to their grades. Schools making decisions about promotion or retention, or about student placement in courses or sections, rely upon additional information about an individual, such as measures of his intelligence, reading ability, or personality, and the recommendations of his teachers.

Employers often demand more than grades, too. Combs, in his book, *The Professional Education of Teachers,* has recently commented on the inadequacy of transcripts for teacher placement. Noting that placement offices apparently learn more about the applicants after a few moments' contact with them than colleges and universities seem able to find out in four or five years, he asks whether we should abandon grades and use placement office evaluations instead.[2] He may be joking, but his point is serious—grades alone do not suffice.

Possibly it is only at graduation time that the grade-point average comes into its fullest flower. The moment of graduation is often the one where schools stand most squarely on hours of credit and averages of marks. However, even here there is much doubt. Consider the discussion which has taken place about the relative "meaninglessness" of the high school diploma. How many people have come to maintain that the fact of

[2] Arthur W. Combs. *The Professional Education of Teachers.* Boston: Allyn and Bacon, Inc., 1965. p. 129.

graduation is itself not sufficient to determine the quality and extent of a student's learning? It seems evident that administrative functions are inadequately served by marks, and more and more these functions require other sources of information.

Guidance Functions. Similar conclusions can be drawn about guidance functions. Few guidance workers are convinced that the grades which a student has obtained are in themselves sufficient evidence for making decisions about his abilities or about the courses he should take. Counselors, far from being impressed by the contributions that marks make to their work, are often more impressed by the problems they provide. Perhaps as many emotional and maladjustment difficulties of students, difficulties which counselors are often called upon to deal with, are caused by grades as by any other factor.

Information Functions. The information functions of marks seem almost like a bad joke. Studies have shown that no two people seem able to interpret a set of grades or even a single grade in the same fashion, and that different persons called upon to give marks to students under standardized conditions tend to vary widely in their judgments. Often a teacher combines into a single grade both the expectations he applies to all students and his individual expectations for a particular one. Many teachers take into account whether a student has been gaining or losing ground during the marking period; and often factors such as attitude and behavior, tardiness and absence, or spelling, punctuation, grammar and neatness go into students' marks, even in subjects other than English.

The typical marking procedure consists of lumping together in a rough average a wide variety of factors chosen individualistically by each teacher from all the foregoing. No one reviewing a grade, however, is able to move backwards and to unravel the single score into the original strands which served to create it, thus making diagnosis of the student's strengths and weaknesses impossible. It might truly be said that a mark represents an attempt to reconcile the irreconcilable, and in the process loses its ability to communicate clearly and unambiguously.

In its simplest form, the procedure leads to the impossibility of knowing whether a "B" grade, say, represents an "A" student who is not working up to capacity, a "B" student meeting his normal expectancy, or a "C" student overachieving. In more complex situations, the grade may well represent an indecipherable mélange of subject-matter achievement, current rate of progress, class citizenship, work habits, attitudes of both student and teacher, neatness, and administrative and community pressure. These are amended by such considerations as the grade level, ability grouping, the vocational and educational aspirations of the student, the time of the year, and the treatment the teacher received from his own teachers. If grades represent an effort to reconcile the irreconcilable, they also result in the ciphering of the indecipherable.

Needless to say, the endless belaboring of students by teachers through the marking-grading system leads to considerable student sensitization. One wonders why teachers should evidence surprise at students' over-concern with grades. The ceaseless over-marking of children can surely result only in their being affected permanently and it may well destroy the taproot of their motivation.

Motivation and Discipline Functions. The motivational functions of grades are very much subject to question, although Wrinkle says, " . . . of all the functions marking and reporting practices are supposed to serve, they actually serve only one with any considerable degree of effectiveness—motivation." [3]

The question lies in the way in which motivation is achieved. The process is based more often on fear—of failure, of humiliation, of loss of privilege—than it is upon the positive desire for accomplishment or reward. Even when the search for a mark is based upon the latter, the emphasis is more often competitive than it is cooperative. That is to say, the view of learning is usually not one of a joint search by teacher and student, or by students together. Rather, it is often one of an ant-pile of scramblers, fighting one another for the few positions of safety, with self-interest the most prominent motive and little room for the luxury of concern about others. To be sure, most people believe that competition is often healthy, and that it fosters the courage and self-reliance of those who engage in it freely and fairly. But if so, it should be competition among equals, and should not be forced upon the fearful and ill-equipped. Certainly, academic competition has little to offer the perpetual loser. For the latter, the motivation is basically one of finding out what someone else wants him to do, so that he can try it—and usually fail. Even for the perpetual "winner," the result is undesirable, if such competition should lead him to become insufferable in his supposed superiority.

Psychologists and psychiatrists have noted the undesirable effect upon the mental health of many children caused by an overemphasis on marks. Educators are acquainted with the distress created during the grading process—distress often evident in teachers as well as students. Is this not too high a price to pay for the "successful" use of marks to fulfill functions of motivation and discipline? Especially when the motivation is negative—a form demonstrated by research to be less helpful than more positive means to the acquiring of learning quickly and permanently.

[3] Wrinkle, *op. cit.,* p. 33.

A Little History

The shortcomings just discussed have not gone unnoticed in the past. Many of the problems described have received attention, and many efforts have been made to change the marking-grading system.

The first such effort was to change the percentage-grade approach to what we might call standard letter grades. The percentage grade, used widely in the early years of this century, assumed that a teacher could distinguish one hundred and one levels of student achievement validly and reliably (although for all practical purposes perhaps only thirty to forty levels were used regularly). Since common sense indicated the difficulty of doing this, many persons recommended that percentage grades be replaced by a system in which there would be fewer levels of achievement to distinguish, with higher reliability as a result. From such proposals arose the letter-grade systems so widely used today, most commonly in the ABCDF form.

Some writers, and indeed many schools, carried the same line of reasoning a step further. Arguing that fewer levels of difficulty would serve to increase even more the reliability of teachers' grades, they advocated a simple two-step system, most commonly S (satisfactory) and U (unsatisfactory). In many instances where this system was used, considerable dissatisfaction arose because of its failure to recognize outstanding accomplishment by better students. Often, therefore, a third level, typically E (excellent), was added to overcome this difficulty.

Still other educators followed a somewhat different line of reasoning regarding the ABCDF system. Dissatisfied with the extent to which it discriminated among students at any given level, they increased the number of categories from five to eleven or thirteen by adding plus and minus signs. Needless to say, this practice served to lower the reliability of the ratings.

The traditional report card has sometimes sought to acquire certain of the advantages of a written letter by providing additional information about students. Generally, this takes the form of a list of social and citizenship learnings or achievements which the teacher fills out, usually by checking the appropriate level of accomplishment in each area included in the list. Most commonly, each learning is reported at one of three levels (often E, S, or U), and the teacher is expected to add some written comment regarding areas in which the student's work is unsatisfactory or in which he needs specific improvement. Often, though, the teacher either writes no comments or makes them too perfunctory to be helpful.

The list of nonacademic objectives or learnings which is added to a report card is often quite long, frequently lengthier than the list of conventional subject areas. The advent of the computer has served in some districts to shorten this list, and may lead to a trend in this direction. However, short or long, there has been the criticism voiced by parents that the information provided in these areas is not sufficiently explicit or clear. Studies have tended to show also that teachers' judgments on different items have been so interrelated that there is little assurance that they are validly reporting distinct, meaningful traits or accomplishments.

None of the efforts to improve grades has been successful enough to achieve universal adoption, though the letter-grade system has been popular. It does not seem possible that any foreseeable changes in our present practices will bring about sufficient improvement to justify the continued use of single grades in each subject as an educational procedure. This most commonly used system in today's schools yields merely an undifferentiated, multi-purpose, non-informative record.

More important, this record is produced at a staggering cost. We do not refer just to the data-gathering, record-keeping, form-making paper work, because vast amounts of information are vital if one is to keep track of such a complex thing as student learning. We refer rather to the cost compared with the outcome. Surely this is an instance of a mountain producing a mouse! Yet most of all we refer to the human cost, the anguish and agony of teachers, the terror and torment of students, and the damage done to learning.

Why Don't We Change?

In spite of many expressions of concern and many recommendations for change, little actual change has occurred. Earlier, we discussed the alleged demands of four outside groups as a possible explanation of this condition. At this point, let us consider in more detail some of the reasons why so many suggestions for modifying or abandoning the marking-grading system have led to so little action.

1. *Inertia and resistance to change are widespread.*

Most people prefer the evil they know to the evil they do not know. Further, there has been little or no agreement on any alternative to our current practices. Hence, a comfortable inertia, coupled with an inability to perceive anything better, has led to a widespread continuance of the present situation.

A large, intertwined system has its own built-in resistance to change. It is very difficult to amend a structure which is widely used, which is thoroughly entrenched, which is familiar to so many persons, and upon which so many practices have been built. For example, our system of credits and units and our procedures for providing transcript information would need alteration if we were to abandon grades or amend them seriously. The inherent inertia of a complex situation almost destroys local control of its form of recording progress and leaves the individual school nearly helpless to change or experiment. A large-scale effort is needed.

Perhaps a word or two more should be said about the influence of the system of credits and units upon evaluation. Although the impact of this system is referred to in other parts of this volume, we should like to state categorically at this time our belief in its undesirability and inherent uselessness. Not least among our reasons for saying this is the rigidity of the structure, a rigidity which spawns countless rationalizations and excuses for inaction. "If we teach each student in a history class individually, how can we tell any one what history he has had, or how much he knows? A 'B' in American History for a year should *mean* something."

In addition to rigidity there is also shallowness. What does one unit in American History mean? Even students taking the same course the same year from two teachers using the same text and the same syllabus in the same school may have different learning experiences and accomplishments. So too, for that matter, may two students who have shared the same classroom throughout the same year. Our credit-unit structure encourages us to deal with superficialities, to state categorically that four units of English are required or should be offered, in the belief we have said something meaningful about the quality or nature of education. This is sheer delusion, though one shared by many prominent figures.

2. *Those who "win" in the system have an interest in its continuance.*

Ambitious and able students (or parents) see in grades a method of demonstrating their superiority (or their children's) and a means of "getting ahead." Generally speaking, those who most vigorously support our present system, or perhaps even call for a more rigorous fulfillment of it, are those who have succeeded in it. They have "won" good grades or see the opportunities to do so in the future, or both. Among this group must surely be included most educators, whose own performance in their school days places them among the academic elite of our society.

3. *Grades satisfy the need for simple, "precise" answers.*

Life frustrates many of us with its unpredictability and complexity. How often have we sought simple answers to difficult problems! How hard it is to give up such answers when we appear to possess them! How often, too, have we accepted simple answers that were not answers at all!

4. *College entrance requirements have tended to perpetuate grades.*

Although college admissions officers insist that they have no require-ments which interfere with high schools' doing as they wish, most high school teachers and principals do not feel secure in breaking a pattern that colleges seem to expect. Perhaps even more important, the prospec-tive college applicant and his parents do not feel secure under such circumstances. In consequence, colleges' demands for transcripts and rank in class have led public school educators to conclude that our present grading system is a necessary evil and must be continued. We have already dealt with this objection.

5. *Teachers feel a need and a wish to justify their evaluations.*

Teachers deal with human lives. Their evaluative judgments may direct or redirect, may aid or may frustrate the ambitions and the life goals of the students in their charge. Conscientious teachers feel humble in the face of this responsibility. They know only too well that they do not possess either the objectivity or the omniscience which the evaluation process seems to demand. So they often resort to somewhat mechanical and arithmetical approaches to grading, in order to be at least as objective and "fair" as possible.

6. *Grading is an emotionally pressuring area.*

People are reluctant to face up to areas of great emotionality. Grading certainly qualifies as such an area. It is human to avoid uncom-fortable or emotion-packed issues, or to rationalize about such issues, or to take arbitrary stands. All such behavior has often been ignored or postponed. Use of some of the "explanations" of the impossibility of change, as discussed earlier, reveals the emotional base of much resistance and much of the support of the status quo.

7. *Inability to agree on a substitute for grades has encouraged the continuance of present practices.*

There seems to be little ability to agree on a feasible professional substitute for grading, possibly for one or more of the reasons already discussed. Most proposals which have been advocated have been quickly attacked, often with considerable vehemence. Combine a complex problem with the emotionalities attendant upon changing an entrenched structure, and one can see why agreement on a substitute for grades has not been easy to reach.

Yet agreement is essential. Since our present marking-grading system is clearly inadequate, we must have at least agreement to experiment with carefully developed alternate procedures. Such procedures should meet the criteria presented in Chapter 1. One plan for a formal evaluation program which we believe to be of this kind is proposed and described in **Part Three of this book.**

Tests and Examinations

*ONCE UPON A TIME the principals in a large school system pro-
posed to the superintendent that all the teachers take an annual examination. The information thus gained would supplement the principals'
classroom visits (which they were usually too busy to make), and would
provide objective data about the qualifications of everyone in the system
It might even show the aptitude of teachers for higher responsibilities.*

*The superintendent found the suggestion excellent, and promised to
present it to the board of education. Indeed, he liked it so well that he
decided to expand the plan to include the principals, too, along with other
administrative persons. The principals had little objection to this last feature, but did oppose an examination for themselves, asserting that the creative and flexible nature of their work was such that an examination would
not give a full and fair picture. And besides, they were willing to rely upon
the judgment of the superintendent and the central office staff who had
selected them in the first place.*

*But the superintendent was still enthusiastic about his idea, and
proposed it one night to the board of education. They were even more enthusiastic than he, and endorsed it wholeheartedly. They felt scores could
be posted and persons getting the highest scores could be formally honored
with a dinner and a plaque. They had only one change to suggest. They
would like to request that the superintendent be examined also, to give an
inspiring example to all, and a challenge to all in the system to equal his
score.*

*At this point the superintendent praised the wisdom of the board, but
warned that refining the proposal, preparing the examinations, and imple-
menting the plan would take some time. Indeed it did, more time than anyone was able to give it!*

Examinations are part of the ancient heritage of education. Today
they have flowered beyond any expectations of the past. Books have been
written about the burgeoning test movements, and the production and
processing of examinations for school use is a multimillion dollar business.
Both in emotional punch and in massive attack, the role of tests and examinations is potent.

Of course, these instruments are not the only forms of educational
data-gathering. There are countless others. However, we have chosen to
consider tests and examinations because they are prominent, potent and
widely discussed today.

We do not intend to limit our comments to commercially produced or
other formally developed devices. By far the most common use of testing
is by teachers, and the most common tests are teacher-made. These range
from 5-minute "pop" quizzes to formal final examinations. Yet since it is
harder to discuss the less visible and more variable instruments created

in individual classrooms, much of our comment will necessarily center about those tests which are published.

Without doubt, the testing movement represents one of the great achievements of education in the twentieth century. The attempt to make the gathering of educational data more scientific has led to many accomplishments, among them the following:

1. Greater awareness of the objectives of education and the need to define these in specific terms

2. Greater awareness of the nature and extent of individual differences

3. Greater consistency and precision in measuring educational outcomes

4. Development of instruments by means of which educational hypotheses can be rigorously tested

5. Acceptance of the possibility of scientific demonstration of educational principles.

In other words, the testing movement represents one facet of mankind's growing awareness that no area is beyond the reach of research, and that human beings and their thoughts and feelings can be scientifically studied. To be sure, educational measurement is still in an early stage of development, and the professional literature abounds with evidence that many instruments now in existence do not satisfy qualified professionals as to their effectiveness. A brief reading of the reviews in any issue of Buros' *Mental Measurements Yearbook* attests to this dissatisfaction.

However, it is not the purpose of this yearbook to examine the difficult and technical problems which examination makers face. Nor is it our intention to downgrade the past successes and almost limitless future potential for education of the testing movement. Perhaps it is sufficient to say that although much progress has been made in improving the quality of standardized tests as measuring devices, much more needs to be done before these instruments can achieve a level of precision and technical excellence which will satisfy both those who construct the tests and those who use them.

The principal concern of this volume will be rather with the ways in which such devices affect educational programs and practices. Is it possible, or even likely, that in the effort to achieve certain goals of measurement, the makers and users of tests may have achieved other purposes besides those they intended? Incidental or unconscious accomplishments are often the side effects of educational practices in a manner somewhat analogous to the undesirable side effects of "wonder" drugs in medicine

Following a brief review of past developments in educational tests and examinations, there will be a consideration of the effects and side effects of these devices in schools.

A Little More History

Dating back at least 4000 years, according to Chinese records, examinations have undergone many changes in the past century. Just over a century ago Horace Mann was influential in replacing oral examinations, then in vogue, with written ones. He argued that many questions asked uniformly of all students were fairer than a smaller number that varied from student to student. Today, when written tests are often criticized, it is difficult to remember that these devices once challenged an existing system.

Until a generation ago, the written essay test was almost universally used. During the 1920s and 1930s, however, essay questions were increasingly subjected to attack, largely on grounds of the subjectivity of their scoring and their failure to yield diagnostic results. Too many irrelevancies were said to enter into the scoring process, and the final outcome usually represented a blending of many diverse elements.

The main recommended substitute, so widely used today, especially in standardized tests, was the so-called objective item (often called at that time the new-type item). This kind of question eliminates variability in scoring although it retains other variable elements such as the effect of guessing and of daring on the part of the student.

To this day, both essay and objective questions have their advocates, and many persons are prone to debate their respective merits. This debate represents an oversimplified view of the issues involved, since each approach to measurement has strengths and weaknesses.

However, the objective item facilitated and encouraged the development of the commercially produced examination which is so common today. Any kind of widespread examination program, with a need for reliable norms or standards, requires a scoring system which is not subject to variations among people and situations. The objective item, most notably in the multiple-choice form, possesses this attribute, and it opened the door to the standardized test.

The standardized test required another essential element beyond that of an objective scoring procedure: namely, a base for comparing and interpreting students' scores. This base was found in national norms (which are not always so national), representing the distribution of scores obtained on a given test by students drawn from a representative sample of American schools. In this way it is possible to locate a given individual or group in relation to this distribution. Although norms have been indispensable to test makers and interpreters, they have long been charged with encouraging undesirable comparisons.

One side effect of the testing movement has been the increasing separation between formal and informal approaches to testing. For instance, the selection and use of commercially produced, standardized tests is called in many a school *the* testing program, although the vast majority of tests used in the school are those produced by teachers. Frequently we see teachers' tests downgraded, even by the individuals creating the tests themselves, as being of negligible quality and value in comparison with standardized tests. The technical gap between the test specialist and the field educator has become so great that the former often patronizes the latter, and the latter accepts the judgment implied.

However, it is clear that locally produced tests are likely to ·fit more closely the characteristics of the local curriculum, and no amount of technical excellence can compensate for the irrelevance of an instrument to a given situation.

Among other aspects of the gap between nationally and locally produced tests is the debate between essay and objective items. Frequently, teachers see the essay question as an area which the standardizers cannot enter (although this is open to question), and the objective question as an area which teachers should leave to the test professionals. In spite of many books and other efforts to help teachers become skillful writers of objective test items, the debate over essay vs. objective tests continues.

To sum up, we have seen a revolution in the development and use of standardized tests in the past half-century. Much of the control of the examining process has been taken from the hands of field educators and given to others more remote from schools and possibly less immediately knowledgeable about instruction. Teachers have tended to become more uncertain of their own skills in measuring educational achievement, and more ambivalent about the relative roles of classroom testing and standardized testing. The result is a situation in which many undoubted gains have taken place, as was mentioned earlier, while at the same time many difficulties have arisen which were formerly either unknown or unnoticed.

Effects and Side Effects

Tests and examinations largely fulfill the same functions as grades. Their widespread use to provide information for grading purposes is sufficient evidence of this. Standardized tests may not usually be so used, but teacher-made tests certainly are.

Of Wrinkle's four functions earlier discussed—administrative, guidance, information, and motivation or discipline—commercially produced instruments are widely used for the first three. Locally made devices are likely to be employed for the last two. It cannot be denied that, in the eyes of many users, standardized tests fulfill their functions with considerable effectiveness. Certainly they are used for many administrative and guidance purposes, and most practitioners in these areas are convinced that the data obtained are greatly needed in their work, as indeed they are. And in spite of abuses, particularly in the form of administrative interpretations and practices, standardized tests will continue to play an important role. It is a role that contributes much, and it is toward the correction of some of the abuses that the rest of this chapter is directed.

The information function is outstandingly fulfilled. Measuring devices are designed to yield more and better information than is otherwise available, and without doubt such instruments have added vastly to our knowledge. Also, shortcomings in the kind and quality of information provided by tests are the concerns of measurement specialists, who work constantly to improve the yield. Once again there are abuses and misuses which demand our attention. Both professionals and lay citizens are often gullible in what they believe test results reveal. The title of a standardized test is assumed to mean what it says, regardless of the varied ways in which the terms in that title are actually understood and applied in schools. Achievement in social studies surely means different things to different people. "Intelligence" does not mean the same thing to all people or to all schools, nor do aptitude or critical thinking or many other terms. Clearly, no test result yields information which is equally appropriate to all situations.

The information yielded by a teacher-made test is even more difficult to identify. The instrument may be quite relevant to the experiences of a class, yet still fail to reveal anything meaningful. Lack of skill in test construction or scoring may have destroyed its reliability. The content may not be compatible with professional consensus (or even the teachers' notion) of what achievement in the particular course should be. However, teacher-made final examinations *do* communicate information very effectively to students, at least as to how well they fit the teacher's expectations.

It is perhaps in the area of motivation and discipline that the effects of tests and examinations are most equivocal. As in the case of grades, many tensions and pressures are created by examinations. Test publishers contend that students feel less anxiety about most standardized tests than they do about teacher-made tests, since the standardized tests seldom enter into course grades and their scores are not ordinarily accompanied by praise or blame. Of course, a few crucial standardized tests may arouse anxiety, such as Regents' Examinations or College Board Examinations, yet it is hard to see how such anxiety can ever be avoided. It is unlikely to do serious or lasting harm except to neurotic students in whom examination pressures may combine with other prior, underlying causes.

Our concern is not so much with the functions fulfilled by tests as with their possible side effects. If undesirable incidental outcomes occur, educators should be concerned with overcoming such side effects, while simultaneously retaining the unquestioned benefits that the testing movement has brought about. We shall study this matter by seeking answers to six questions about the educational impact of published tests and examinations.

1. *Have such instruments tended to influence the content and emphasis of the curriculum or the plans and activities of teachers in any undesirable direction or to any undesirable extent?*

It is evident that the things which are easiest to do are likely to be those which are done first. In education, this means that simpler learnings are more likely to be measured through tests than more complex, the tangible before the intangible. However, the simpler and more tangible are not usually the more important. For instance, where are the tests to measure such vital outcomes as citizenship or cooperativeness or social effectiveness? Critical thinking is another learning of great importance; only a few instruments exist designed to measure it, and they are variable in both quality and nature, with a low intercorrelation.

It is too easy to blame test publishers for this condition. Perhaps one had better look to the schools themselves. Producers of tests for sale have to satisfy their public. One representative of a publisher phrased it this way, "It is a fact of life that anything unconventional in a test battery will lower sales, and anything very unconventional will kill them." Doubtless commercial houses would produce almost anything for which there is a demand, and it is probably not very fair to expect them, rather than individuals who bear the prime responsibility for education, to provide leadership in breaking new ground.

Teachers and administrators often choose the easy way. Administrators buy tests which are available and give considerable emphasis to the results. Teachers use information which is obtained from the school's testing program, and either consciously or unconsciously stress the areas emphasized in the program. In consequence, two kinds of distortion may and often do occur in a school. The first is the emphasis on certain kinds of learning to the detriment of other kinds *within* a given subject area. The second is the partial or even total neglect of important learnings which cut across subject areas, and for which reliable measuring devices are not readily available.

The first has been more successfully fought than the second. Test makers work very hard to insure that the emphasis in the content of a given test reflects consensus of leaders in that subject field, as well as the most typical practices of the best schools. However, consensus is not a universal, and vast individual differences exist among school programs. Inevitably, the content of a given test at best approximates the content of the subject field as taught either at a specific school or by a particular teacher. It is up to the curriculum planners of the school to determine its "closeness of fit," and to decide what emphasis should be placed upon its results.

Any test fits more closely the pattern in some schools than it does in others; it fits more closely the emphasis and concerns of some teachers than of others. It is not easy to determine the extent to which a discrepancy occurs in any individual instance, and the assumption is often made that the result yielded by a test in a specific subject area is a valid indicator of achievement in that field. In consequence, teachers subjected to the knowledge that their students will be taking a particular instrument, tend to insure that their teaching and the student's learning are adequately oriented. In such a case, the test maker has in effect become a curriculum maker for that school and that teacher.

Not only is it important to examine coverage of topics by a test; it is vital to consider its coverage of a range of learnings. For instance, knowledge is easier to measure than understanding; skill than ability; content than appreciation. Where is the test that determines a student's willingness to use the learnings he has acquired, or his motivation to continue to learn after his schooling is completed, or his ability to direct his own learnings? And yet, these are often the outcomes most earnestly desired by the teacher, at least ostensibly. Emphasis upon data which are readily acquired may well lead to practices which interfere with more vital learnings, while the absence of data regarding these latter obscures even the fact that interference has occurred.

In brief, the method by which learning is evaluated influences the way in which that learning takes place, from the point of view of both the teacher and the student. The use of a true-false test covering a textbook determines the way students will read that book. Such a test will often cover a large amount of minutiae, since it is easier to write difficult questions by searching out obscure facts than in any other way. In consequence, students often read, not so much seeking important ideas or those which will be valuable to them, but rather looking for statements which would make good examination items.

The nature of test items themselves has come in for a lot of attention recently. A number of popular books have appeared attacking the claims of test publishers and calling attention to presumed shortcomings of items on objective tests. One of the best known of these publications is *The*

Tyranny of Testing by Banesh Hoffmann.[4] Hoffmann basically maintains that multiple-choice items tend to penalize the creative individual and to reward persons who have a tendency toward a trite, superficial approach. The merit of Hoffmann's attack has been much debated, and there is considerable reason for believing that he selects items to suit his purposes. The overall effect of standardized tests upon students is doubtless not nearly as great or undesirable as he indicates, or else our prestigious universities are loaded with plodders. However, his basic point is representative of an important concept, namely that the effect upon learning of specific types of examination questions should be studied.

One example of an effect upon learning lies in the difference between "recall" and "recognition" items. This difference is somewhat analogous to that which exists between an individual's reading and writing vocabulary. We all know that we can recognize and understand, when we encounter them, many words which we would never use in our own writing or speaking. They are words we can recognize upon demand but cannot recall as needed. An item which calls for the student to recognize what is right or wrong or to determine the better among two or more choices is a different challenge from one which requires him to dredge up from his own memory the knowledge which is needed to answer an open-ended question. An important challenge confronting those who would use evaluation intelligently to influence the curriculum may well be that of determining what information all of us should, so to speak, "carry around" with us, and what information we need only to recognize when the occasion calls for it. Probably we have in the past required too much memorizing on the part of students, particularly of details which often decay rapidly in the mind. We ourselves use our learning in important problem-solving situations invariably by referring to appropriate reference material to support our remembrance.

The emphasis provided by a question furnishes another way in which influence can be viewed. Many items limit themselves to information or routine skills; others deal with increasingly difficult discriminations and judgments, up to some exceedingly comprehensive challenges. The history department of one of our leading institutions once gave as a one-day comprehensive examination to its majors the following: "Write a history of the world to date."

In addition to considering the influence of subject-matter tests, it is both important and difficult to know how to place evaluative and curricular emphasis upon learnings which cut across subject-matter lines. Except for intelligence, most school testing programs are almost exclu-

[4] Banesh Hoffmann. *The Tyranny of Testing.* New York: Crowell-Collier Press, 1962.

sively focused upon subject areas. Still, such outcomes as critical thinking, good work and study habits, and the acquisition of citizenship values
and skills are vital to an informed and effective people. Doubtless, much
learning of this sort takes place, but where is the evidence, and what
systematic efforts are made to determine areas of strength and weakness? Perhaps curriculum committees should be named to study and improve school practices, including evaluation, concerned with specific goals
of education which cut across subject lines.

Perhaps the foregoing discussion has centered too greatly on standardized tests. Doubtless this is because these are so well known that they
afford an easy basis for communication. Our comments, though, are ap-
plicable to *all* kinds of measuring devices and data-gathering procedures.
It is tiresome but necessary from time to time to restate the fact that the
vast majority of tests used in schools, and an even greater percentage
of all data-gathering, represents activities of teachers using devices or
procedures they have constructed, selected or devised on the spur of the
moment. Under such conditions, even more than under the highly visible,
technically skilled circumstances of "testing programs," it is essential to
guard against imbalance or distortion, both conscious and (more probably)
unconscious.

In summary, the existence of measuring devices in some areas but not
in others, the emphases provided by the content of tests, and the nature
of the test challenge itself—all these affect the curriculum and should
be the concern of instructional leaders. The influence of tests and examinations upon the activities of teachers and schools must surely be
enormous, and it is frequently unrecognized.

2. *Have standardized measuring instruments led users to place
greater reliance upon the results they yield than their quality and capacity justify?*

The results of group tests may have a high degree of reliability for
groups, but much lower reliability for individuals. More precisely, the
standard error of group means is smaller than for individual scores. Presumably we use such information only with caution—only as indicators,
and only in conjunction with other data—when dealing with individuals.
In reality, the opposite often occurs: teachers and administrators accept
individual scores from single administrations of group tests with unjus-
tified confidence. Students are sometimes grouped on the basis of evidence
which, though it would not stand up in a law court, is used to justify decisions that often have a greater impact than a court judgment.

Decisions made about boys and girls in school frequently have lifelong consequences. It is crucial that every effort be made to avoid inadequate bases for decision. Curriculum workers have a responsibility
both to inform themselves of the adequacy of data they use and to help

teachers perceive the limits and the values of such data. Test publishers issue warnings in their manuals regarding proper and improper uses of test results and disclaim responsibility for abuses. Yet assessing responsibility is not enough. What is needed is joint action on the part of test producers and school people to plan appropriate lines of action and appropriate safeguards.

Frequently, the change of only one or two responses on a particular instrument can mean switching a student's score from acceptable to unacceptable, or vice versa. "Cutting" scores are established even for such important matters as military service, when a second administration of the test would cause some of the previously rejected examinees to be accepted. In draft deferment, for this reason, either a passing score on the test or a satisfactory record in college is usually accepted.

It is argued that this is true—but unavoidable. The argument states that whenever a line is drawn across the distribution of scores on any one test or on the combined results of several tests, some of those who stand just below the line might stand above it if the testing continued indefinitely. In practice, of course, the testing cannot continue indefinitely, and some lines have to be drawn. It may still be argued, however, that *no* decision about a matter of vital importance to a human being should ever be made on the basis of a single item of information.

Even in colleges and universities, where presumably the greatest understanding exists regarding the imprecise nature of test results, an indefensible use of cutting scores exists. It is intellectually dishonest for anyone to assume greater validity or reliability for an item of data than he knows this item is capable of sustaining. It is professionally incompetent for an individual using a piece of data not to be acquainted with its reliability or standard error. It is indefensible for educational leaders not to give a high priority to in-service education designed to overcome both kinds of inadequacy.

3. Have the existence and availability of published devices discouraged educators from investigating ways of developing or improving their own techniques of evaluation?

There has been a startling absence of creative efforts to devise evaluation instruments and procedures at the local level. There has even been a notable reluctance to establish local norms for standardized tests—in spite of publishers' urging that this be done. Apparently the ready availability of published instruments and supporting services has often stifled local evaluation initiative.

One reason for the lack of such efforts at the local level is the obvious discrepancy between the technical proficiency of the test specialist and that of the field educator—a discrepancy often reinforced by the test specialist himself. The practitioner feels as though he were challenging

General Motors with a machine "made at home with loving hands." It is unfortunate that so many educators have become convinced of their own amateurishness in test construction.

Another reason for a low level of local activity is the lack of training of many teachers. Measurement and evaluation are problem-solving challenges requiring a high order of professional insight as well as knowledge and skill. Often, particularly for teachers prepared in a university or for liberal arts graduates working on a fifth-year program, the only attention paid to the topic of evaluation is that given in a single unit in a single course. Often, too, those who supervise the work of student teachers are not equipped to provide expert assistance in this area. It is not too strong a statement to say that teachers are less well prepared in the field of measurement and evaluation than in any other professional competence.

Concurrently, very little is done in schools through in-service education to improve skills and understanding in measurement and evaluation. Perhaps this is because instructional leaders themselves lack technical know-how; perhaps they do not perceive the deficiencies clearly; perhaps they defer to the expertise of test specialists, and do not possess confidence in their own convictions. Possibly it is because schools are reluctant to spend money for consultants or in-service education. Perhaps the administrators believe that a standardized testing program is an adequate evaluation system. If anything, the more a system uses formal instruments, the more its teachers need help. In any event, little in-service education in this area takes place, and much is needed.

Still another explanation for a dearth of local activity is that many of the areas inadequately covered by published tests are among the most difficult to measure. Teachers are understandably reluctant to try to measure citizenship, motivation or honesty. Indeed, they often consider such items as incidental to their main business of teaching subject content, and would not be interested in trying such measurement if they could. Besides, they say, if specialists avoid such challenges, how can amateurs hope to succeed?

The individualistic tradition of classroom testing also tends to inhibit cooperative work on local evaluation programs. Teachers traditionally make their own quizzes, tests and examinations. As long as such instruments are treated as the individual responsibility of each faculty member and are not considered part of an overall program, teachers will use their energy on their own devices. Further, if they feel defensive about the quality of these, free discussion of tests and their improvement may be inhibited. It is essential that instructional leaders aid teachers with their classroom evaluations and seek to develop coordinated evaluation programs.

4. *Have test publishers or their representatives wielded undesirable amounts and kinds of influence on educational practices, or allowed their own concerns to take precedence over legitimate educational needs?*

It is always difficult for an individual to deal professionally with conflicts of interest. A test publisher or representative has a legitimate desire to see his own products used widely in the schools. Yet he may often be in the uncomfortable position of knowing, or at least suspecting, that a competitor's material would be more appropriate for a given school, or possibly that no existing material is appropriate. The professional representative so reports to the school, even to his own disadvantage. However, not everyone is equally professional or equally insightful. In addition, school people are often not sufficiently sophisticated in measurement to be independent of representatives' recommendations. For both reasons, too much influence may be exercised by a salesman, and sometimes this influence is not conducive to the best interests of the schools.

The better publishers seek to moderate this situation. They select, train and supervise their personnel carefully. They sponsor conference and other in-service education activities; and they produce materials designed to help field educators choose and use tests intelligently. Schools should make at least an equal effort to choose. tests that best fit their own curriculum. The most serious mistakes are made when administrators alone make these decisions. They should be advised by test committees made up of experienced teachers.

5. *Have tests and examinations tended to encourage undesirable forms of competition or comparison among students, teachers, schools, and communities?*

Although test manuals warn against the practice, and professors and textbooks do likewise, there is an unfortunate and widespread tendency for school people and lay citizens to make inferences about the quality of education by comparing test results. Test specialists warn that a difference in scores between two students or groups may be less than the normal variation due to chance, or may be based on a wide range of causes other than a difference in the excellence of the instruction or curriculum. Among possible explanations for such difference could be one or more of the following: difference in students' abilities or in their prior experiences, difference in the circumstances of test administration, difference in the amount of preparation for the test, variation in the instruments' appropriateness for the two situations, different sequences of topics within programs, and different times at which the devices were administered. Indeed, specialists warn that every other possible explanation for differences in scores should be examined and discarded before one reaches the conclusion that there is variation in the quality of the program or instruction.

And yet, the tendency is to make such judgments. School superintendents, boards of education, and school patrons boast about the superior performance of their students on standardized tests, or they criticize if the opposite occurs. Further, examinations concerned with college entrance or selective service lead students into a fever of competitive activity. Competition itself is not presumed to be necessarily undesirable, and certainly life includes competition which students must learn to accept. However, competition should be fair, should match persons with reasonably equal capacities to deal with the challenges they face, and should be oriented to educational goals of the highest priority. It is questionable that our present situation achieves these standards.

Test specialists have long urged that school districts develop their own norms and use test results as profiles for diagnosis. That is to say, charting performance in several subjects can enable the teacher to see in what areas a student or class is doing best or poorest, or in which the most or least progress has been made. This is not the same as using individual items or subdivisions of an instrument for purposes of diagnosis. Although the latter might yield some useful clues, it should not be regarded as definitive, since the reliability of the parts of a test is usually too low for dependable conclusions to be drawn.

However, little effort is made to establish local norms and diagnoses, even among our larger, richer districts. Possibly this is because local educators prefer to leave such matters to specialists. Maybe it is because test people themselves have unintentionally implied that the comprehensive type of service they provide leaves little or nothing for the schools to do (athough this is certainly not what the test people say). It is clear that local educators have at least as much responsibility to maintain their own evaluation specialists and programs, or at least to obtain effective consultant service, as they have to provide any other forms of educational leadership.

The curriculum director or one of his staff should take responsibility for leadership in measurement and evaluation. Each school district should employ, either full- or part-time, an individual who is technically proficient and who knows the problems of the instructional program and the teacher. Ideally, there should be persons familiar with the problems of measurement in all areas of the curriculum, possibly obtained on a consultant basis. Principally, however, there should be someone close to the instructional program who bears responsibility for improving evaluation in the district, and for seeing to it that evaluation is an aid rather than a hindrance to learning.

Such a person could help provide in-service opportunities and assist teachers with their own measurement activities and devices, to make these as valid and reliable as possible. He might take as his ultimate responsibility that of developing a full-fledged, well-balanced, comprehensive program of evaluation and measurement, within which the standardized testing program would take its part, but within which all other measurement and evaluation activities of the school would also be included.

6. *Has the use of standardized tests brought undue pressures for conformity and uniformity?*

Many states have organized state-wide testing programs; college entrance and selective service activities have encouraged widespread use of examinations; and increasingly there is the imperative to build "sound" evaluation procedures into proposals for federally supported projects. At present, there is debate regarding a proposed national assessment of education.

Two conflicting values are involved, each of them legitimate. On the one hand are those who maintain that an activity sponsored generously by the public should be willing to present evidence regarding the quality of its product, and should be willing to undertake systematic and comprehensive evaluation. On the other hand are those who believe that the great strength of American education lies in its local control; these persons believe that the maximum of individual freedom for teachers is our best guarantee of continued improvement. Supporters of the latter position hold that any widespread testing program might dull the edge of growth. Supporters of the first point of view believe that local control can be converted into a license for mediocrity if its results are not carefully evaluated.

It seems reasonably evident that the present national assessment of education has been seeking to avoid the extremes of both positions. A careful effort is being made to obtain a picture of the present state of education throughout the nation without providing opportunity for pressure to be exerted against individual schools or communities. However, it is still not clear whether or not an activity such as this might be the opening wedge for a more massive attempt at evaluation, and one that could lead to uniformity and conformity. Neither is it clear whether the philosophy behind the national assessment program represents a fully representative planning procedure or instead a belief in planning by an elite group.[5]

It has been recognized that some experimental programs are not fairly evaluated through measuring devices designed to deal with more traditional curricular forms. For example, the first students who took the

[5] For a further discussion of "National Assessment," see Appendix A, p. 243-53.

experimental physics course developed by the Physical Science Study Committee made lower scores on the College Entrance Examination Board's examination in physics than did those of equal aptitude who were in conventional courses. Because of the prestige and national scope of this experimental program the scores of these students were adjusted to the level predicted by their aptitude scores, and a more suitable examination was prepared for the next group. But have similar safeguards been provided for students in other experiments, undertaken without the same degree of prestige behind them? Probably school districts undertaking anything very unusual should devise special measuring instruments and procedures.

Certainly public education cannot tolerate a situation in which experimentation and improvement can take place only with difficulty and in the face of resistance and rigidity. It is therefore important that schools, colleges and testmakers agree on procedures and policies which will enable thoughtful, conscientious experimentation to take place without the hazard that students and districts may be penalized. College admissions officers and regional accrediting associations both assert their willingness to modify any procedures that interfere with the opportunities of local schools to experiment, and test publishers affirm that such experimentation rarely influences adversely a student's scores on standardized tests.

Nevertheless the fact remains that these statements are viewed with skepticism by local educators, and external evaluations are seen as discouragements to change and experimentation. We must insure that examinations do not become straitjackets, yet we must also not use examinations as an excuse for inaction. Those who are most concerned with the supposed restrictive effects of examinations are often those who may have no original ideas that could possibly be jeopardized.

The Challenge

The foregoing discussion leads to one major conclusion and one basic challenge. Evaluation is central to curriculum development, and its influence must be better understood and used.

Evaluation is central to curriculum improvement because it is close to the emotional areas that motivate much educational activity. Curriculum improvement implies change in the habits of people. Habit alteration is tension-producing, as anyone knows, for example, who has tried to stop smoking. Emotion may be considered the motive power or force which is channeled and directed by our intellect. Often, then, curriculum development demands that feelings, as well as insights, be influenced.

Evaluation influences motivation and thereby affects instructional programs. Probably no program is really altered as long as it is evaluated in the same manner. It is equally likely that change in evaluation processes will inevitably lead to change in the curriculum, whether or not such change is intended.

The challenge comes in knowing how to study, understand and use the role of evaluation in curriculum improvement. This volume constitutes an examination of this challenge, particularly in areas concerned with evaluating students and programs. Some of the directions in which instructional leaders can work are the following:

1. Course grades must be replaced with something more informative, more diagnostic, and more harmonious with students' own motivations.

2. Instructional leaders and testmakers should join in (a) finding safeguards against undesirable practices, (b) encouraging better use of tests through greater insight and understanding on the part of field educators, and (c) engaging in continuing communication intended to insure that instruments meet instructional needs, and meet *all* such needs.

For example, some of the changes we should consider making include dropping the name and the whole concept of the I.Q. and getting rid of grade-equivalent scores. Both of these have led to more heedless acceptance of unsound concepts and to more spurious certainty than they have contributed in usefulness. Even if their past contribution was more useful than not, the time has come to "put aside childish things" and develop more mature conceptions.

3. School districts should regain control of their own evaluation programs by (a) employing consultants who are knowledgeable in both measurement and instruction, (b) developing local evaluation programs which integrate all forms of evaluation used locally, (c) using standardized instruments in terms of local needs and norms rather than making regional or national comparisons, and (d) undertaking in-service education activities to improve the evaluation practices of local educators.

4. Instructional leaders should study the whole problem of interaction between evaluation and curriculum development, and should plan ways to insure adequate feedback of evaluation into the program. Consideration should be given to the effect of evaluation on students, teachers, administrators, and curriculum workers, and plans should include systematic and continuing attention to all major objectives of the educational program.

In brief, the challenge is one of studying and dealing with something as complex as life itself. Indeed, as John Dewey stated, education *is* life.

Understanding the role of evaluation in education is no less a task than learning why men act as they do, how they can learn to act differently, and how we can aid this learning. The task of evaluation is no less than this, and we cannot settle for less.

Part Two

Evaluation and the
Teaching-Learning Process

We ARE all so used to thinking of evaluation in terms of judging and grading and testing and measuring that it is hard to shake off this set of our minds. Nevertheless, in this Part Two, we do ask you to shake it off. More precisely, we ask you to suspend it for a while.

We are quite aware that there are real needs for testing and measurement and the systematic compiling of records, and in Part Three we shall face up to these needs directly; at that point we shall try to demonstrate how the necessary jobs can be done without the undesirable side effects we see in the present system. But, for the moment, we want to push all that aside in order to take a deeper look. For a little while let's act as if we simply did not have the whole superstructure of assigning grades, granting credits, filling out transcripts, etc. Let's assume that all we have before us is a learner —or a group of learners—and a teacher, and that the only question is what will contribute most to the learning and the teaching.

Stripping the problem down like this permits us to conduct an inquiry into the essential nature of the process. We shall look at it first in terms of the student—what part evaluation plays in his becoming. To analyze this we have found it necessary to go even beyond shaking off concerns for grades and credits, etc. We have had to go outside the schooling situation altogether, to ask more fundamental questions: Why does the human organism learn at all? What forces impel a person to a lifetime of becoming? How does his own ceaseless evaluation shape this becoming? To deal with such questions we have developed a construct which might be called a theory of learning but might better, perhaps, be called a theory of becoming. It is not the only possible construct or theory. Not everyone will agree with it, or agree that it is totally adequate. It has been a matter of some controversy within the Committee preparing this book. But its set of assumptions does put into perspective the cease-less involvement of every human self in a constant aware-ing and evaluating which guides the way he acts, learns and becomes.

The ensuing chapter then goes directly at the teacher's use of evaluation. Again we ask you to assume for the moment that the teacher is not driven by any external pressure to produce grades, and all that. His problem is simply to maximize his effectiveness in teaching the children or adolescents he has before him. His first concern, then, is for diagnosis—clear, precise diagnosis that keeps him aware of all the variables that matter and helps him know how to go on. Yet inevitably he has another kind of concern, too: how to handle the whole process so that, for the learner, it leads to challenge rather than threat, to encouragement rather than defeat, to a richer, more valid self-image rather than need-distortion, and to the involvement of the learner in a cooperative, ongoing inquiry rather than to imposition by the teacher. The problem is not so simple as merely getting a wealth of precise "objective" data; there is a human problem, too.

We hope we do not sound as if we mean to take the reader by the hand and lead him step-by-step. But Part Two does go into questions a bit different from those one might expect in a volume on evaluation. If it is to serve its purpose, it is important that the reader be willing to hold in suspension for a while a host of customary "practical" concerns that have already dictated our actions far too long.

3

Learning and Evaluation

Rodney A. Clark and Walcott H. Beatty

THERE are many ways of looking at learning but the understandings
that grow out of them are often hard to translate into classroom procedures. Mechanistic stimulus-response explanations of learning have never
appealed to most teachers. Neither have laboratory findings about conditioning, trial and error, reinforcement, extinction, reward, etc., which have
seemed to have little to do with the way boys and girls really act in the
classroom. Most teachers now know that older notions of training the
mind, mental discipline, and transfer of training were based on a kind of
mythology. However, while these notions were in command they generated
methods of teaching and ideas about school organization which have been
in practice so long that they now seem natural and sensible; thus the
procedures linger on, long after their rationale has faded. Besides, many
teachers have come to feel that it is not their province to try to understand learning, that whatever the mystery of the process, the teacher's
job is to teach and the student's job is to learn.

Evaluation Is Essential to the Learning Process

Coming into prominence recently is a different approach to explaining
how humans learn, one which takes into consideration the learner's motivation, his values, the uniqueness of his perceptions, and the social nature
of man. This kind of explanation ties directly into the activities of live
boys and girls in a classroom and therefore makes more sense to teachers.
And it makes it clear that all learning involves evaluation. Let us briefly
summarize one of these new descriptions of the learning process, which
may be called a self-concept theory of learning (Wilhelms *et al.*, 11).

Each person is continually developing more and more of his potential
self. All his life he is purposely becoming what he believes will most ex-

press his self. He is not the circumstantial, mechanical pawn of external forces. He is not the accidental result of what happens to him. Man is a choice-maker! He strives and believes and hopes and cares. His becoming is in the direction of effectiveness in the best way he can define effectiveness. Child or adult, at any moment of his life, he is doing his utmost to be his most effective self. Bruner (1) has discussed this in connection with the role of language in development, and the researches of Piaget (Flavell, 3) give concrete examples of how this development proceeds. Through such development man transcends the limitations of his biological inheritance.

It Is Man's "Nature" To Evaluate

As a living organism, man inherits the potential to become involved in a great variety of processes. He will grow according to a more or less predictable pattern. He will have the same kind of arms and legs and teeth and hair as other humans. He will probably walk upright, talk, use tools—because he is equipped to develop these skills just as are the other humans with whom he lives. He will probably develop the ability to discriminate sensations of pressure, temperature, pain, light, sound, taste and smell. His brain will enable him to remember, to plan, to reason, to abstract, to conceptualize, to understand far past the capacity of any other animal, though his mental ability will not be exactly like that of any other human. He will be able to process data at amazing rates and in amazing amounts—and develop computers to do it even faster—without yet knowing surely how he does it. And he will be able to learn from the data after they are processed. He will become hungry when he needs food, thirsty when his body needs liquid, and he will desire sexual expression.

Man is, of course, limited in his potential, too; but, compared to his assets, his limitations are so few, and he is so creative in compensating them, that they hardly matter. All these organically based assets may be termed man's "process potentials." He does not choose to have these process potentials, but he does choose what he will do with them, how he will develop them. Each man is born with the potential to be a fully functioning human, but he expresses this potential after the fashion of his own choices.

There is a reason why man never ceases his efforts to become more effective. Unlike other animals, he is born with little in the way of automatic, built-in manners of dealing with his environment. He must build his relations with the world. He keeps feeling his way into his physical and social environment, trying out ways of relating to it. And he is the most powerful of all animals in his potential to learn the meanings of his experiences. He not only keeps trying ways of doing things but he also constantly judges the results. Experiments in which human subjects are deprived of sight, sounds, tactile cues, tastes or movement indicate that when a person is cut off from a "real" environment to relate to, he tends to hallucinate some relationship to which to attend (Hebb, 7). Thus, it is the "nature" of man to relate and constantly to test and judge the results of the relating. If we think of this constant testing and judging as evaluation, then, in an abstract sense, evaluation is the process of *making meaning out of experience.* It is an essential part of the learning process; for no one could learn from his experiences except by utilizing the feedback from these experiences and converting it into meaning for the future.

Becoming

Through his efforts to evaluate his effectiveness in the world, each man's becoming is unique. No two people see "effectiveness" as the same goal.

At the same time, people share certain kinds of experiences as they mature physically and socially. From the way each person uniquely knows these shared experiences he learns to value certain kinds of relations with his world.[1] Thus, he expands his first responses to being mothered to a great variety of ways in which he wants to be loved, to share a closeness, to be important to someone. However we define acceptance, we all test our effectiveness in some terms of acceptance.

We also want to be coping, skillful users of the things in our sur-roundings—even builders or creators of things. We grow up in a culture that supplies us tools and processes for effectiveness. We want to be able to use this heritage, which is a part of our environment. We want to make the physical world contribute to our well being. We want to be unafraid in the world.

At another level of aspiration, we want to push further and further into the realm of knowledge. We want to know what the world means to us, and what we mean to the world. From a direct, one-to-one relation between ourselves and things, we move to the examination of relation-ships between the things themselves. At first we need to know, "How am I related to *this?*" and "How am I related to *that?*" Then we must continue to explore, "How is *this* related to *that,* and how does the result-ing relationship affect me?" So, from what we know, we reach toward expanding relations, concepts and integrations. At the same time, we must

[1] Throughout this chapter the term "world" is used to indicate the environment with which the child interacts, including things and people and the culture. Thus, at times, "world" may refer to a tiny factor of the total "real" environment; at other times it may refer to something large-scale.

continually establish new firsthand relations so there is an ever-expanding new basis for further knowledge.

Through each man's efforts to express his effectiveness, as he weaves together meaning from his experiences, there threads the ultimate question: "What am I? What is the scheme of things that yields me significance?" For each human, his becoming goes on and on. He is always expressing what is changing for him. He is always in the process of building a new, more effective relationship with the world.

The Self-Relating-with-the-World

From his very first efforts to investigate what is going on, an infant begins to develop a conception of his self-relating-with-the-world. Everything he does elicits a response in the world. People and things nurture him, irritate him, attract him. Some phenomena he can control, but others are independent of him. The world is dynamic, eventful, changing. All these interactions help to define what he is in the world. The infant learns about up and down, far and near, hard and soft, smooth and rough, hot and cold. He learns these meanings because he is acted upon by the world and he must interact. Knowledge comes to him as he gradually interprets his experiences, and each piece of data has meaning only in reference to himself. He must learn to differentiate pain, fear, anger, pleasure and love; and each emotion takes on meaning in terms of what happens to his person as he matures.

The child develops identity as he experiences separateness from other selves and other things. (Perhaps it would be more true of some cultures to say that identity is the sense of being different or unique, not necessarily separate.) The child learns his separateness, or uniqueness, by being dependent, and probably this is the beginning of his realization that being a self is a complicated business. The world known to each person is unique since he is the only one who has evaluated experience in just his way. Much of what happens to one person is much like what happens to other people, but each person uniquely develops the meaning of what happens, because each is his own evaluator. The world of each self is, then, rather like the world of other selves who have had similar experiences. The similarities and differences depend on how the individual evaluates the experiences, not alone on the experiences. The extent of similarity and difference is not fully communicable.

For each of us, then, our sum of experiences has meaning as it relates to what we are trying to become. We know we are selves who (a) relate to people and are supported by people, more or less; (b) use things more or less skillfully and know what things are useful; (c) extend the self's meaning until all the self is being expressed in a full relationship with the world; and (d) make our own choices in becoming, although the self's becoming contributes to a larger organization of meanings of which the self is a part. Adolescents and children, more than adults, are still beginning to know their selves in these areas. Nevertheless, each child in school has some concept of himself-in-the-world which includes the meanings he has developed from these four kinds of experiences.

Concept of Adequacy

These same experiences also supply the data from which one builds a concept of adequacy. As a person learns what he can do to things and what things can do to him and to each other, there is a parallel learning about what a more effective relationship would be. The learner realizes, "*If* I could do this, I could control that. *If* I could become this, I could overcome that." As he is relating to the world around him, he senses that there is potential for greater self-expression, for fuller becoming, *if* he could alter the relating somehow. By the time a child, say at six or eight years of age, has a concept as to what kind of self-relating-with-the-world he *is,* he has also built a concept of the kind of self he *needs to be* in order to be effective (as he conceives effectiveness).

The concepts of self and of adequacy are, of course, both ever-changing. In a circular effect, a person's perception of the self-relating-with-the-world grows from his efforts to become effective, while at the same time his becoming self is the basis for his concept of adequacy. Each, by way of his unique definitions, builds a set of standards so he can say to himself: (a) I am worthy, valuable, lovable, as is being shown in my relations with people. (b) I am using things skillfully, effectively, as is shown by my successful coping with things. (c) I am fully interacting with the world; I am counting for something; what I mean in the world leads to behavior, is tangible in the world, so that the world and I are fully, freely, satisfyingly open to each other. (d) I am autonomous, fully determining my becoming in line with my understanding of the scheme of things. These criteria of adequacy are stated in the order in which they probably develop. But some aspect of each will be critical in even a young child's evaluation of his becoming.

Harmonizing Perceived Discrepancies

As has been pointed out, the driving power for the process of becoming is the person's need to be effective. The learner evaluates his effectiveness by comparing his self as he perceives it to his concept of what would constitute adequacy. Whenever the self-system perceives that its relationship with the world meets its concept of adequacy, the system strives to maintain the relationship. If, however, the relationship does not harmonize with what is defined as adequate, then the system must strive to alter the relationship toward adequacy. The greater the discrepancy perceived between the relationship with the world and the concept of adequacy, the greater will be the force organized in the system to harmonize the difference. This is the general explanation of human motivation.

Perhaps it should be stated that the sense of discrepancy need not always be conscious, and that the strategy for harmonizing a discrepancy need not always be thoughtful or deliberate. Sometimes it is, as when a student says, "If I'm going to be a teacher, I need to be able to write better, so I'm going to take another composition course." But much more commonly, the image of what would constitute adequacy, the sense of inadequacy, and the "plan" for remediation may all lie deep in the background, unnoticed. The whole process may go on below the level of deliberate or conscious thought—but that does not make it less real or powerful.

Some schemes for explaining human motivation have bogged down in the effort to provide an appropriate place for organismic drives (Cofer and Appley, 2). As discussed previously, the human inherits mechanisms which automatically signal the system about organic needs. In the becoming of the individual human, however, the automatic signaling about needs takes on meaning only as the self-system relates the satisfaction of organic needs to the whole complex of adequacy. Human motivation is not solely toward satisfying organic needs but toward the development and maintenance of satisfying relations with the world in terms of becoming adequate, which, of course, subsumes or sublimates the satisfaction of organic needs.

At any one stage in an individual's life his concept of adequacy is made up of attitudes and goals similar to those which have been labeled as the "developmental tasks" of that stage of life (Havighurst, 6; Tryon, 10). In other words, adolescents define adequacy as becoming more independent, deepening their same-sex, peer relations, becoming attractive to members of the opposite sex, and so forth. Children include the same kinds of relationships in their concept of adequacy, but they define the processes in different terms. That is, they also define adequacy partly as becoming more independent. But they tend to define independence in terms of skillful control of themselves in physical relations with the environment while adolescents define it in terms of dominance-submissive relations with people and "authority." Nevertheless, every child, adolescent and adult, each in his unique way, has a developing concept of adequacy and is striving to harmonize specific discrepancies between this concept and his perception of his self-in-the-world.

While patterns of motivation are shared by people at certain stages of development, each individual's behavior springs from his unique evaluation of whether or not things "are" as they "should be." Whenever there is a discrepancy, it must be harmonized.

The most common discrepancy with which the self-system must deal is the special case in which some aspect of the perceived world is appearing not to be in line with what the self has come to expect of the environment. The concept of adequacy demands that the data feeding into the system "fit"—the system has to trust itself. Therefore, if things move which "should" be stable, if things bend which "should" be rigid, if things fade which "should" be permanent, if things disappear, or pop into being, or turn into something else—all these phenomena must be explainable in the self-system or the self cannot form an effective relationship with them.

Other discrepancies which are recognized in the process of becoming are more intrinsic to the self-system. For instance, if a person begins to feel that he is not being accepted by others, he must try to be more acceptable. If one realizes that he lacks the skill to accomplish what he is trying to do, he must strive to become more skillful. If one begins to lack identity, he will try more to express his individuality, to seek the full meaning of self-ness by testing the world with it.

We all strive to harmonize these kinds of discrepancies between our perceived selves and our concepts of adequacy, but each makes the effort according to his own unique definitions. What constitutes being acceptable, skillful or meaningful is built for each of us from our particular becoming. We grow in a particular culture; we are exposed to certain models; we have some tools available, and not others; there are special expectancies, demands and sanctions which we share with other people. So we are never alone in our becoming. We can be somewhat understood and somewhat understanding. We can be helped and we can be helpful. We must participate in social efforts. And we must communicate. We value most of the same kinds of things as do the people with whom we live. Yet there is still difference in our behaviors, as well as similarity.

Motivational States

Whenever a discrepancy is recognized between the self-relating-with-the-world and the concept of adequacy, becoming effective demands that the discrepancy be resolved. The demand for resolution is expressed in the self-system as a motivational state.

A motivational state is made up of organic hungers and hormone-controlled reactions such as alertness, fear, anger, attraction or repulsion. This organic basis, however, is thickly overlaid with complexly organized associations, some preverbal, some unreal, some distorted, all stepping up the original organic charge. The overlay is, of course, unique to the individual, who has drawn it from his own uniquely experienced self and his concept of adequacy. The importance of the organic basis remains, however, because it is through the organic mechanism that all the forces of the organism are brought to bear on the resolution of the motivational state, even though the result is a matter of meaning and concept rather than a physical, or only organic, satisfaction.

Again, though definitions are private and extremely varied, it can be expected that each person has motivational states "like" those of other people. These will be of four kinds: The self-system will be motivated to preserve relations as they are, to change relations, to explore, or to express.

When there is harmony between the self and the concept of adequacy —when things are going as they should be going—the system preserves and protects what it has. Any threat to break down this balance produces a *maintaining* motivational state. The self defends itself from threat or pain. It provides and safeguards. It may try to ignore change. In a special case it may hide or run away, to preserve or continue as much of the existing relationship as possible.

When the self and the concept of adequacy are not in harmony, then the system must exert energy toward change. This is the *changing state.* Aggression, competition, conquering and taking may be ways of changing the relationship with the world in an attempt to make the self-system more adequate. In some situations, and particularly for some people, adequacy is largely defined in terms of the *things* one needs in order to be adequate. The self-system may develop all kinds of skills to cope with the world in order to change the relationship to a more satisfying one. Usually, in these cases, the world is changed to better satisfy the self. In some other cases the self has to change to better fit the world as it is perceived to be.

The *maintaining* state, described above, is aroused when the self's "defenses" are threatened. The *changing* state, on the other hand, is aroused when the self's power or possessions are threatened. There are two other motivational states which come into effect when there is no sensation of threat. Many recognized discrepancies, especially unexpected phenomena in the perceived world, arouse the state of *curiosity.* In this state the self finds some satisfaction in exploration *per se,* but the resolution of the motivational state comes when collected data can be fitted together to explain what was previously surprising. When curiosity is open, not entangled in defenses, it may be the most powerful of motivational states for involving the self in new experiences. Under its influence, newness, unexpectedness, strangeness—even the bizarre—is not threatening to the self-system.

The remaining motivational state is *expressiveness.* There are many recognized discrepancies in the self-system which can be resolved only as the self is made known to the world, as the self is tested for meaning by being given to some relationship.

For instance, the need to express love and to expand fully the loving relationship may come from the motivational state of expressiveness. For humans, even that part of love which is sexual activity has meaning in the self-system which moves sexual activity from its function as coping with an organic drive. Like any other behavior, sexual expression is motivated by the necessity to make the perceived self adequate. Sexual activity could express continuing satisfactory relations, could express a motivation to change, and certainly could express curiosity. But love, as more than sexual activity, as the need to complete oneself in the effectiveness of another, comes from the motivational state of expressiveness.

Teaching is another activity which often comes from the motivation to express the self fully. Teaching as "expressing" makes one self helpful to another as the teacher makes his relation to a learner part of the significant experience of the learner.

The need to paint, compose, write, design or perform creatively largely springs from the effort of the self to be more complete by externalizing certain feelings, meanings, values, and thereby "knowing" them better. As the expressed aspects of the self become tangible in the world, the relationship of the self with the world is fuller. The product of the expression is not intended to change the world—although it does— but as the relations between self and world are put in form to be touched, heard, seen, the relationships are more richly experienced. Appreciation of other people's artistic expression serves the same purpose. One's self is clarified as it is examined by relating to the tangible statements of others. To participate in the flame of sunset, the tranquillity of a lake, the loneliness of a mountain peak, or the violence of a stormy sea is to know the self more fully expressed. In all these activities the spiraling need of the system to experience the world → in order to better know the self → in order to better know the world for greater effectiveness → builds up tremendous force behind the motivational state of expressiveness.

At any particular moment a person is acting out of a complex of motivational states. He is trying to resolve a variety of discrepancies at the same time. The important thing here is not that we know what motivational states are moving a person at a given time, but that we recognize that the forces exist.

Through a continual process of evaluation, dissonance in the self-system is revealed and generates motivational states which organize organic forces toward resolution. We should realize that, whatever we see a person doing, there is a driving need being expressed. The self *must* resolve its motivational states; and every act is, at the time, the best thing the self can find to do to become more effective. Whether we approve of a person's activity or not, we must accept his *need* to be acting toward his definition of effectiveness.

Strategies for Becoming

Although a person chooses each of his acts purposefully, he builds from his perceptions of the world and his concept of adequacy certain continuing criteria which enable him to make choices in a sort of pattern, without starting the evaluation from scratch each time. He organizes strategies for becoming. He defines certain kinds of satisfactions as appropriate to his self-system and tends not to consider others. He does this in two ways.

Many persons structure a way of determining what is "right" and what is "wrong" by resting in an external authority such as a father figure, a church or tradition. When faced with a choice of activities, such persons will select the activity dictated by the authority.

Some persons who do not accept an external authority for their criteria of "right" and "wrong," nevertheless allow a set of criteria to become fixed. From their own experiences they build their own authority. They then react to new situations in the same manner as the persons who take their criteria from an external authority. What they will do in the new situation is determined by prejudged patterns that may or may not apply to the situation.

There is another orientation toward criteria that is quite different. Some people seek to draw out of the data coming from each new situation an interpretation of "right" and "wrong" which is specific to that situation. They do not carry prejudged ways of responding into a new relationship, but determine "effectiveness" anew with each expanding experience. This orientation allows the greatest freedom to discover one's potential for effectiveness; one's values remain related to reality, and experience is more richly consistent with the self-system.

Besides developing these kinds of orientations, a person also patterns strategies for becoming by adopting long-range goals and by accepting roles. One might, for instance, decide to become a teacher; then many kinds of choices would fall in line. An adolescent's determination to be a "clown," a "hood," "one of the gang," or a "student" is the adolescent's strategy for becoming. It directs his choices in the same way that "being a teacher" directs the choices of an adult.

A person's strategies for becoming are close to his everyday behavior. If we know a person for any length of time, we can begin to predict the pattern of his activities. But this is not as important as is our recognition that a person's seemingly varied activities are not whimsical or random. According to his evaluation of his becoming, his activities fit together in a pattern leading to effectiveness. There is strategy, purpose, long-range planning, behind all that each of us does—even though we may rarely be aware of it, and never be aware of some of it.

Choosing Effective Actions

Because the self-system is in the process of becoming, it is involved in an *action space* that is developing as part of the process. A self's action space is all that part of the physical world, the people, society, expectancies and roles with which the self is in relationship at a given moment. The action space exists according to the self's perception of it; but the action space is nevertheless "real"; there is a "real" world to be perceived.

In choosing to act toward more effectiveness in the world, each person must choose an act in the action space as he understands it. If curious, he will try to explore the action space; if satisfied, try to maintain it; if not satisfied, try to change it; if acquisitive, try to take something from the action space; if protective, try to defend against the action space or flee from it; if expressive, try to make some aspect of his self tangible in the action space. The specific act he devises to carry out any of these motives depends on the self's understanding of the action space and how to relate to it.

No self ever knows all the possibilities of relationships that are the "real" potential of an action space. The self's action space has become, out of the self's experience in a culture, a given life style, a particular family. A male self knows one kind of action space while a female self knows another. The strength, health, and body type of the self have to some extent determined what the self could learn about actions. No self learns all that could be gleaned from each experience. Nevertheless, the self chooses the act which according to its best guess is the act most appropriate to a strategy of becoming. But the act must be chosen from those available in the self's understanding of the action space.

Acting

The aspects of self which have been described cannot be observed directly. They are all inferred from the observed behavior of the individual. They are hypothetical constructs which are intended to help us make sense of the observable physical and verbal actions of a person. Our only source for understanding an individual is the interpretations we make of these actions.

The acts of an individual are more complex and provide more data than an untrained observer realizes. It is possible to see and analyze behavior at at least two levels: in terms of the *content* of the act and the *intent* of the act. We all respond to some parts of the content of another's act. We hear the words a child speaks or we see him push another child. This is what we generally respond to in terms of what we have already learned as to the meaning of such words or actions. Such judgments rarely give us any understanding of why the child spoke or acted as he did. Yet, unless we have some understanding of what the child was trying to achieve by his actions, it is impossible to be sure we are making a helpful response.

A fundamental postulate of psychology is that all behavior is caused. Within our framework here, the cause of an act is the intent which lay behind it. In order to infer this intent we must pay attention to the context within which the act occurs and especially to aspects of the content of the act which are frequently ignored. Some of these aspects are tone of voice, gestures, bodily tension, changes in the skin coloring such as blushing, facial expressions, and the choice of particular words. In evaluating this content we are asking: Within this context, what was the person trying to accomplish by this behavior? The answer we come up with will determine the response we make, and this response becomes the consequence, or one of the consequences which the person experiences as a result of his act.

The importance of this point cannot be too strongly stressed for teachers. Through observing more of the total content of a child's actions, a teacher can evaluate the meaning of these actions more accurately and then make a more appropriate response. It is the teacher's response to the child which determines what the teacher helps the child learn. A child learns the relationship between his act and the consequences which follow. By being able to change these consequences, through responding differently, the teacher has the power to influence learning.

Aware-ing

The meaning of the consequences of action feeds back into the perceived self because the system is constantly *aware-ing* the environment in order to determine how the system is fitting.

Aware-ing, we feel, is a useful label for an otherwise unnamed process. It holds, in one term, ideas about readiness to relate, attending to stimuli, processing data, finding relations, and making unique meaning from experience. It is the process by which the self system gives value to experience. As such a process, it includes "evaluation."

The aware-ing part of the process of becoming is complicated and certainly not altogether understood. As has been pointed out, the organic process potential includes equipment to process data coming into the self-system all the time from the environment. The data about sights, sounds, smells, textures and so forth, enter the system as single sense modes and by the time they reach the higher nervous system they have been simplified to the "outline" of information and then somehow stored.

Before the data from the environment can be used by the self-system, however, the data must take on meaning by being fitted to what is already perceived by the system. Nothing can come into the system that is not consistent with what is there. The addition can be new or different, but it cannot deny previously developed meaning. It can conflict with previously developed meaning only if there is an existing basis for dealing with the conflict. New data can be accepted only if they·fit, clarify, augment or change consistently the old meanings in the system. As information, data may be stored indefinitely and remain only a potential for meaning until the self needs them or discovers their pertinence creatively.

Some data will never become meaningful. Somewhat as the self-system expedites becoming by organizing long-range strategies, the system also builds defenses which keep certain definitions of the perceived self or of adequacy from being brought under examination. Certain elements of becoming are blocked off and remain static because at some phase of development the self was too severely disrupted. The system maintains these defenses by refusing to fit data to them. Information which would cause the self to change such a defense is not admitted to a relationship and therefore does not acquire meaning in the system.

For example, most of us have built defenses which protect us from examining our relationships with authority figures. This is because many of our attitudes toward authority were formed in infancy, before we had verbal symbols for expressing relations with parents and other adults. Whatever our relations with adults were at the time, we needed the relationship too much to dare question it. The infantile procedures which we developed to avoid examining how we felt about authority at that stage have lingered on, because we cannot examine them.

In occupations other than teaching it might not matter so much if a person never reexamined his infantile reactions toward bosses and other authority figures. In teaching, however, the role of authority in the teacher-pupil relation is forced into prominence, and the relation is part of what every child must be learning if he is to be effective. Most teachers deal with each problem of authority relations by the same prejudged, impersonal devices. Since these stereotyped reactions do not recognize the individuality of given children, they do not help children learn. They may actually constitute areas in which the teacher is refusing to allow children to learn.

It is not our intention in this discussion to belabor the description of aware-ing. We wish only to make it clear that in this phase also the key to becoming is a judging, comparing, guessing, estimating, testing, fitting —in short, evaluating.

Learning

Man, unlike other animals, must build his relationship with the world into which he was born (Fromm, 4). Through their reflexes and instincts other animals are integrated with nature and must only engage in rather simple learnings about their innate skills in relationship to their surroundings. Man, on the other hand, is both of nature and outside of nature. He is born with the minimum internal integratiôn necessary to stay alive, but even his survival needs must be met by others. He must learn how to relate to nature in such a way as to survive and continually transcend his biological beginnings.

This learning is a three-step process. He must first learn what he is, then he learns what he can become. Finally he learns the means by which this can be achieved. There are important differences between these two kinds of learnings. Learning what one is and can become involves taking on goals and purposes and giving direction to the general motivation to survive and find satisfaction.

Learning the means of achieving these goals involves skills and knowledge which make possible psychological growth. The first kind of learning will be called *intrinsic* and the second will be called *instrumental*. Intrinsic learnings become the criteria for selecting the instrumental learning to be achieved.

Instrumental Learning

Even when processed data become meaningful as relating to the self's becoming, it is not necessarily true that learning has taken place. Data that become meaningful because they aid the relating of the ongoing process as it is already known are necessary to maintain the system on course; but they do not expand the potential of becoming. However, some data can fit the system if some altering of the system is allowed, and this brings new meaning. This is learning. The system finds a new part of the world to relate to, acquires a more skillful way to relate, recognizes a new approach to becoming effective, or defines effectiveness differently. Learning always is change in the system.

For example, if the consequences of acting feed through the system so that new choices of action are recognized in the action space, then instrumental learning has occurred. The self-system is more effective because it recognizes more ways to relate to its environment than it previously knew. The greater the variety of choices of action that are open to the system, the more specifically the complexities of motivational states can be resolved.

It is an instrumental learning, nevertheless, if the action space is perceived as having previously unrecognized limits on choices of action. The self-system "knows" that in òrder to achieve effectiveness it must use the world differently than it had intended before the constriction for action was revealed.

Besides recognizing that there are more, or fewer, choices of action available than it had known about, the self-system may also recognize that there are more skillful ways to perform the available actions. Each of us by very early in life has built an amazing repertoire of intermeshing skills, and from these we go on all our lives mastering more and more skills. We do not stop to realize that a large part of what we are learning is the mastery of a better way of doing something we can already do. For instance, consider mathematical calculations. If a person can add, he can solve laboriously any problem involving multiplication. But this would not be an efficient way to deal with quantities. Therefore, most of us learn the special way of adding which we call multiplying. We are still doing the same thing, but we are using more appropriate skills.

A third kind of instrumental learning grows out of any change in the understanding of the consequences of action. Curious children spend many hours just exploring the concept of "consequences."

—Tip over the first domino in the row and see what happens to the others in the long curving line!

—Hit the board here and watch the marbles jump over there!

—Things are related.

—There are forces.

—There is more happening than at first appeared.

The child has a great deal more control over the world if he considers more the consequences of his actions.

The expanding recognition of consequences of action, however, does not grow just because phenomena are obvious. It took man a long time to master the use of fire. A child can sail a paper plate, but we are just now understanding the potential of the airfoil. The recognition of consequences must be part of the resolution of a motivational state or the sensing of data about phenomena will not become meaning in the self-system. And only new meaning is learning.

Intrinsic Learning

There is another kind of learning that does not have to do with *how* the self acts in the world. This second class of learnings is concerned with changes in *why* the self is acting. *Intrinsic learnings* change the internal self-system at the deep level of strategies, motivations, perceived self, or concepts of adequacy. When any of these aspects of the system changes in relation to another aspect (or the world), the self is a different self, becoming for different purposes, toward altered goals.

For example, at some phase in his becoming, a male human chooses a sequence of actions which changes his perceptions so that he stops seeing himself as a *boy* and sees himself as a *man*. Broadening experiences are timed with changes in the organic process potential to affect what the boy is aware-ing. Consequences of action come into effect that have not happened to him before. He has to recognize that he is now different; therefore, he builds the difference into his notions of what it would take to be adequate. New motivational states arise when the perception of self (as man) and the concept of adequacy (as man) are not in harmony. Strategies of becoming will be organized now toward becoming a man by new definitions, and even though the same choices for action are available in the action space and acted with the same skills, their consequences will be evaluated by altered criteria. New instrumental learnings will result, and, from these, experiences will open the way for further intrinsic learnings.

In all the previous descriptions, the changes in the process of becoming involved examples of intrinsic learning. It was pointed out that each of us learns some notion of being a relating self, a self using the world, as valuable, lovable, skillful, meaningful. These learnings determine *why* we act and are intrinsic.

In the process of becoming, both instrumental and intrinsic learnings are necessary. The self-system must expand toward its potential effectiveness, and this necessitates both learning new ways to use the world and new reasons for relating to the world. The developing of an intrinsic change necessitates instrumental changes as ways of expressing the new intrinsic meaning. Until appropriate skills or knowledge are developed to bring a balance between the intrinsic meanings and the ability to express them, further self-development is not possible.

The two kinds of learning play into each other in a circular effect. For example, when a child is learning to read, much of what he learns is an instrumental skill. Yet intrinsic learnings are essential from the beginning and the child should have reading experiences which enable him to perceive himself as a reading person—one who uses reading to be a more adequate self—and to include in his concept of adequacy some notion about the kind of reader he needs to be in order to be effective. Unless both the instrumental skill and the intrinsic motivation grow, the child will not continue to learn to read.

The instrumental skills, *per se*, are ephemeral. They are task-oriented so that when the task is accomplished there is no further need for the skill. Some routines go on and on, but once established we do not learn much regarding them—we do not change, that is. If being a skill user is intrinsically learned, however, motivational states will call up the need for the skill again and again because one perceives himself as adequate when he uses the skill, and aware-ing the consequences of using the skill will keep open the potential for always using the skill more effectively. It makes a difference if one *can read* or if one *is a reader*. In the process of becoming, both instrumental and intrinsic learning must be fostered by the learner and by those trying to help him.

Teaching

It was intended that the preceding analysis of the learning process should be very strong in its varied implications that much of what we do as teachers must be reexamined. It seems obvious that our traditional curricula—our time-honored notions about the structure and sequence of content; our preference for seated, indoor verbal learning activities; our defensive notions about control; our limited respect for the human potential; our undemocratic manipulation of other people's choices; our procedures for being helpful; our concept of the teacher's role—these deeply entrenched aspects of teaching grew out of archaic notions about human behavior and human learning that are no longer acceptable.

We are at a crucial moment of social evolution when the future of mankind can be influenced greatly by teachers. A large segment of our society is afraid of change. Particularly, people are afraid of *open* change —afraid to foster growth without knowing for sure what the growth will become. Some teachers are among those who fear what the next generation will decide to do if we freely open the choice-making process to them now. In the face of these fears, however, we must take one of two mutually exclusive routes—society must go one way or the other! And the choice is largely up to teachers.

It is clear that what we do in controlling human behavior is one of the major issues of our times (Rogers and Skinner, 8). Either we must learn to foster the full human potential for open change and trust what humanity's search for effectiveness will find; or we must decide that man has already achieved the potential of humanity, that teachers know what is right, that they know what man should do, that our present values must be preserved, and that, therefore, we must teach young people in such a way that they will accept our decisions about the potential of man.

A number of times in history people have decided to take the second route and have failed. Perhaps the human potential for open change is so strong that it cannot be long smothered in the dictates of prejudged values. But individuals do succumb and lose their freedom to be fully themselves—and perhaps this time it could happen to all of us. For it may be that we now know enough about manipulating learning to destroy the full realization of human potential.

At no time in history have we tried wholeheartedly to foster individuality, to open choice-making, to support the uniqueness of becoming effective, to demonstrate real faith in the potential of humanity. We have accomplished something of these all along because the strength of individuals found effectiveness, but development has been haphazard, by chance and good luck, and in spite of many blocks to learning set up by schools. Even now we could not be altogether successful immediately, but we do know enough about the learning process and how to establish helping relations between people to make a good start.

Each teacher should realize that he, too, is in the process of becoming effective by his own definition. A teacher has chosen teaching as a strategy for patterning a sequence of activities for moving the perceived self into harmony with the concept of adequacy toward expanding effectiveness in the world. A deep understanding of why the teacher has chosen this strategy, in what way teaching makes the perceived self adequate, what the teacher is trying to get from teaching—such insight would expedite the process of becoming and probably clarify the teaching relationship.

It is certain that such an analysis would make it clear that out of the teacher's becoming there are not too many ways the teacher can affect the becoming of a student. The teacher has no direct access to the student's perception of self or concept of adequacy, nor can the teacher directly influence the student's motivational states or strategies for becoming since these are drawn by the student from his perceived self and his concept of adequacy.

The teacher does have access to the student's action space. The teacher may limit the space or open the space by controlling the resources for experiences in the space. It is up to the student to choose what act he will perform in his action space, but the teacher can so restrict the possibility of action as to all but determine what the student will choose. Or, the teacher can make the action space so rich in possible experiences as to guarantee that choice-making, exploring, evaluating, all will be satisfying intrinsically so the student will not only learn but will also learn to know himself as a doer.

To some extent the teacher can also affect the evaluation a student makes of the consequences of his actions. The teacher can simplify the environment in which the consequences of the student's acts occur so that certain effects stand out noticeably; or the teacher can emphasize certain consequences by demonstration or by selective reactions. In addition, if the relationship is close enough and the self-system of the student allows it, a teacher can be a direct consequence to the student through the quality of the relationship. The teacher's support, or approval, or lack of approval, will be seen by the student as a consequence of his actions.

If these are the only ways a teacher can affect a student's learning, what about all the lecturing, the homework, the drills, the repetition? How about all the pressures of grades, threats and punishments? How about the expensive school buildings, the texts, the libraries, the laboratories, the gyms? Only to the extent that these open or close the learner's action space or help him attach meaning to what is happening to him do they contribute to a student's learning. In the final analysis, the student will learn only his own choices out of his own motives according to his own strategies.

In what way can the teacher guarantee that efforts to help the student meet with more than chance success? If we are willing to determine what the student is to become, to manipulate him according to our values as to what he "should" learn, then we control his action space so that he has only certain experiences and comes to define effectiveness in the world without knowing how limited his world has been. However, if we hope to open the world so that a student can stretch toward his potential with no prejudged limits to that potential, we must become a resource for help to the learner in a relationship such that he can take the help without its imposing any limits between teacher and learner.

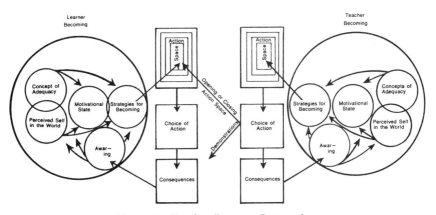

Figure 1. Teacher-Learner Interaction

The basis of this relationship between teacher and learner must be the faith that no limits to becoming effective are intended. The teacher must have faith enough to let students make mistakes. There will be complications, however, when the teacher tries to protect the student from some consequences of action which the teacher can recognize but which are as yet not knowable to the student. The teacher will attempt to sequence some experiences so that the student can best relate to the consequences of meeting them. This kind of protection will at times seem to the student like a restriction on his becoming effective, and his faith in the relationship with his teacher will abide only as long as the process of communication keeps the relationship testable.

The burden of communication must rest with the teacher, of course, because the teacher should have mature skills in communicating, while the student is still learning them. Therefore, the teacher must tune very sensitively to what the student is trying to do as the student expresses himself in word, deed, gesture, pause, stammer, laugh, frown or smile. The teacher should be able to empathize with how the world is to the student and how he is relating to it. Sometimes it may be enough that the student know the teacher is *willing* to empathize and that the teacher will empathize when their perceived worlds become congruent enough. The teacher must share all of his self that is appropriate to the student's needs. It must be certain that in the relationship the teacher's values, motives, feelings, words, and actions all express the same unrestricted willingness to help the student become effective. Rogers sees the "helping relationship" as being made up of empathic understanding, unconditional positive regard, and congruence in relation to the learner (Rogers, 9). The effectiveness of this helping relationship in assisting learners has been borne out by research (Halkides, 5).

With the process of communication maintaining the teacher-student relationship as a helping one, what can the teacher add? As the student reveals the direction of his becoming, the teacher comes to recognize what experiences can be supplied to the student's action space. Then as the student uses these provisions the teacher sharpens the learner's evaluation by questioning: What is this to you? What are you to it? What is this to these other things you've been learning? What? How? Why? Over and over, further and further into the meaning of becoming effective in the world. The teacher cannot know the answers for the student! The teacher can only help the student to develop answers.

Teaching has so far been described as a one-to-one relationship between a teacher and one student. Ever since Rousseau wrote *Emile*, theorists have wondered if a teacher can teach more than one student. The answer is obvious—we must. What is more, there is evidence that major learnings in relating to the world are fostered by the interaction among peers (Fromm, 4).

There is nothing about the above description which implies that a teacher has only one student. The description only makes it clear that the teacher must have an individual relationship with each student. Every action on the part of a teacher must be constructive in relation to what some learner is doing. The wise teacher will develop class experiences which are richly pertinent to many things in the world and appropriate resources to the becoming of many students, each in his own unique action space. As the teacher maintains effective communications with individuals, what is more, the basis for individuals to communicate with each other is established, and they learn to help each other as part of becoming effective in the world. This is not demanded of the students as a price for their learning; rather it is predictable that effectiveness will go in this direction. In order to help each other, the students will develop group projects out of which they will all grow.

The Evaluation Program

Now we are ready to return to the topic of evaluation, *per se*. We hope it is obvious that we have been considering evaluation throughout all the processes that have been described. We have tried to show in some detail that the very distinction of being human rests in the need for, and potential for being evaluative. All becoming, all learning, all teaching rests on evaluation. Learners and teachers are evaluating all the time. But how should what they are doing be organized into a program?

To be comprehensively useful, the school's program of evaluation must be organized at four levels. There are judgments to be made independently by (a) the individual student, concerning his becoming; (b) the teacher, concerning an individual relationship with each student; (c) the teacher and students, concerning how to organize all the relations which must be maintained in a class; and (d) all the resource people —administrators, supervisors, coordinators, counselors, researchers, lay boards, and citizens' committees—concerning the facilities the teacher uses to help the student toward his becoming effective. At each level of evaluation the process of making judgments is much the same, but the questions asked and the data collected are of a different order.

At the first level stands the individual learner. He is building his values from his perceptions of how things are related in the world. His purposes, goals and needs arise as motivational states. He chooses the actions, of those he perceives to be available, which seem to him most appropriate; and he tests the consequences of his actions against the harmony between his perceived self and his concept of adequacy. The learner brings this process to school with him, of course, and maintains it because of his own need to become. The contribution of the school's program at this level is to guarantee that provisions are made for thorough evaluation by individual learners.

At the second level of evaluation, the teacher must continue to seek insights about how the teacher role pertains to the perceived self and how relations with students are used for the teacher's own becoming. In addition, the teacher should have well organized concepts about the nature of learners. The values pertinent to these understandings should be systematically and periodically reconsidered. With these values as background, the teacher should form hypotheses about what each student is working toward and plan procedures to help each student be successful. In a following chapter it will be shown how a teacher should record his plan of action and include with it an answer to the questions: What will the student be doing if he is successful? What data must I collect to know whether he is doing this?

At the third level of evaluation, among the teacher and members of the class, there must be continual development of shared values. In most classes, as these values begin to build, the students will undertake to help each other and their efforts will materialize as group projects. The plans for these projects should include ways to test their contribution to the needs of group members and each project should conclude with a consideration of what to do next to further the effectiveness of the participants.

At the fourth level of evaluation, the major problem is to clarify values about what schools are for. It is generally recognized that we can answer questions about our programs only in terms of what we are trying to do. It is not a general practice, however, to plan programs which steadfastly aim at a consistent set of values. It is almost impossible to find a program in a school today that does not straddle some value conflict. This state of affairs produces curricula which leave the individual student stranded in his private efforts, confuse the relation of teacher to student, and limit the plans a class or group can make.

The time has come for each group of resource people, wherever there is a basis of communication in shared needs, to come to grips with a reevaluation of what they believe in. The issue must be faced: Do we shape learners according to our values and teach them what they "should" know? Or, do we foster the potential effectiveness of humanity by opening choice-making, problem solving, creativity, and autonomy, and following the results wherever they may go?

References

1. J. Bruner. "The Course of Cognitive Growth." *American Psychologist* 19: 1-15; 1964.

2. C. N. Cofer and M. H. Appley. *Motivation: Theory and Research.* New York: John Wiley & Sons, Inc., 1964.

3. John H. Flavell. *The Developmental Psychology of Jean Piaget.* Princeton, New Jersey: D. Van Nostrand Co., Inc., 1963.

4. E. Fromm. *The Sane Society*. New York: Holt, Rinehart and Winston, Inc., 1955.

5. G. Halkides. "An Experimental Study of Four Conditions Necessary for Therapeutic Change." Unpublished doctoral dissertation, University of Chicago, 1958.

6. R. J. Havighurst. *Human Development and Education*. New York: Longmans, Green & Co., 1953.

7. D. O. Hebb. "The Mammal and His Environment." *American Journal of Psychiatry* 111: 826-31; 1955.

8. C. R. Rogers and B. F. Skinner. "Some Issues Concerning the Control of Human Behavior: A Symposium." *Science* 124: 1057-66; 1956.

9. C. R. Rogers. *On Becoming a Person*. Boston: Houghton Mifflin Company, 1961.

10. C. Tryon and J. W. Lilienthal. "Developmental Tasks: I. The Concept and Its Importance." In: *Fostering Mental Health in Our Schools*. Washington, D.C.: Association for Supervision and Curriculum Development, 1950. Chapter 6.

11. F. T. Wilhelms, W. H. Beatty, R. A. Clark and B. L. Taylor. "Teacher Education and Mental Health." *Monograph*, San Francisco State College, 1963.

4

Teaching and Evaluation

Dorris May Lee

W<small>E</small> ARE going to shift now, to look at evaluation more completely from the classroom teacher's point of view and to focus more closely upon the evaluation of academic matter. Let us remind the reader, however, that we are still talking about a teacher who is free to use evaluation purely for the good of his pupils, to enhance their learning. We are still shaking off the usual preoccupations with marking and grading and the granting of credits, so that we can take a deeper look at evaluation as an integral component of effective teaching.

Therefore, this chapter will not concern itself at all with techniques of testing and measuring, such as are discussed in many textbooks and manuals. What we are after is a conceptualization of what evaluation is like if its sole concern is the facilitation of teaching and learning.

But, of course, we do *not* see our teacher free of other, more demanding tasks. We do not, for example, see his only task in the evaluation related to arithmetic to be that of getting precise, diagnostic data on each student's arithmetical skills and understandings. He will have to do that. But we shall also demand that he do it in ways that respect the integrity of the learner. While the evaluation must help the pupil toward a realistic appraisal of his progress and needs, it must not make him think less of himself as a learner. It must not violate his individuality. On the contrary, even though the pupil is having difficulties, evaluation must build up his confidence and increase his desire and ability to move on to his next steps.

Furthermore, the process of evaluation must involve the pupil himself. It cannot be carried on for him by the teacher, though the teacher must help him in important ways. It must be done in such a way that the pupil not only can attack the subject matter more intelligently but also can play a large part in setting his own goals.

Finally, we shall insist that the program of evaluation reach out beyond the technicalities of the immediate subject matter to embrace all the goals that are important at that time and keep them in perspective. Evaluation that produces precise, objective data on the technical side is indispensable; but there is also a human side and attention to this side is also indispensable.

Obviously, to satisfy such stringent criteria, many of the usual evaluation procedures will have to be changed. A different approach is demanded. Let us now look at one conception of such an approach.

Diagnostic Teaching

What we are trying to conceptualize is a system of evaluation so integrally related to the teaching process that the necessary kinds of feedback flow to both learner and teacher right out of the teaching-learning situation. We do not mean to imply that there should not be any of the more "external" sorts of testing and measuring. These have important functions, too. But they constitute a kind of superstructure, and we are concerning ourselves with the foundation.

Rationale

Before they come to school, children have different experiences from which they learn different things in different ways. They have differing perceptions of themselves and of their worlds. They value different goals and purposes. After they begin school the same thing is true, both inside and outside the classroom. For these reasons different "school" and "non-school" learnings are acquired in different ways and the range of differences grows consistently greater, not only through the school years but for the rest of their lives.

Therefore, any program which plans to teach the same aspects of any curriculum area to all learners (as is done in so many classrooms) is wasting the time of many learners. If it teaches this same curriculum to all *in the same way* (again the usual procedure), it is that much more wasteful. We can no longer tolerate wasting children's time teaching them what they already know or trying to teach them what they are not ready for, or concerned with. Neither can we afford to teach them in ways which do not result in effective learning for them. The learning situation must be tailored to the specific needs and styles of specific learners.

Children and youth learn most effectively what they know they need, what they choose to learn, and what they have a part in planning —i.e., that with which they become involved. But it is very difficult in a group situation to shape each child's curriculum so that a high proportion of it meets these tests. It can be done only if there is continuous evaluation of the child's learning and needs both by the child himself and by his teacher.

Evaluation in this sense must be in terms of specific and immediate as well as long-range purposes. For the learner it means: "What do I know?" "What does it mean?" "What do I need to know to get where I am heading?" "What is my next step?" For teachers it means: "How clear is the learner's immediate purpose?" "What meaning does it have for him?" "How can I help him analyze his difficulties and recognize his next steps?" "How can I help him see possibilities and meanings of which he is not even aware?"

The process by which teachers help students identify specific learnings they need, and then help them plan and set up experiences to achieve these learnings, may be called *diagnostic teaching*. Crucial elements in diagnostic teaching are that:

1. Each learner must learn how to establish his own goals and purposes.

2. He must be steadily aware of these goals and purposes.

3. He must devise for himself as well as plan with the teacher ways of achieving each goal as well as ways of recognizing the accomplishment.

4. Within reasonable limits, each student must be self-directing, self-pacing, and free to choose immediate goals, materials and procedures.

5. As far as possible, both teacher and learner must be aware of longer-term goals and larger frameworks of concepts to be developed, so that these may be used as guides to more immediate steps in teaching and learning.

Diagnostic Teaching as Continuous Evaluation

Most skills do not need to be tested out of the context of the ongoing activity in which they are used. In fact, any valid test should involve ability to use the skill in an appropriate situation. If the learner can use a skill for the purpose for which he learned it, and perhaps other purposes as well, that is the most significant evaluation. The evaluator needs to cultivate a sensitive perceptiveness to assess skills—or the lack of skills—in reading, oral language, writing, penmanship, spelling, mathematical reasoning and computation, research, group leadership, human relations, and thinking in each subject area—and to do this right while the actual process is going on. (Once again, this is not meant to imply that the teacher or the school system will not use formal devices such as paper-and-pencil tests to measure breadth or depth or degree of competence in any area as a supplement to the teacher's observational data. But the heart of the evaluative process lies in the diagnostic teaching itself.)

Diagnostic teaching, therefore, requires a radically different kind of evaluation on the part of teachers from that in operation in most classrooms:

1. It requires teachers to be aware of the skills—all the skills for which they have accepted responsibility, not just those arbitrarily assigned to any one grade or performance level, and not just those identified with the content of each area.

2. It requires the ability to see evidence of competence or lack of it in behavioral terms.

3. It requires awareness of concepts, understandings and generalizations which are important for learners in accomplishing their purposes and goals.

4. Again, it requires the ability to see evidence of the mastery or lack of mastery of these elements in behavioral terms.

5. It necessitates watching learners with a seeing eye and listening to them perceptively rather than merely "talking at" them or asking them memoriter kinds of "checking" questions.

6. It necessitates much self-evaluation and self-direction by learners on the basis of their awareness of their needs and purposes, which the teacher must help them to cultivate.

7. It requires teachers to look at the specific learnings, skills, competencies, concepts and applications of each learner rather than at general levels of learning, because the latter give little or no guidance in determining needed next steps.

Diagnostic teaching makes use of many of the principles of learning which are otherwise difficult to put into effect. Such teaching makes it possible for individuals to learn more effectively since they are learning what they have decided they need and have a use for ("use" here in the broad sense of what has value for them). When they help establish the objectives, plan the learning, set it up and carry it out, the learning has far more personal meaning for them.

Of course, as the teacher helps learners evaluate and plan, it is important that he keep in mind broader and longer-term goals than the learners may be able to see. Little by little, the teacher can help them to see more by providing experiences which will create an awareness of needed learnings.

If, even then, the learners cannot recognize needs which the teacher believes to be important, the provision of more experiences calculated to raise the level of awareness is far more effective than simply going ahead and requiring the "learning" anyway. And it is always possible, after all, in spite of the teacher's conviction to the contrary, that this particular learning is not needed by this learner at this time!

Self-direction Essential for Diagnostic Teaching

It is essential that each pupil in the group be encouraged to exercise as much self-direction as possible, within the framework of the group. This may be threatening to the teacher who still sees his role as that of controlling all learning procedures and activities in the classroom. However, it is an essential element in helping children and youth learn what will be significant to them in living most effectively in their own worlds. If, when they are on their own, tomorrow's citizens are to keep themselves knowledgeable and informed so that they may continue to be effective citizens of their world, they must begin to learn self-direction now.

Self-direction is also essential from another standpoint. As a student learns to be responsible for taking the initiative and carrying out his own learning, his whole point of view changes. Before this he may have been a more or less passive recipient. The teacher decided what he was to learn; made the assignments, usually in a common text; chose the questions to ask and the persons to ask them of; and at stated intervals made up a test, scored it, and made a judgment as to how much each had "learned." The student could make only rather minor modifications, if any, in the process. He had to take whatever satisfaction he might have from this experience mainly as he was able to satisfy teacher demands in reaching teacher purposes. To the extent that this was true, he was likely to take away with him almost no ability or desire to have these "learnings" modify his behavior, now or in the future.

As a learner is encouraged to be self-directed, he becomes involved in the purposes of his study and work. He grows more aware of the value of his learning and how it makes a difference in his day-to-day living. By definition, the learning must be important to him at the time or he would not have chosen to work at it. As he continues in this fashion over time, he comes to understand, through his planning for himself and with his teacher, the interrelatedness of his learnings. They become naturally the means of changing much of his behavior so that he can be more effective in his own world. This and the inherent involvement insure learning that makes a difference and learning that lasts.

Another aspect of self-direction is creativity. By their very nature creative thoughts or actions are initiated by the learner and carried out by him. It follows that as self-direction is encouraged there will be more tendency toward creative thought and activity.

However, the essential contribution of self-direction in diagnostic teaching is that, within the guidelines and purposes established by teacher and learner together, it enables the learner to recognize his own immediate needs. Then, to the extent that he is self-directing, he can move to take the indicated next steps in his quest for increasing adequacy.

As the children or adolescents in a group grow and learn, it is totally impossible for any teacher to know just what is most needed by each and every one. For years we have assumed that they all need about the same thing; we have operated on the idea of putting all children through the same paces at the same time in the same way. We now know that the necessary alternative is to come closer to helping each move ahead fairly continuously at his own growing edge. Yet we are still faced by the virtually insoluble problems of providing so much differentiation if the teacher has to plan it all. Self-direction, within a reasonable framework, seems the most effective solution. For it adds the learner's perceptions and diagnosis of his own case to the teacher's broader understandings of the field as a whole.

All Persons Want To Learn. This point has been so thoroughly documented in the previous chapter that further discussion would serve no useful purpose. However, there is one question which could prove helpful to discuss: If all persons want to learn, why do teachers meet so much resistance and have to work so hard to get children and youth to learn? The key is really fairly simple. *Everyone wants to learn that which has personal meaning for him and which he sees as making him a more adequate person.* He resists when teachers make two mistakes: when they neglect to take the learner's perceptions into account to guide him to what seems truly relevant to him; and when they insist on using a curriculum and materials which have become traditional and rigid and often remote from real life.

Far too often children are forced to learn what we as teachers, supervisors and administrators want them to learn. We lack confidence in the tremendous energy youngsters display in their efforts to achieve adequately, as they see adequacy. Furthermore, we even blunt their drive in school by failing to help them enrich and focus their perceptions of adequacy. They need opportunities to explore and identify, to question and choose, after meaningful consideration and inquiry. But we are so sure we know what they ought to want that we skip the foundation-building. This is not to say that we do not have understandings beyond theirs or that we should not provide active leadership. It is rather to argue that we need to put their insights and our own together to achieve something superior to what either could achieve alone.

There is another point we commonly fail to see: the really significant learnings cannot be avoided if there is freedom to consider all concerns and if no generalizations and understandings are accepted only on the "authority" of the text or the teacher. If some traditional curriculum content never becomes involved in any exploration or study which has personal meaning to an individual or group so that they wish to become involved with it, we must certainly question its value, at least at that time, for those learners.

Each Must Learn at His Growing Edge. One implication of this statement has already been assimilated into our common sense. We have fairly well accepted the idea that a learner will not choose to operate "above his head." To be sure, there are individuals who sometimes *seem* to do just this. Some youngsters who are having little success yet ask for the most difficult learning tasks. When we explore into this we invariably find some outside pressure which makes it unacceptable for them not to "try for the top." Or, we see the one who is practically a nonreader "eagerly" volunteering to read. One such, now a fine teacher, confessed the she always volunteered for two reasons. First, knowing she was going to have to do it sometime, she wanted to get it over with; and second, she wanted to control what it was she was going to read. Nevertheless, the basic generalization holds true. A child cannot learn effectively what he does not yet have background or readiness for, and ordinarily he will not choose to try.

The other implication of the growing-edge concept is that youngsters will not choose, either, to work at what they already know, what is "too easy," what they have already grown beyond. Here there are more doubters. Many teachers are sure that if they did not push and require, some students would do nothing constructive all year. They "document" this by the fact that some do not do anything constructive anyway! These teachers simply do not trust pupil motivation enough to be willing to depend on anything but their own directions.

Other teachers do try taking the pressure off and moving toward self-direction. Yet they become frightened or impatient before any real change in the learner's concept of himself and the situation has opportunity to develop; they start imposing requirements again, and this, of course, defeats the whole purpose. Students who have spent years doing what someone else has required of them, even though they viewed such assignments with little concern and less purpose, have built up a resistance to "school" tasks. They may do the tasks—even do them rather well—and yet not throw themselves into the work as learners. In addition, some of them have learned very effectively that they will not be able to satisfy the teacher's expectancies. When suddenly the situation is reversed and they are given a chance to help establish learnings useful to them and to choose to work at levels where they feel confident and capable, it takes time for them to learn to trust the reality of the change and to reorient their whole way of thinking about learning in school.

However, a number of teachers have had the courage to provide a rich environment, to wait, to encourage, and to permit self-selection and self-direction to operate. So far, in these situations no learner has failed eventually to move on his own in a constructive direction although his first reactions may not have seemed promising. Often, for example, children who have been pushed in reading, hanging on for months or years "by their fingertips," actually regress for a while as to the difficulty of the books they choose to read. They may stay at the lower level long enough to try the patience and confidence of the teacher to near the breaking point. But when they finally develop confidence in their ability to try something new, they suddenly move ahead into other material. They begin to make progress. This growth may not be exceptional, but over a few months the kind of real and solid learning occurs which teachers recognize is greater than would have occurred under the assignment-requirement procedure. In addition to their technical gains as readers, they often change their concept of themselves as readers and read with far more confidence and more zest for further learning.

Another evidence of the importance of permitting each learner to work at his growing edge lies in what happens to the abler children when the teacher's expectancies are the same for all in a class. Often those who would be able to move to more complex studies learn virtually nothing and become bored with the whole situation, with varying results. Particularly at the younger levels, if this situation continues, children may temporarily (or, depending on what else happens, permanently) reduce their rate of learning in school, sometimes markedly. They may develop habits of inattention and daydreaming. Needing adventure and excitement and not finding it in the learning situation, they may push the limits of forbidden behavior. Out of sheer frustration they may react in ways neither they nor others approve.

We must understand that when school learners have a significant part in defining their areas of study, in setting their own tasks, and in directing these tasks with the assistance of self-evaluation guided by the teacher, each will work at his own growing edge. If this does not happen after a reasonable length of time, some pressure from inside or outside the school must be preventing it from happening.

Developing Self-direction. In initiating a program of self-direction it may be wise for a teacher to begin in one area at a time, an area in which he feels especially comfortable. In elementary classrooms, this might be in arithmetic or reading or spelling. At the high school level a teacher might prefer to start with a project in one class. When it becomes evident that learners actually can direct their own learning effectively in this one area, without upsetting the classroom, the teacher will probably grow in acceptance of learners' self-direction in other areas.

An essential in the development of self-direction is planning with children and encouraging them to plan for themselves. Naturally, planning must be done in terms of significant purposes. (Planning how many pages a week they must cover to "finish the book" by the end of the year is scarcely significant!) As learners become aware of real purposes through planning to satisfy them, each easily begins taking more initiative and responsibility for his own learning. As they make personal meaning out of the experiences they plan, they become more capable and more desirous of planning further experiences, thus becoming increasingly self-directing.

If children in elementary schools do not have these kinds of experiences, they will be unable to cope with the secondary curriculum, the flexible schedule, and the self-directive activity expected in independent study. Innovative secondary programs are advocating independent study by providing time and space for this activity. These programs are in great jeopardy if students have had undeveloped study skills or no previous experience with self-directed activity.

The teacher encourages self-direction by changing statements such as "Now do this" to questions such as "What do you think we (you) need to do now?" He then must listen and accept, raising further questions to be helpful but not pushing decisions in a direction he may have had in mind. These questions are appropriate at any instructional level.

At first, the learners are apt to "give back" the sorts of responses teachers have previously expected or required. When this is recognized or suspected, teachers should question the responses rigorously and should not accept them until learners document them from their own point of view. (Teachers need to be very perceptive here, knowing that it is satisfying personally to hear children say back to us what we have been saying to them! It sounds so natural and proper that it is hard to remain wary.)

Another useful procedure when pupils raise questions such as, "What shall I do?" or "What should I do?" or "Is this right?" is to respond with another question such as, "What do *you* think?" The learner may be unable to deal with this, at first, but it is worth investing some effort to help him find his own answer rather than give him ours. If he asks, "What do you want me to do?" we should respond with some variant of "What seems most important to you?" Again, he may need help, this time in terms of establishing or becoming aware of his own purposes.

It is important not to rule out arbitrarily any suggestion or idea of a student. To be sure, in the busy life of a classroom, not every suggestion can be put into action even if it may be good in itself, but the student will be likelier to go on being constructive if he knows his idea was not simply rejected. If our greater experience leads us to question a suggestion, we can and should raise questions about it which will enrich the student's thinking. We might ask, "What about ....?" or, "Have you thought that .... might happen?" If such questions do not influence him, it may be best to let him go ahead unless the proposal seems to involve serious consequences such as physical or psychological harm to himself or others. We must recognize that in spite of our misgivings the idea may work out very well. If it does not, the pupil is in a most favorable position for learning—that of learning from his own mistakes. This we must accept without comment, resisting the impulse of an I-told-you-so attitude.

Learners must be free to make mistakes without punishment. If their ideas do not work out, this is in itself some penalty, but it is a natural one and one they can live with. If, in addition, they see themselves losing favor with the teacher, or if they are "punished" by more work they see no purpose in, by words, by "looks" or by low grades, they will freeze up and be reluctant to "stick their necks out." It requires very sensitive consideration of our procedures to be sure we are not *discouraging* self-direction by what we say and do—and by what we communicate non-verbally.

A Healthy Self-concept Must Be Built and Maintained. To the extent that a learner respects himself as a person, believes he can develop in a positive direction and can learn what he needs to learn, he becomes increasingly able. There is some confusion about what a positive self-concept and self-acceptance mean. They do *not* mean that a person is self-satisfied, feels no need to change, or thinks he "knows it all." Rather these terms mean that he has confidence that he can do and be better.

In fact the apparently self-satisfied "know-it-all" is maintaining defenses against a world which he feels he cannot deal with effectively. Since such a perception is too threatening to face, he spends much time and energy trying to convince himself and the world that he *is* what he feels he is expected to be. He has less time and energy for learning. He dares not evaluate himself realistically. And his inability to arrive at a realistic appraisal of his needs cuts down his effective learning even further.

The manner in which a teacher handles his system of evaluation can have a great deal to do with whether a given student will become so fearful that he has to cover up, or so confident that he can look at himself with clear, insightful eyes. Teachers need to be aware of all the outcomes of the evaluative process, those which contribute positively and those which are defeating.

Factors Which Inhibit Realistic Self-evaluation

Many procedures—organizational, instructional and evaluative—commonly used in classrooms hinder a learner from facing himself realistically without severe damage to his self-concept and hence his ability to learn.

Classroom organization may lower the self-concept when learners are grouped on the basis of a prejudged potential for progress. When a group is formed because school people believe the individuals involved have little ability, have not learned much, and will not learn much, a situation is created in which the sad predictions are more or less foredoomed to come true. The learners involved become convinced that they cannot learn well, and so they become less able to. It may be that some of them would not learn rapidly under any circumstances; but if their self-concepts could remain intact, they might be able to move ahead rather effectively when they had developed other needed skills and felt a real purpose in learning.

One first grade teacher had grouped her children into slow, average and fast reading groups. Nancy, in the slow group, did almost nothing; the teacher, feeling she could not reach her, feared she would "fail" at the end of the year. About midyear this teacher came to see another way of working with her children; she abandoned the groups, and worked with the children largely in an individualized fashion. The change in atmosphere and expectancy made an almost immediate change in Nancy, and within a month she was reading almost as well as anyone in the class.

Being in the "top group" may put pressure on some learners which will also hinder realistic self-evaluation. They feel so much is expected of them that they are afraid they cannot measure up. Meanwhile those classed as average proceed to be satisfied with mediocre performance.

The usual alternative is whole-class operation where the same teaching is "done" to all and the same expectancies held for them. This obviously is no solution, since the wide range of individual differences cannot be taken into account, except as a sensitive teacher does make adjustments and allowances. However, there are other possibilities, notably the emerging program of "diagnostic teaching" which we have been discussing and will discuss in more detail later in the chapter.

Instructional procedures. Among the factors calculated to lower the self-concept and minimize learnings is the use of a set curricular program, devised by the school district, school or teacher and imposed on the learners, who have had no part in the planning, no choice, and little opportunity even to modify any part of it. This tells the learners that "we" know what "you" need; "you" don't know and have no ability to contribute or make a useful choice. In this day and age, when knowledge has increased phenomenally so that no one person in a lifetime can hope to encompass more than a small part of it, who has the temerity to say, *all* shall learn *this*? Communication skills, learning and thinking skills, and human relations skills are about the only specific content which seems essential to all, and these may be acquired in so many ways with such a great variety of materials and procedures that they do not require a pre-set curriculum.

Another defeating aspect of instruction is that which depends solely upon rote memory. The only reason for learning anything is that it is useful to us. It need not be useful in an immediately utilitarian way. It may, rather, help us understand ourselves or others or to appreciate beauty of sound or line or color. But assuredly such learning must have meaning for us. Rote memorization has little relation to meaning and readily downgrades the importance of meaning. Thus as the memorization of information takes on increased importance, meaningful learning is by necessity minimized and the value of individual wants and needs is belittled.

Teacher evaluation is usually very closely related to instruction. What a teacher feels is important to teach he usually also feels is important to measure. Teacher-determined learnings portend teacher-determined testing. As a teacher feels no need for nor confidence in pupil participation in planning, neither does he feel they have any place in the evaluation of the results. If we believe, as we have verbalized for so many years, that learning is changed behavior, then how else can we evaluate learning than by setting up situations in which the desired behavior has a chance to operate, in which each individual has an opportunity to see how he can operate in a real situation, try out his newly gained skills, know for himself what he can do satisfactorily and what he cannot? More than anyone else, the learner needs such information on which to base his next choices.

If self-evaluation is essential and must at least accompany all useful evaluation, we need to be aware of the effect of external evaluation. By external evaluation we mean the teacher's making judgments about the extent to which the learner has met the teacher's goals. Whether the judgment is expressed in grades and marks or only in the teacher's praise of a desired answer or condemnation of a "wrong" one, the recipient learns to look to someone outside himself for judgment as to his worth, his success, his goals. As much as any practice can, this leads the learner to belittle his own judgment, to lose confidence in himself, and to be less able to depend on himself to make worthy choices and decisions.

When an individual's adequacy is to be judged by some outside agent, person or thing, he may well feel threatened and belittled. He can be sure that the outside agent can know only a small portion of the pertinent data—quite possibly the least significant part. He feels at the mercy of an outside force whose goals and purposes for him may be far from his own. The more this outside judgment can affect or control his future opportunities, the more detrimental it may be, because it will exert greater pressure on him to give up his own purposes and values and work to adapt and conform to those of the outside force. Since these other-directed goals are not his own, they will tend to become superficial and extrinsic. If he tries to maintain both his own and those of others, there will inevitably be conflict which will produce anxiety and contribute to his confusion as to who he really is and what he really believes and values.

On the other hand, if there can be significant communication between the evaluator and evaluated, common goals can be identified and common purposes accepted and progress toward these recognized by both. To the extent that this occurs, the evaluation can become useful and can contribute to further development in line with the individual's goals. As the evaluator respects the individuality and purposes of the learner, the evaluator's reactions can be contributive rather than harmful.

Evaluative interaction can be a positive force in personal development:

1. When that evaluation is in terms of what is important to the learner

2. When it is a means which he can use for directing his future study

3. When it gives him feedback to help him know his competencies, where he is, to what point he has progressed

4. When he feels that the teacher is helping him evaluate himself and improve his perceptions as to his next needs

5. When it helps him see next steps and opens doors for him to move forward; *not* when it stops study and closes doors to future learning in the area

6. When it helps him gain personal meaning in an area of learning

7. When it helps him see progress and thus feel good about himself, even if he realizes he still has some way to go

8. When it encourages rather than discourages further learning

9. When it is set up so as to be a challenge (leading to what he believes he can do), rather than a frustration (convincing him he cannot succeed)

10. When in one form or another it is continuous

11. When the learner comes to see the behavior valued by the teacher to be his own realistic self-appraisal and self-direction, rather than convincing the teacher of the amount of information learned.

If instruction based on individual evaluation by teachers and self-evaluation by learners seems to be a step in the right direction, what does it mean for everyday classroom operation? The first response by most "practical" school people is that such instruction is impossible. Such people might be believed if a group of regular teachers in a typical school in an average neighborhood in a large city had not proved differently. With a minimum of guidance, the support of the principal, and their own increasing understanding and satisfaction as they have seen the program develop, these teachers have established situations in which the children are learning much more effectively. Other individual teachers in school after school, some in deprived areas, as they begin to see the possibilities, have moved toward such a program with great success.

Using Diagnostic Teaching in the Classroom

However, a program which requires such great change cannot be developed overnight. It is better if teachers move into one area after another as they feel comfortable, starting wherever they feel they can. Let us now look at what is necessary to initiate the development of such a program. What might it look like when in operation?

The *first* requirement is a thoughtful look at the fundamental purposes of the school and the major derived goals. For years it has been a voiced, though often ignored, basic principle that evaluation should be in terms of the objectives. Objectives were also supposed to be criteria against which to test content, teaching procedures, and materials. Diagnostic teaching requires that the principle be turned from platitude to reality. When we inquire as to which historical, sociological and political concepts and understandings are most likely to help a child live more effectively in his world, we arrive at quite different learnings from those usually taught.

The *second* step must be a new look at the curriculum to see how well it squares with the major purpose of helping each child to live more effectively in his world. An incident illustrates how two teachers helped their children develop respect and appreciation for others, realize the satisfaction of being helpful and contributive, and at the same time increase their skills of significant communication.

In the teachers' room one day a first grade teacher was complaining that there just was not enough reading material of appropriate interest and difficulty for her children to read. A third grade teacher saw an exciting opportunity to have her class write materials for the first graders. Her children had been doing considerable writing but were losing interest and needed a real purpose for writing. They were most enthusiastic over the new project and did some important planning under the challenging questions of the teacher. They talked about the competencies and needs of their audience; they analyzed their own procedures to make sure the material would be readable and would communicate important ideas in an interesting way. They set up "readers" in their group who acted in an editorial capacity both as to content and mechanics.

The final draft was read by a child who determined whether the manuscript writing was easily legible or whether certain letters needed to be erased and re-written. Relevant illustrations were prepared to interest the reader and help him interpret the meaning. Finally covers were made for each story, with an appropriate picture, the author's name, and the illustrator's name on the front. When all the stories were finished, the pupils paid a call on the first grade group during which they explained how they had written the stories and made the books. Then each of the third graders put his book on the shelf in the bookcase so that each first grader might choose the one he wanted. The excitement of the first graders and their comments kept some of the children involved in the project off and on throughout the year.

Here no test was needed to identify writing skills. Each child had a reason for doing his very best, and it was amazing how well most of them could identify their own needs in improving their various skills. Many of them took constructive action to meet these needs, though others appealed to the teacher for help. This truly was diagnostic teaching. The completed booklets were the best possible evidence of progress, and as the process went forward both the teacher and the young authors were receiving abundant feedback.

In connection with its science program one school has helped the students in the upper grades build a greenhouse against a south wall of the building. The students did the planning and building of the greenhouse, taking into account the need of plants for heat and light. They mixed the soil, planted the seed, and cared for many flats of a variety of plants both useful and ornamental. The extra plants they sold and plowed the money back into the project. Records of the financing and the decisions as to the use of the money in further development of the project called on many important principles and procedures in economics. Together with the increased understandings and skills in various areas of science, the economic learnings more than justified the project. At each stage, learners identified their own needs through planning in a real situation. In addition, the students had fine experience in cooperative planning and performance. Altogether, they gained many practical skills at the same time that they experienced the reality of an area of aesthetics.

None of this needed testing by paper-and-pencil tests. The pupils' performance, the improvement of their judgment in decision making, and the need they saw for correcting mistakes by modifying procedures the next time constituted a running evaluation of real learning. The enthusiasm, effort and involvement were obvious as they responded to life-related problems. As they proceeded with their project, a student here and there would recognize a problem he faced or information he needed which he did not have. The resultant learning, both self-directed and guided by the teacher, was an excellent example of diagnostic teaching.

A high school class in American Government began exploring ways in which other governments differ from our own. In discussing the advantages of an autocracy they decided that it was far more efficient. So they organized themselves on an autocratic basis, and things went fine for a while. Soon, however, a dissident group developed, recruited some converts, and overthrew the leader in power. When this was discussed and the reasons were brought out and generalized, they began seeing relationships with revolutions throughout history in various parts of the world.

As a reaction to the autocratic government, the group decided to establish a democracy. Again trouble arose. Action was too slow; some felt they were hindered by a minority who were very vocal; and they all wanted equal say regardless of their qualifications. Finally, someone proposed they try out communism to see if it might solve some of the problems. This lasted a shorter time than either of the other governments, and the unanimous decision was that with all its problems each of them could live most effectively under a democratic government.

As each different organization of the class was tried, a great deal of research was used as a basis for operation. Abstract statements and generalizations were not enough. The students had to know how to implement general ideas in everyday living. And the payoff came near the end of the year when, having moved back to being a democracy, they realized that in the previous try at it they had not really understood the implementation of some of the basic principles. They felt that they could understand these much better after their other experiences.

Here again, paper-and-pencil tests, while they might have been useful to probe certain kinds of developments, would have been, at best, only a secondary source of insight. Direct analysis of each student's ability to operate in the terms of various forms of government was far more valid, and the learning that resulted from it was more meaningful. As inconsistent behaviors showed up in individuals, diagnostic teaching by self-direction and teacher guidance was again a natural solution.

These three illustrations bear upon curriculum and instruction as well as evaluation. They show how, when learning is significant and life-related and when it is seen to be important by the learner, self-direction and self-evaluation take place naturally and diagnostic teaching is a normal development.

The *third* step in initiating a program of diagnostic teaching is to take a fresh look at the diversities of the children in our schools. Meeting "individual differences" has been a major verbalized concern of our schools for forty or fifty years. For an even longer time, sincere attempts have been made to solve the problems involved. Although these efforts have certainly produced improvements, none has been altogether successful. Two major factors probably account for most of the lack of success: (a) a lack of consideration of *what else happens* when certain procedures are put into effect; and (b) the fact that major attention has been given to only one kind of difference, usually called "ability" or "achievement."

We must be very sure that whatever provisions we attempt to make to provide for individual differences do not, as a side effect, harm learners in other ways. For instance, many schemes of ability grouping are conceived as ways of adjusting the curriculum more nearly to the differing abilities of student groups. But one side effect may be that many children are taught that they are not expected to learn much; another may be that the teacher, assuming that he now has before him a "homogeneous" group, lessens his efforts to accommodate the wide ranges of differences which still exist in a group. Even without ability grouping, when some pupils have difficulties, a frequent solution is to bear down hard on "remedial" reading, arithmetic, etc. While such efforts certainly have some benefits, they often have the unfortunate effect of narrowing and constricting the remedial pupil's range of experiences. He may face a veritable mountain of drill work.

Situations must provide the greatest breadth, depth and richness of experiencing possible. Such experiencing can provide learners bases for later understanding, and it can open doors on hitherto unknown fields of exploration. It can enrich the pupil's perception of the alternatives which are available to him. If not all of this is usable at the moment, at least it can increase learners' awareness of other aspects of their world. Furthermore, such experiences can be managed in such a way that each learner feels better about himself than he did before. He feels more self-worth, more confidence in his ability to do what seems important for him to do, and more able to take charge of his own life space. All in all, he becomes a more capable person. Efforts at "meeting individual differences" which concentrate on narrow academic skills, excluding all else because "what this child needs is to learn his spelling" run great risk of killing individuality for the sake of reducing a few deviations from academic norms.

When we consider the differences in young people we must consider all the differences which are learning-related, not only "where they are" on some academic skill or the rate at which we can expect them to move. We must consider differences in what they bring with them, the directions in which they hope to move, the kinds of knowledge and skills they will value picking up along the way, the ways in which they come to understand most effectively, and, particularly, differences in perceptions of themselves and of their worlds.

Since all learners vary in all these respects as well as others and since progress is always uneven for each child, there can be no way to organize on the basis of "ability" or "achievement" which will by itself be more than temporarily useful. Utilizing the diverse resources of children and youth and altering the program to each one's needs and purposes will take something far more sensitive and creative than any mechanical system of grouping. It is important that a group enjoy living and working together and do so effectively as in a sociometric grouping. Such a group might include those of approximately the same age or it might deliberately include those of different ages, abilities and concerns. (For further discussion of this point see discussions of multigrading.)

What Is Important To Evaluate

Much evaluation or testing has been concerned more or less exclusively with facts and information. While no one questions that pertinent facts are essential in learning, they are not valuable in and of themselves, but only as they increase understanding and contribute to effectiveness of living. Hence effectiveness of living—not the facts and information—needs to be the focus of evaluation. This makes evaluation not only more difficult but also far more significant.

Are There Essential Sequences in Learning?

The traditional school program has been established on the basis of scope and sequence. While, obviously, there is some needed sequence to learning, teachers have been badly misled as to which learnings are essentially sequential and which are not. In courses of study, textbooks, and teachers' manuals, many learnings have been set up as sequences which are not necessarily so at all. It sometimes happens that several bodies of material which are generally considered in sequence actually constitute alternate ways of learning the same thing. Thus, some of the learning tasks commonly found in the sequence may never need to be considered at all by some learners, if other media produce the basic competency and understanding which are the goal. Much of the confusion here arises out of a tendency to consider the subject matter itself the goal, rather than to see it as a means to an end.

Much school learning has been established by adults on the basis of their judgment. This may seem a reasonable procedure, since teachers do watch the learning which results. Yet the inclusion of all the material or its presentation in one particular order has seldom been checked out with learners. Very few learners have had the opportunity to participate in determining their own goals and purposes and then to do only those learning tasks which they find necessary to reach their goal. As this now occurs somewhat more often than in former years, we shall almost surely find that many learnings will need to secure other defenses and that much sequencing will be altered.

At first thought, it may seem odd to the reader that we are dwelling on the question of essential sequencing at this point in a discussion of diagnostic teaching. Yet the question is highly germane. If it is true that there are set bodies of materials which have to be presented in a certain sequence, then a teacher and a pupil have very little room for maneuver.

They can make only small modifications—such as going through the materials faster or more slowly—in a program which has to remain essentially what it is. We have argued, on the other hand, that: (a) Very few bodies of content are in themselves essential; generally there are many choices among bodies of subject matter, any of which may be used by a child or a group to move toward the same goal; and (b) the sequence in which these units of subject matter are taken up often matters less than has been thought. If these two things are true, then the room for maneuver is very large. Then a child—or a group of children —and a teacher can reshape the program in significant ways to meet discovered needs. Only then can the ideal of diagnostic teaching have much reality.

Much research is needed in this area, with experimentation with a variety of sequences. Recently, an author of one of the "new" mathematics texts stated in an address that he felt the mathematicians had had little to go on when putting concepts and skills in sequence. He urged teachers to try different orders and organizations when these seemed useful to children.

To illustrate further, let us examine the field of communication, focusing on reading because this skill is so important for learning at all stages and because schools are still not coping with it adequately. Here the ideas concerning necessary sequence in learning are particularly confused. Some still believe that knowing the names of the letters must precede reading. More still want children and adolescents to know the sounds of letters and phonemes as *the* way of moving ahead with communication skills. Teachers at all levels may insist on the learner's developing ability to identify a basic list of words in isolation as a part of the process.

All of these ideas are based on an assumption that reading is the ability to translate symbols into sounds. This interpretation impoverishes the meaning of reading which, as one aspect of communication, is essentially dealing with ideas and meaning. The successful non-oral teaching of reading has shown that the symbol-to-sound procedure is unnecessary. The use of children's own writing and of trade books as the substance for reading has denied the necessity or even desirability of a basic list of words to be learned so they can be identified in isolation. Instead we now know that children quickly recognize those words and can read those materials to which they can bring personal meaning.

What Sequence Is Important?

So we really have quite a different sequence of needed learnings. First, a learner at any age must be able to talk about the content he is to read. This requires some relevant experience, vicarious or firsthand. Most of the words need to be a part of his speaking vocabulary. These help to insure that he can bring personal meaning to the material so that through reacting to it cognitively and affectively he may expand his store of experiences from which meaning is built. Thus one genuine essential in determining sequence is that oral communication precedes written in each area. Another factor is the learner's concept level in relation to the concept level of the material. This aspect of a piece of reading material may or may not be related to any of the usual measures of difficulty. Concepts must be developed to some level before young children read material involving them; if the concepts are available, the usual criteria of vocabulary difficulty may be less important than they have seemed.

If oral communication is taught within a general framework of diagnostic teaching, it can be evaluated in terms of familiarity with ideas and development of concepts in the areas a student or group has chosen to study. When lacks and gaps which block progress are noted, steps can be taken to fill in what is needed. To the extent that a child understands his lacks and converts them in his mind to learnings needed to accomplish his purposes, he will move ahead. If, however, he can accomplish his purposes without certain learnings, then they may only have been part of the traditional sequencing rather than something essential to him.

A common problem at every learning stage is sequencing difficulty of material read. For instance, common procedure for assessing a learner's progress in reading is to identify his "level" of reading. This evaluation is often made by having him read, usually orally (which is a separate skill), and finding the graded level he can read without missing more than a certain percentage of the words, usually five percent. His comprehension is also checked, usually by evaluating his ability to tell what the material says, rather than what it means. When his reading "level" has been identified, the learner is put into other material which has been graded at the same "level," and he is asked to read it and answer questions about it to indicate whether or not he understands it. Since most of the questions can be answered by identifying appropriate words or phrases in the material, only a low level of thought processes is required, and there is no evaluation as to whether the reading has added to his store of personal meanings.

Evaluating Ability To Bring Experience To Bear

A more helpful consideration of sequence would be to explore the kinds of experiences which have built understandings so that the learner can talk about the content, situation, ideas or feelings to be reacted to in the material, so that he can bring personal meaning to the material and thus enrich personal meanings by means of the material. What is his stage of development in the various thinking skills which are needed to deal adequately with the material to be read? Judging by his reaction to his reading, which skills show need for increased development? What kinds of questions need to be posed to help this learner with this development?

The "difficulty" of material cannot be identified apart from the skills and attitudes of the reader. It has long been recognized that readers can profit greatly from material of greater concept load and increased vocabulary when it deals with fields to which they can bring a rich background of experience, while at the same time they are unable to profit from simpler materials in some other fields. We know, too, that a person can read meaningfully material he has a great desire to read even though it is very difficult. At the same time he may fail to read other material perhaps because it has merely been assigned to him and he has no special interest in it.

Evaluating Increases in Meanings

Since reading is dealing with meaning, the getting of meaning must be our first concern, over and above exact accuracy of word identification. When meaning is significantly distorted there is reason for concern and for identification of the cause. But when the getting of meaning is relatively adequate, we must have confidence that as the pupil continues he will refine his word identification skills, just as little children refine their speech skills.

As we note which skills of word identification a pupil does need at a particular time as well as which reactions to ideas he is unable to use effectively, we have a basis for specific teaching attuned to his needs. It helps us see what the learner can cope with and what his next steps must be. Identification of a general "level" provides no such useful evaluation or basis for instruction.

Evaluating Self-concept

Another factor which needs continuous evaluation is the learner's concept of his own competency and progress as a reader. As he is aware of progress in specific skills identified through continuous evaluation with the teacher, he can gain a feeling of increasing adequacy which in turn will promote greater growth. If "levels" are used as the basis of evaluation, progress is much less easy to identify and it takes longer to make a noticeable difference, because of the global, non-specific character of the evaluation. Since study and testing materials are not scaled on the same bases, moving from one set to another may show wide gains or even a loss, all very disconcerting.

In order to gain confidence in his ability to learn and to have positive feedback into his self-concept, a learner needs to see for himself his progress toward his identified purposes. Involvement in the cooperative evaluation in diagnostic teaching provides opportunities for learners to look at themselves and become aware of their increasing competence and self-confidence.

Organizing for Diagnostic Teaching

One reason teachers have not developed more specific evaluation is that they have not found ways to organize their classroom to make use of the information it would yield. The general practice of trying to teach the same thing to all children at the same time, or at least to those grouped together for the year, has prevented many from meeting the needs of individuals. However, if we accept the previous discussion, diagnostic teaching—specific teaching to the specific needs of individuals or fluid groups—becomes reasonable, logical and manageable. It may be that we need to look at ways of organizing and working in the classroom so that the needed procedures can be effective.

At any school level diagnostic teaching employs a combination of total group, ever-changing small groups, and independent study, with the needs, concerns and learning style of the individual always highly visible to the teacher. This is true whether the group is in a self-contained classroom, in a team teaching situation, or in a departmentalized program. In most traditional classrooms, the largest part of a day or a period is involved with total group activity—all doing about the same thing at about the same time. Diagnostic teaching devotes more time to a combination of independent study and activity, to small self-organized groups which proceed while the teacher is working with other individuals, and to small groups brought together temporarily for a specific purpose. The chief purposes for which the total group is involved are planning together, the sharing of products, and appropriate horizon-raising experiences.

Teacher Role in Diagnostic Teaching

By encouraging the students' self-direction, self-selection, and responsibility for their own learning through guided self-evaluation, the teacher frees himself to perform his most effective roles. Less preoccupied with his traditional tasks, as presenter, corrector of papers, order-keeper, and disciplinarian, he can spend more time being a resource person. He can increase the materials and sources of information available to the learners, can enrich their environment and help to bring their real world and the school world into closer congruence.

The teacher in such a free role can provide means by which learners can get their own feedback, such as balance beams,[1] answer books, slide rules, globes, maps, charts, experimentation with many types of materials and situations, and all the wide variety of books and materials which learners can use as resources and for checking their ideas and information. He can also participate with individuals or groups in their explorations, inquiry, and theory building, as well as in their development of skills in thinking and learning, human relations, and democratic action. Above all, he is also freed to carry on individual conferences, which are the backbone of a program of diagnostic teaching.

Individual Conferences: Their Purposes and Use

As teachers stop using up most of their day in making general presentations, and as learners assume more and more responsibility for their own classroom activities, there is more time for individual conferences. Teachers who have made extensive use of such conferences cite many dividends in addition to the primary purpose of evaluation. They consistently feel that they know the students much better and have a better relationship with each of them. They gain many leads as to areas or ideas individuals might explore with special profit.

Still, the main purpose of the individual conference is evaluation. Where are we? Where have we come from? Where are we headed? What are the next steps? The teacher and learner look at the situation together and develop the learner's skill at self-evaluation. In terms of subject matter, the teacher raises questions, through relating not so much to information as to understanding. With his eye on the pupil as a person, he

---

[1] The balance beam is an ingenious contrivance, a three-foot long stick balanced on a point at the center. Metal points at one inch intervals along either side of the center hold weights, e.g., washers or drapery weights. This provides an equation whereby a washer on 3 and another on 5 will balance one on 8 on the other side of center. Or two washers on 5 will balance one on 10 and so on. It is a vivid and kinesthetic aid to mastery of concepts of the number system and provides its own feedback.

initiates questions and discussions that relate to purposes and goals and reality testing. The teacher helps the student identify lacks and needs in following out his specific purposes. Together they arrive at direction and next steps. If, after discussion, the learner still wishes to follow procedures or directions different from those envisioned by the teacher, he should be free to do so, unless of course, they could involve serious harm to someone or something. Since learning is building personal meaning out of experiences, what the learner sees as valuable to him is likely to be more valid than what someone else sees. If it does not turn out that way, he is still in an excellent position for effective learning from his experience and mistakes.

Records should be kept of these conferences. These are mainly for the teacher's use in guiding instruction, but they may also be helpful in evaluation for the record. As the teacher looks over these records for the individuals in the group, he can identify the learners who at the moment have common needs. These can be brought together at the first opportunity for short teaching sessions or seminars focused directly on the point of need. Such teaching has maximum effectiveness as it centers upon the present need of each pupil in the group.

Both the individual conferences and the group seminars may deal with concepts, understandings and skills in any of the content areas, or the interrelationships among them; with the development of thinking skills such as seeing relationships, generalizing, hypothesizing, testing hypotheses, applying generalizations to specific situations and the like; with human relations skills, including understanding oneself and others; with research skills; or with any other learning that is important to the learner at that time or which the teacher feels he needs to explore in order to provide more effective help.

To be more specific, let us look at the sorts of things which might well be a part of an individual conference in reading. Since reading is dealing with ideas and personal meaning, the conference should be focused on what the material read means to the child. If meaning seems to be minimal the teacher goes to the important sequencing aspects (see p. 91). If the reader can bring no relevant experience to bear on what he has read, then such experience needs to be planned for if desired by the student or felt essential by the teacher. Otherwise, a different choice of material should be made. It may be that the needed vocabulary is lacking even though experience and understanding of the general area are adequate. Or it may be that the thinking skills needed to relate the ideas read to the personal meaning of the learner are lacking, in which case the particular skill needed should be identified and procedures should be set up to develop it. But it may also be that more maturation and wider experiencing are needed first.

Thus, the first task is to explore the pertinent aspects of comprehension of the material read. Incidentally, it is not essential that the teacher have read the material before holding the conference. A great deal of understanding of the learner's reaction to his reading can come from asking him to summarize, to discuss important points, to document why he saw these points as he did by finding and reading aloud the key portions. The pupil may also be asked to predict on beyond where he has read, if he has not finished the material. In some cases it is wise to have him indicate the personal meaning the material has for him. Such personal meaning can be discovered, for example, by exploring with the pupil his identification with a character, or by asking how he might have responded differently than the characters in the material did.

During this exploration of what the material means to the pupil, it may become clear that a lack of certain mechanics of reading is getting in his way. If this is the case, the pupil may be helped immediately, or a note may be made to include him in a skill group dealing with this particular learning. Any of his other lacks—of experience, of vocabulary, of thinking skills and the like, may also be noted with a view to his inclusion in a group experience focused on this area of need.

Developing Confidence and Skill in Self-evaluation

Whether it is organizational, instructional or evaluative, any practice which limits the opportunity or lowers the confidence of the learner in evaluating his own progress and purposes is detrimental to his development and learning. The "giving" of grades and marks is the most obvious offender. Since these represent judgments based on the teacher's values in relation to how well the teacher feels a learner has met teacher-determined requirements, they cannot help playing down the values, self-direction, and self-evaluation of the learner. Since, as research has shown, the reliability and validity of such grades or marks are low anyway, their use is hard to defend.

Continuous evaluation, however, is essential as a basis for further learning. To be usable for this purpose it must be specific, pinpointing specific understandings and competencies as well as needed next steps. Teachers need such evaluation in order to plan for useful learning situations. Each learner needs this kind of evaluation to give him a realistic basis for his self-directed activity and for his involvement in his own learning.

Self-evaluation is always present. However, when a learner finds that the teacher's or the school's evaluation is quite different from his own, he must either reject the former (thereby downgrading any effectiveness the school may have in working with him) or else downgrade his own ability to evaluate himself. When it is his own judgment in which he loses confidence, the pupil has limited his most powerful learning tool. If one can never decide for himself the direction or effectiveness of his own learning, the amount and usefulness of that learning is, for him, inevitably decreased. If learners find it prudent and profitable, in the coinage of grades, to forget how they feel about their learning, they look to outside authority for direction. By this very act the meaningfulness of their learning is eroded away, their own sense of importance lessens, and their alienation increases.

In order to develop and improve self-evaluation in learners, we educators need certain attitudes, and then we must develop techniques appropriate to such attitudes.

1. We must respect and believe in the learner's ability to evaluate himself and his learning and to improve his evaluation if he has reasonable support and assistance. The longer the learner has experienced only outside evaluation the harder it will be to get him to take the initiative. If, for this or any other reason, he lacks a healthy self-concept, the task will be still longer and harder.

2. We must be willing to accept, at least temporarily, somewhat different goals than those we had in mind, particularly specific purposes of the learner. Perhaps, as illustrated in "The Poor Scholar's Soliloquy," [2] a boy may want to explain about diesel engines and make a tailgate for a truck rather than do abstract experiments on air pressure or make a broom holder.

3. We must be willing to accept the learner's own sequencing and his elimination of those parts which he can demonstrate he does not need. Many of the skills, in particular, are taught in some adult-determined sequence which often has little relevance to learners' needs. When children are free to be self-directing and self-evaluative, they make progress in quite different sequencing and often apparently leap over many "steps" through intuitive learning.

4. We must be willing to accept the learner's vehicle for gaining understanding and competencies. Needed skills, since they will be used in many ways and in many contexts, may be developed in a variety of ways which the learner may choose. Since the main problem is to arrive at learnings in such a way that they will be meaningful to the learner, it seems axiomatic that when a learner sees a certain context as meaningfully related to a learning, we might well encourage him to use that context.

[2] Stephen M. Corey. "The Poor Scholar's Soliloquy." *Childhood Education* 20(5): 219; January 1944

A girl wishes to understand living in Ecuador—rather than Peru, which the others are studying—because an uncle lives there and writes and sends her things from there. It seems inevitable that through a study of Ecuador she will not only have a more meaningful experience and achieve greater learning, which she can share with the group, but also that evaluation of this learning will be constantly taking place in a most realistic way. A boy may wish to develop arithmetic skills by keeping his dad's business accounts. This will certainly have, for him, far more value from any point of view than review exercises on computation, banking, and income tax procedures as these can be taught out of a textbook.

5. We must directly encourage self-evaluation not only by accept-ance, but also by providing specific opportunities and helping learners to build their skills through experience. A start can be made by talking with the total group. After the stage is set, individual conferences provide op-portunities for the teacher and learner to evaluate together; to look at the learner's goals and specific purposes, to decide where he is, what has been mastered, what is in process, and what are his next steps.

Most learners will continue to need occasional teacher assistance, and some will need considerable help for some time. Little by little, however, they will all learn to depend more on their own judgment, partly because the experience will have improved their judgment. As time goes on, they will have clearer conceptions of their goals and pur-poses, and they will learn to value their own thinking as the cornerstone of decision making.

Looking Back Over Chapters 3 and 4

Dare we remind the reader once more of the terms on which the inquiry in this section was conducted? We deliberately turned our backs for the moment—knowing full well that we could do so *only* for the moment—on the whole paraphernalia of marking and grading and grant-ing credits and filling out transcripts. In a sense, we entered the private world of the individual—and the almost equally private world of a teacher and his class—and we asked ourselves a fundamental question: If evaluation had no function except to help the individual learn well and the teacher teach well, what would evaluation look like then?

As we focused our attention on the individual learner, leaning heavily on modern perceptual psychology, we found a few fundamental gen-eralizations that we could depend upon:

1. Every human being is always *surgent*. He is always trying to make himself more adequate, as he defines adequacy for himself. He cannot stop this any more than a young oak tree can stop growing.

2. Every human being is always *evaluating*. He cannot stop this either. He keeps receiving feedback from the world and the people around him, as well as from the results of his actions. From this he keeps building a conception of himself as he now is, a conception of the self that would be more adequate, and a conception of ways to move from where he is to where he wants to be.

3. The crucial element in his becoming, then, lies in the *feedback* he receives and in his *perceptions* of it. The feedback to which he has access may be meager, if his environment is poor; it may even be distorted, if the people around him have distorted views. The interpretations he makes of whatever feedback is available to him may, in turn, be unperceptive or even distorted, for a number of reasons. As a consequence, his perceptions of himself may be meager or distorted; his conception of adequacy for himself—of the self he might desirably become—may be equally faulty; and his tactics and the strategies that guide his becoming may suffer the same lacks.

4. The function of school-assisted evaluation, then, is to aid his becoming by providing rich, valid feedback and by helping him perceive and use it. It must offer him ways of perceiving himself more validly, especially of sensing his underappreciated strengths; it must reveal possibilities of improvement which he has not seen; and it must clarify the action choices before him. Particularly, in terms of the school's function, it must work toward relevance between the curriculum and his goals— and make that relevance clear to him.

When we turned to the teacher, we found ourselves virtually talking more about a *changed way of teaching* than about evaluation as a separate thing:

1. We want an organization of instruction in which evaluation is built right into the teaching itself. We have called this *diagnostic teaching*. (In this connection, we have ignored the more formal devices, such as paper-and-pencil tests; we are not hostile to them. Undoubtedly, in the process of diagnostic teaching, there would be many times when a teacher's reading of a student's paper or the use of a test would provide the feedback both he and the learner need. We have probably leaned over backward in our emphasis on the less formal and more personal elements.)

2. The organization of instruction must be such as to bring the individual learner into high visibility. This applies to his developing knowledge and skills; and the system must provide opportunities to see these *in action*, in a kind of test-as-you-go plan. It applies with equal force to the individual's attitudes and purposes and goals; and the system must be designed to get these into plain sight for both the learner and the teacher.

3. The system must strive for full and open communication as the key to both teaching and evaluating. One important means to this end is a high degree of pupil participation in planning work and later in reviewing it. The group as a whole or small groups can bring much into the open just by talking things over.

4. Above all, we have placed reliance on a heavy use of individual conferences.

5. Finally, it seems to us, the whole system must consciously work its way toward a high degree of self-direction, with active but relatively nondirective participation by the teacher.

At this final point, especially, our separate views of the learner and of the teacher merge into an image of the two together. The central figure is the child, progressively seeing himself more and more clearly, sensing his latent powers and abilities, discovering more and more choices and opportunities open to him, exploring freely and opening himself to a flood of stimuli, little by little taking charge of his own life space and moving ahead on his own energy. But beside him stands the teacher, a mighty force in his life, wise in providing him data about himself and the world and helping him see what the data mean, sensitive in shaping the school's subject matter to his needs, open in offering himself for all the help that he has to give.

We may have seemed, at times, far from the topic of evaluation, as it is usually understood. We ourselves do not wish to say that we have presented the whole of evaluation. We do wish to say that, in the relatively private world where learner and teacher meet, what we have sketched is the essential foundation upon which the other necessary superstructure can be built. We go on now, in Chapter 5, to move a little bit closer to the traditional tasks of testing and grading and reporting. Only, we shall still insist on examining what testing *really* means and how one opens up communication. In effect, then, Chapter 5 is an extension of our treatment of diagnostic teaching. From there we shall go on, in Part Three, to see how other portions of the evaluation system we need can be built, without distorting the open, unpressured position we have so far envisioned.

5

Mr. Newman and Joe

Rodney A. Clark

IN HELPING each student evaluate his unique becoming, the teacher's behavior will vary to fit the individuality of each relationship. This means, certainly, that the method of helping each student must grow out of the specific help the student needs, and most procedures will be effective only once. Certain principles about the process may be generalized, however, and furnish guidelines for making the teacher's help more likely to be completely pertinent to the student's needs.

Helping Students with Personal Evaluation

Consider, for instance, the following episode in which an English teacher is working with Joe, a boy who has difficulty with all aspects of communication. (Let us assume that the statements of such a boy can be written in something resembling conventional spelling!)

What Does Joe Need?

When the students had settled to their various tasks, the teacher asked Joe to sit with him at the corner table.

"Do you have your list of objectives?" the teacher asked.

Joe took a much-folded sheet of paper from his shirt pocket and smoothed it on the desk. From where he sat, the teacher could not read the paper, but he could see there was not much written on it.

"I saw you writing on a long list the other day. What happened?" he inquired.

"I still have the other list somewheres. D'ya want it?"

"Not particularly. I'm just curious about the two lists."

"Well, when we were all talkin' about objectives in class, I'd hear someone tell an objective and I'd agree. 'Yeh, I want ta do that.' And then I'd hear another, 'n'another. So pretty soon I had a long list of things. But when I got ta thinkin' it over I knew I'd be kiddin' myself. All those things would be nice. I'd *like* to be all those things. But I'm not really tryin' ta do 'em. So I made this list of things that I *am* tryin' ta do— or be. Ya see, there's all kinds of things I know I *should* do 'n' I'd be nicer if I did 'em. But I'm not."

"I think I understand, but try that last phrase again. You're not what?" the teacher urged.

Joe took a deep breath and stretched his arms out straight on the desk. "It's so much easier that way." Then he grinned and went on. "What I was hopin' you'd guess I meant was, I know there are objectives I'm s'posed to have. There are things I'm s'posed to want ta be or do. But I haven't agreed yet that they're *my* objectives. Whether I'm s'posed to or not, I still am not headin' for those things."

"Yes!" the teacher exclaimed. "I understand that. So now you have a list of objectives that state what you *really* are trying to accomplish."

"Yeh—six things." Joe's hands were still smoothing the list.

"I gather you don't expect me to read that paper. Are you going to read it to me?" the teacher asked.

"I'm still not sure what happens to this list," Joe answered.

"You're not sure you want me to know your objectives."

"I *want* you to know 'em and I want you to help me with 'em," Joe answered, but he still was hesitant.

"You're afraid I won't help when I hear them," the teacher tried to finish for Joe.

"Sort'a. I still can't help feelin' that if somethin's real important ya hafta hide it, and people don't like ya if ya need help." Joe added, almost as a question, "I guess I'm still not sure you'll help." He slowly looked up at the teacher. The teacher smiled, but he made no comment. "I guess the only way I'll know is to try you?"

The teacher agreed, "Even though I promise to help, you still have to try me and see."

Joe began to read from his list. He had written a run-on paragraph and read it as though it were one long sentence: "First, I want to talk to any person whenever I need to and, second, I want to make good sense saying the things I'm thinking. Third, I want to know some girls who could go on a date with me and act like I'm grown up. (I can dance, sorta, but I'm willing to work on anything like this that helps.) Fourth, I wanna act so people will know more sides to me. I don't wanna stop believing things I do, but I'd like people ta know there's more to me than just what they already think I believe in. Fifth, I'd like ta know about imagery, maybe even get ta be able ta write a poem. Sixth, I'd like to—"

Joe hesitated finally and then explained, "This last one's a little dif'rent and it doesn't—but it's still what I want—sixth, I'd like to let my dad know I think he's all right. I've never even told him so, but I'd like really to do somethin' so he'll know what I think."

The teacher commented, "You haven't talked about this before."

"Well, in a way, I have. I just haven't said it was Dad I talked about. Way I feel 'bout it, he's kinda mixed in all the other objectives. Like wantin' to talk to people. Quite often I'm thinkin' of somethin' ta say to 'im—Dad—but by the time I kin get ready ta talk he's gone or he's talkin' ta somebody else, or about somethin' else. And I wanna get to know girls and all that just 'cause I do, but I think if girls began to treat me grown up, maybe Dad might, too. And you know what he thinks I'm like? He thinks the only thing I'm interested in is horses! That as long as I have a horse to ride I'll be happy. Just last night he was tellin' people that. An' I do like horses, but I like a lotta things he never knows even."

"You seem to be saying he doesn't understand you. What is this in your sixth objective, letting your father know you think he's all right?"

"That's the objective. He doesn' know I think that. In fact, he thinks I don't feel that way. I don't think even you could explain it to him. I mean, it isn't just that I don't communicate so good. He don't hear much of what we say to 'im 'cause he has this other idea. But if I could do the other five things, then gradually I might get so's I'd do the sixth one somehow. So what I want help with is the first five objectives."

"All right. What help do you need as you see it?"

"I need you to keep on practicing with me, keep on talkin' to me, and tellin' me if you understan what I'm sayin'."

"But you stated in your objective you wanted to talk to *any person*. How are you going to transfer what you and I develop together to interactions with other people?"

"I think I know. You see, I watch what it is you do to let me know if you understand. An' I know you understand when we keep on talkin' 'bout what I'm tryin' to say. So I figure when I'm talkin' to someone, and we keep on talkin' 'til we're finished—not just quit—but finished talkin' 'bout the thing, then I must be makin' sense to that person."

"Why don't we try that as a test and see what we learn from it?" the teacher agreed.

"That would tell about the second objective. How about the first?" Joe asked.

"You'll know if you do better with the first, of course, because you'll begin to get more of what you need from people. I think I can help you check on the first just by watching whether you do talk to people more. Would you accept that as a test for a while?"

Joe chuckled. "It's a test, 'cause that's what I need. I need ta talk to people."

"And number three? What am I supposed to do about that?" the teacher asked.

"You know I'm not expectin' you to 'range a date for me. Anyway, the whole point is that I can *arrange* a date of my own. But you could keep on havin' us do things in class like talk ta girls."

"All right. I think that procedure is good for many members of the class. But you'll have to talk to a number of girls and not get exclusive. That way you'll be working on objectives three and one. Now, about four. How will you test to see whether you're achieving that?"

"I thought maybe you would tell me if people change their ideas 'bout me. You know, if someone tells you they are thinkin' sumpthin's different 'bout me."

"That's kind of tricky. You don't want me to tell others what you say about them. You must be pretty sure I won't, or you wouldn't tell me the things you do. And why is my word any more important than the word of others?"

"What others?" Joe snorted.

"The ones whose opinions of you change. If they begin to think of you differently, won't they tell you so?"

"I hadn' thought of that," Joe mused, pleased with the idea. "Maybe they won't exactly say 'Joe, you're diffrn't,' but if they *think* I'm diffrn't they'll hafta *treat* me diffrn't."

"So the real test of objective four will be when you can tell me who has seen a new side to you! Now, what is this one about imagery?"

"The other day when you were readin' us some poems, I really knew that the poet was tellin' me sumpthin'. You said it was imagery. An' I thought 'bout some ideas I've had like that. An' it would be really good to be able to write out some of these things and see if they'd make other people feel like I do 'bout 'em."

"So your objective isn't to *know about* imagery. Your objective is to create poetry."

"Yeah! And you don't hafta sock me with it. The test of that is to write a poem. That don't seem very likely."

"I think it's altogether likely. Others in the class are writing poetry. When we get a collection, you can test each other on what kinds of response the poems arouse."

Four Guiding Principles for Personal Evaluation

Joe and his teacher have already established a working relationship in which there is mutual trust, and Joe is convinced that the teacher can help him. It can be seen in the episode, however, that the trusting, helping relationship is reaffirmed and retested as the two work together. The first two guiding principles for personal evaluation have to do with guaranteeing that the teacher and student continue to build and extend a personal interaction which binds the teacher's resources directly to what the student is working on. In summary, the two principles make up the "helping relationship" previously discussed. However, since one principle derives from the student and the other from the teacher, the principles are listed separately.

1. *The student must recognize a need and look upon the teacher and the school situation as a source for the satisfaction of his need.*

Such a recognition by the student does not come about automatically. It is the teacher's responsibility to provide learning situations through which students will experience acceptance of their needs as legitimate concerns for class time and effort. In the preceding episode, Joe was not sure what would happen to his list of objectives if he read them, but he knew he could ask. He knew he could legitimately discard one list for another that would be more personally real to him. He did not suppose the teacher would arrange a date for him, but he did feel that increasing his skills for knowing and relating to girls could be an accepted class activity.

Joe's awareness that the English class was a place for him to satisfy his needs came about because he *experienced* the acceptance, not only because he was told so. Even his awareness that the teacher would keep a promise came about, not because of the promise, but because the kept promise was experienced. The list of objectives Joe read to the teacher was the outcome of some activity in which the whole class seems to have participated.

2. *The teacher must be willing to help the student satisfy the need the student recognizes.*

The teacher must be sensitive to all the student is trying to communicate and must empathize with the student's estimate of his needs (although the teacher may also recognize that the student's evaluation is not yet complete). It is the teacher's *willingness* to help that is emphasized. The resources of a good teacher are vast; with imaginative, divergent thinking, who knows the full potential of a teacher's resources for helping students? Yet a teacher is not omnipotent and will sometimes have to say to a student, "If I could help, I would," or *"When* I can help, I will," or "To the extent I can help, I will." When a student experiences the willingness, he can appreciate the reality of what resources are available.

When Joe talked with the teacher about his father, he knew that the teacher could help only indirectly. Yet from his relationship with the teacher, Joe was learning a larger concept of communication and experiencing more accurately what was lacking in his relation with his father. To talk about the need was appropriate class activity, whether or not the need could be satisfied in the class confines.

Certainly activities to satisfy Joe's other felt needs were all being included as class activities in the context of Joe's own definitions. This is true, even though in Joe's list of objectives, perhaps only his interest in imagery might be thought of as appropriate to the traditional English class. Even in this regard, Joe is talking about writing imagery, not writing about it. Joe's concern is neither academic nor mechanical. He has some feelings he wants to share with other people. He sees in poetry, particularly in the use of imagery, a technique for communicating about these feelings. To him the important goal is a response to the feeling he is communicating.

3. *The teacher must help the student experiment with different ways to satisfy his needs and to devise means of testing results of each experiment.*

As Joe described each of his objectives, the teacher asked him to explain how they could tell whether or not Joe was accomplishing the objective. A consideration of the conversation between Joe and his teacher makes it obvious that it is natural for a student to talk of objectives in terms of some new activity he thinks will get him something he needs. It is also obvious in the conversation that one cannot think of objectives without also thinking of testing. Most of our daily activities are trying and testing—indeed, most of our trying is also testing! Our efforts to achieve are automatically combined with ways to tell whether we are achieving. We continually ask whether or not we are getting to where we are trying to go, and whether or not what we are getting is what we want.

A test is, and is only, a way to tell whether an objective is being reached, whether a skill is being mastered, whether a hypothesis can be accepted. Testing is almost constant. Therefore, a student is much involved in selecting and undertaking tests. Almost always this kind of testing is a satisfying experience. The tests which have to do with personal satisfaction of needs are rarely administered to groups. There are many important and appropriate reasons why teachers and students need to participate in the development of group statistics and to contribute data to group testing programs. It is necessary, however, that these efforts not take precedence over each student's need to test what he is accomplishing in all the ways he can devise.

The students *and* teachers must constantly grow in the skill to devise simpler, more exact and more valid ways to test each person's becoming. The time and effort for both the testing and the improvement of testing must be legitimately part of class activity. Whenever a teacher encourages a student to try something new, there must also be a plan for the student to tell what results from the new activity. That the activity must supply data for the test is one way to know that the activity is pertinent to the individual's goal. It is clear, then, that externally imposed tests will not be valid.

4. *The student should keep a record of what he is trying and how he is progressing. In a separate record, the teacher should record how he is trying to help the student and how he tests the effectiveness of his help.*

Perhaps the teacher should give precedence to recording what Joe says directly about himself. Yet Joe is always telling about himself indirectly, too, in every activity he undertakes. If some of these activities begin to show a pattern, then the teacher can hypothesize about what Joe, by his pattern of behavior, seems to be communicating. For instance, it happens that Joe did undertake to write some themes. In his own peculiar style he told about a little boy longing for something in a store window. Several days later he wrote about a trip to the mountains and emphasized his thrill at standing on a great height and gazing into the far, vast distance. Finally, he wrote a story about a submarine that became stuck at the bottom of the ocean. He described the horror of the predicament and ended with a rather strange thought. "Suppose," he wrote, "that the submarine sank at a shallow spot. Then the periscope would go up to the surface and the sailors could see out, but they would still be stuck!"

Here is a pattern about gazing at unobtainable things. No one could *know* what Joe is trying to say here, but any careful teacher could make a guess by putting this theme with Joe's other behaviors. Perhaps the teacher might guess that Joe is afraid of getting what he wants. With such a hypothesis, the teacher would probably help Joe think about ambivalence. Perhaps this would be an individual problem for Joe, or the teacher might decide such a consideration would be an activity appropriate for some group in the class. Private discussion, group discussion, role playing, selected reading—with a hypothesis about a need, the teacher's resources for meeting the need are extensive. If the hypothesis and activity fit the need, then there will be feedback from the students that reveals their satisfaction. There will be less ambivalence, more of the activity will be sought, and specific ambivalence will come into the open. If the teacher's hypothesis were recorded, his choice of activity would be specific to his guess about need, and he would be alerted to the probable data telling him what came of the learning experience he provided.

It would be ideal, if while the teacher is making a record of how he tries to help Joe, he could also keep a record of how he is helping each of the other students in his class(es). Like many ideals, this one is probably beyond reach. Teachers have found, though, that in turning to this kind of record about their efforts and encouraging the kind of testing discussed in the previous section, the nature of the work they do changes.

There is less busywork to attend to, more communication is oral rather than written, much less time is spent judging student products, there are fewer written group tests. Therefore, time is gained to hypothesize about individual needs, to plan with individuals, to respond personally to individuals, to keep records rather than grades. In addition, since the effectiveness of the individualized efforts to help is more satisfying than traditional norm-oriented or content-limited teaching, the work does not seem so hard.

Even by keeping such a record on only a few children, the teacher can become more sensitive to significant data which will become part of the teacher's interaction with all students.

Grading Is Not Evaluating

In the introductory anecdote, neither Mr. Newman nor Joe mentioned grades. Nevertheless, this description of a teacher-pupil relationship does highlight, though partly by the omission of the expected, the aspects of evaluation which must underline the effective use of grading.

At the risk of once again belaboring the obvious, it is important to emphasize here that grading is not evaluating. What Mr. Newman and Joe are working out together are steps in the evaluating process. They have been at it for quite a while, and they have built an open, communicative relationship, even if Joe still does hang back a little. At some time, after this process is completed, Mr. Newman and Joe may summarize their evaluation and record the summary in some symbol like an "A" or a "C." However, (a) doing so is not a necessary part of the process of evaluating; (b) doing so is entirely dependent on the fact that the process of evaluation is completed first; and (c) no one symbol can possibly reveal much of what came of the evaluation process.

It should serve both as a guide and as a source of security to teachers to keep this distinction constantly in mind: *Grading is not evaluating; grading is one way in which one reports an evaluation.* A grade symbol has no meaning except as it shows that all the steps of evaluation have been completed: an objective has been selected; it has been decided what evidence will indicate the attainment of the objective; the evidence has been collected; the evidence has been analyzed; and next steps have been selected. Even so, a grade symbol has no meaning except as those interpreting it have agreed to define it.

When one thinks about this, it becomes evident that most of the things we are constantly evaluating are not, cannot be, summarized in grades. The practice of summarizing evaluations in grade symbols has, at best, a very limited practical value. Let us consider examples of situations not graded in order to more wisely review those situations which usually are graded in schools.

For instance, almost every school staff is involved, in one way or another, in making evaluations of the needs of its community. A staff sets out to collect data, and, having collected it, frames hypotheses about the needs of the community. Then the school tries to establish some kind of program to meet these needs. A school does not go around grading the community. It just tries to find out what the community is doing. It reports back to the community by taking some kind of action in reference to what has been learned. School staff and community members agree, "If this is what we found out about the community's needs, then this is what we have to do." How could one presume to summarize this process by an "A" or "B" or other grade!

Another kind of evaluation shows up in a staff's concern for conducting action research. Professional groups of teachers participate in trying out certain notions, putting these to some kind of test. Ideas that this or that would be a good way to operate are put into practice in such a way that the group can collect information about what happens and make some decisions. Action research is a scientific procedure for finding out things and turning the results into immediate action. The report of such an activity is built into the ongoing consideration of the data. If a final summary report is prepared, it is rather comprehensive. No one would try to symbolize the report in a letter or a number or even in a short statement or phrase.

If one were going to report an action research project, he would certainly explain what he was trying to find out, how he thought he was going to find it, what data it would take to answer the questions, how he collected the data, and then eventually the data he obtained and the conclusions he came to from analyzing the data. The account would be fairly long and detailed because only as each part stands in context to the rest would any of it make sense. Once again, one would completely skip over any notion of giving the action research an "A," "B," or "C."

It may not be so quickly recognized that a great part of the personal evaluation that goes on in the teaching-learning situation would also appear very foolish in summarized grade form. For instance, even in a teacher-directed curriculum where the teacher sets objectives for students, the teacher must make some estimate of how well he is fulfilling his task. Yet he would not be likely to give himself an "A" or other grade. And, if he faces the situation realistically, he will not turn around and grade the student "C" or "D" because the teacher did not supply enough material for the student to accomplish what the teacher wanted him to do. Such a mix-up cannot occur if the teacher clearly recognizes what evaluation is and what the summary of evaluation is as recorded in grade symbols.

Situations in Which Grades Are Inappropriate

Another kind of confusion can be avoided if evaluation and grading are held distinctly separate. This is in the area of learning about a student's needs and helping him satisfy these needs. By definition, a need is a motivating force that must be met. A student does not choose his needs; the needs are part of his self-system. There can be no question of judging his needs as good or bad, as "A" or "F." One cannot judge the needs of others. One can recognize another's need, accept it as reality, work with it.

Now, after a need has been recognized, and ways to go about satisfying the need have been selected, it *may* be appropriate that a teacher be asked to summarize his evaluation of how well the necessary learning tasks have been accomplished. This evaluation conceivably could be in the form of a grade. The reporting of a need to a student could not be in a grade form, but a judgment about how well he worked at meeting his need could be.

The discussion to this point suggests that only evaluations which result in judgments can be summarized in symbol form. (Evaluation as measurement is discussed elsewhere.) Now, then, with a clear recognition that teachers should strive always to reserve judgments as much as possible, a teacher can determine how most effectively to relate to the requirement of issuing grades.

Reporting by Grades

At present, grading is a requirement with which most teachers must go along whether they like it or not. There are ethical, professional procedures for changing school practices. Until such procedures affect grading practices, however, the teacher has to go along with the requirements of his school, because he is hired to do so. The teacher's great responsibility is to consider thoroughly the local requirements and to work out specific methods of abiding by these, while at the same time keeping faith with the basic commitment to be a facilitator of learning. Because of this, a teacher should hold steadfastly to one overriding requirement: *Before any evaluations are reported to anyone in grade form, be sure the student concerned understands what the grades mean.*

This rule reminds us that, if only communication between teacher and student were concerned, grades would rarely be used. However, there are three other consumers of grades. Before we return to reporting evaluations to students, let us consider reporting to these other consumers.

Two of these other consumers are usually mistakenly lumped together in grading practices. It is supposed that high school records of a student's grades are equally useful to other high schools and colleges and to prospective employers. This is untrue at two levels. First, professional educators are supposed to be better trained and much wiser in the use of information about people than are most employers. Therefore, teachers are qualified to use a different kind of information about a new student than is an employer about a new employee. Second, an employer has the right to choose those people who have certain skills. He has the right to know what a school can tell him about what a student can do. What has gone into making up the learning sequence of a student's becoming skilled is of little importance to an employer and probably none of his business at all.

However, unlike employers, teachers are responsible for working with students whether the students are skilled or otherwise, and the information about what has gone into the student's becoming is usually more important than just how skilled he is at the moment. And even without a recorded history of a student's experiences, the teacher needs to know more about him than just his skills. This kind of information should be of concern to teachers who undertake to facilitate a student's learning at a different school or as he goes on to a more advanced school.

What an employer would like to know, then, is quite likely to be such items as the speed at which a student can type, how fast he can read, an estimate of his vocabulary, whether he can independently use a vertical milling machine, whether he relates to strangers easily, whether he has a history of acceptance by peers, or whether he can compute with a slide rule. If the forwarded record of a high school student explains the symbols sufficiently, an employer may be able to interpret course credits and grades to answer these questions. It would be easier for him, if he could read the answers directly from written statements without having to guess about grade symbols!

In regard to what employers do with school grades, it is likely that most teachers greatly overemphasize their present importance. It is true that employers would like to know about the skills of prospective employees. Few of them think records of grades tell them this. In the author's case, he has had twelve jobs since graduating from college the first time, and never once has he been asked about a grade! In all the professional jobs a transcript has been available to employers, but if they examined it they did not ask about it.

The third important consumer of evaluation reports is the student's parents. Certainly, what a parent needs to know about the development of his child is quite different from what other teachers need to know or what employers have to know. It would make perfectly good sense to have separate records for parents.

Teachers know that different schools require teachers to report to the parents in different ways. One is the parent-teacher conference, which at its best presents an effective procedure for establishing a working relationship between homes and school. It has been easier to use in elementary schools than in the typical secondary school, because each secondary-school teacher deals with so many students. There are ways of getting around this difficulty by having each teacher responsible for all the information about one group of students. But, at best, parent-teacher conferences require skill and forethought.

By sitting down together to communicate their common concerns, parents and teachers can better understand the objectives of a student and what has been set up to facilitate the student's learning at home and at school. They can share information about the extent to which a student is accomplishing his objectives, and come to grips with better ways to live with him. Once again, this procedure cannot be recorded in grade symbols. One cannot put this on a transcript and send it to a college. But certainly there must be a record if the discussions are to be followed up and the relationship is to grow. It is another point in favor of maintaining two sets of records.

Another kind of reporting that appears every now and then requires that teachers write a letter to parents. Most of the schools recognize that it is inefficient to write an original letter that is a specific consideration of every single child. To do so would take at least as much time as a parent-teacher conference, and the face-to-face situation avoids many dangers of misunderstanding which tend to result from the written word. Therefore, the so-called letter becames a form through which there are a variety of blanks to be filled in to personalize a description of what each child is doing in school. Most teachers soon run out of colorful terms to insert in the blanks, and the letters become trite and not personalized at all. If such a letter is used, it communicates much more if each teacher sets up a form very specific to the objectives of his class. Even this form begins to lose sight of the individual unless it is constantly revised as the objectives of the class change.

The most common kind of report to parents is the report card.

Around the country one can find every kind, size, shape and color for a form called a report card. Most schools experiment with novelties and then return to a form that lists the high school subjects with a space beside each subject where a symbol summarizing an evaluation is to be recorded. Many schools use a card for each class instead of one card for all classes. Most report cards have spaces for written comments of some kind, a summary of attendance, and a space for parents to sign an indication that they have examined the card.

Perhaps the most current pattern in the constant revision of report cards is an effort to break down the one summarizing symbol grade into several for each subject. That is, a grade for a subject such as English is not reported in one symbol but will be reported as a grade in spelling, a grade in composition, and a grade in the appreciation of literature. This system does tell a parent more than one grade per subject does, if only to give the parent a better idea of what goes to make up the content of the courses offered in today's high schools. Since this is what a parent will read into the form, the school staff members must be pretty sure that they can stand behind the oversimplified printed breakdown of course objectives.

Whichever of these kinds of report cards the teacher is expected to use, the problem remains that the symbols used are supposed to summarize something. In the particular school, what is the teacher expected to summarize?

If the school does not require that grades compare each student with some kind of norm, then the teacher does not have much of a problem. If the stated definitions of the grade symbols are published in statements such as "has developed—," "has changed—," "has accomplished this or that goal," [1] for example, the teacher is not trying to summarize how one student compares with another but how the student has gone on from a previous report. This is not, however, the usual type of definition for grade symbols.

Most schools stipulate that the "A," or "B," or "C," means a student has done a certain quality of work as compared with the way other students are working (or have worked). There is an expectancy established and this student has performed at the level of the expectancy, above the expectancy, below the expectancy, or not at all. Any kind of percentile system is a forced comparison of some kind. This system may be a comparison with local, regional or national norms; but in some way the individual student is being placed on a scale as to how people are expected to perform.

The teacher does not ordinarily get to choose definitions for the report symbols. These are stipulated on the form itself; or, at least, they

[1] How much? Very difficult to say without comparisons that are at least implied

are part of a local value-attitude system. It is the new teacher's responsibility to learn what the symbols "mean" locally and to use them accordingly.

There is no need to let the comparison type of grade be frustrating to the teacher or student. Even though what the student has been working on is unique to his relationship and involves no comparison with any other student, the comparison may be meaningful if the student understands it fully. What the teacher may be saying to him is that one way to measure him is to compare how he does things with how others do the same thing. He can understand that such information does not at the time tell him much about his objectives, but he may want to know the information anyway. As long as there is no confusion that this comparison is supposed to tell him about his objectives when it does not, little harm will result.

Let us return to an aspect of grading that occurs before the summaries are reported to other teachers, schools, employers or parents. This is the kind of grading that takes the form of ongoing reports to the student. In the usual situation a student sees many grades other than the report card. Almost everything he makes, does, writes, plans, says or admits to thinking is subject to grading in most schools.

As we have tried to show, if teachers think carefully about why students are doing the activities, the teachers will be less likely to grade them. If a teacher asks a student to communicate, and if the student tries to do so, the teacher should be careful to respond to what is communicated and only incidentally to the skill with which the communication is formed. The response should be in such terms as "I understand," "I think you mean some other thing than you are saying," or "I can accept the fact that you have that value." What can the student do with the response, "You have communicated a C's worth"?

Another thing that teachers might consider in regard to responding to student work is that there are many reasons why a student may legitimately be asked to do something that may not involve a response from the teacher. Many times a teacher may need to know only that a student has done a certain thing. Skills practice usually has this characteristic. Both the teacher and student are aware that the student must practice. Both teacher and student need a record that the practice is going on. Why grade such practice? Can we honestly form a *judgment* about the practicing? Do we need to? Sometimes we do. *Right* practice makes perfect; *wrong* practice only confirms errors. Someone should at least observe practice. For example, all coaches do; and they do form judgments about it. Yet this does not mean that every piece of practice needs to be graded.

There is another way in which teachers frequently confuse objectives and thus grade the wrong things, so that the report to the student becomes a misleading communication. In most classes a series of performances is required. For instance, in a speech class a student gives speeches; in an art class he paints or models or creates things; in an English class he writes themes. These performances are representations of the student's efforts to accomplish objectives. Most teachers grade these performances. They tell the student that his speech is an "A" speech, his painting a "B" painting, his theme a "C" writing. This, however, is not what the student needs to know! He needs to know whether or not he has changed since the last speech, painting or theme. He also needs to know that measures of progress in speech, writing or art cannot adequately be reduced to A B C's or other such codes. The teacher should be grading the spaces between the performances, so to speak, not the performances alone.

Sometimes teachers put both a grade and a comment on papers. If the teacher who does so will watch closely, he is likely to find that the closure brought about by the grade will supersede any effect of the comment. If the teacher submits only comments to the students, without confusing the comments with grades, the students have a point from which to continue progress. Of course, if a student's objective is only to pass the course, all he wants to know from the teacher is whether or not he is passing. To have no grades on his paper frustrates such a student. The teacher will have to work with him to encourage him to use school classes for more significant learning. Perhaps withholding grades from papers is one beginning step to help students recognize the teacher as a resource for significant learning. The teacher will have to make an individual decision each time the problem arises.

Teacher-made Tests and Communication

Before leaving this consideration of reporting test results to students, let us point out some important aspects of classroom tests as such. The chapter's introductory anecdote describes a way of looking at testing that varies radically from the kinds of tests generally used in schools. The reader will have lived through years of school experiences in which a certain type of test has been a most emphasized feature. For many students it seems very difficult to realize that the "tests" so much a part of school life are only a very limited use of all the available ways to find out whether or not a goal is being reached.

Any situation which serves as a trial to tell whether a desired accomplishment has been achieved is a test. Or, any device which gathers data enabling one to verify or discredit a hypothesis is a test. By such definitions as these many of our daily activities are tests. We spend much of our time deciding whether we have achieved something or whether we can accept certain hypotheses. The simple tests we use are quite valid and reliable. They are direct and firsthand. Yet these tests are usually ignored in classrooms, or even prevented from occurring, while teachers turn to complicated, limited, indirect precedures of doubtful validity and reliability. Most of the school "tests" measure only what facts a student knows and are quite far from testing the extent to which the student is a fact-using person or whether he is effective in any regard. If such tests are attempts in these directions, they are almost always indirect. They produce an artificial situation in which the student pretends to use some knowledge or skill. These "tests" rarely yield data about the effectiveness of the student in his real life.

In the introductory anecdote, Joe and his teacher are discussing a series of situations which will serve as trials of Joe's mastery of certain skills. The implication is that Mr. Newman may use only the procedures he and Joe describe to tell what Joe is accomplishing in sophomore English. Much depends on the objectives of Mr. Newman's sophomore English as to whether or not these particular trials are the appropriate ones for estimating success in the course. They certainly are appropriate tests of whether or not *Joe* is accomplishing his objectives; and in Mr. Newman's sophomore English, *for Joe,* accomplishing Joe's objectives is the course.

If one considers all the suggestions that have been offered in the preceding chapters concerning ways to improve communication, ways to foster discussion, ways to gather and analyze data, it can be seen that each of these is a test when looked at from that reference point. Any time data are gathered and examined something is being tested, and such tests are essential to need-satisfaction. When needs are being satisfied, the test experience is pleasant. The experience is sought by the person who is testing his efforts. Testing goes on constantly.

On the other hand, most of the usual quizzes, exams, tests—whatever the written exercises are labeled—have very little to do with significant learning. It is a rare event to find in one of these instruments any indication that the examiner is concerned that a student has changed. In fact, it is easy to show that, many times, the taking of "tests" prevents a student from engaging in activities that would have enabled him to change in a developmental way. Such "tests" are usually interruptions to regular procedures, requirements of outside forces, not experiences sought by the persons being tested.

Most discussions of evaluation in the schools include descriptions of how a teacher should construct "tests." They include instructions about different kinds of items—alternate-response, multiple choice, matching, free response, and completion items—and instructions about when these varieties of items are appropriately used. There is little more that can be added to the available discussions about item construction.

The present discussion is an attempt to decrease concern about this problem. Teachers are urged to put "tests" made up of such items "in their place." It is much more important to think of each student's objectives and what data it would take to tell whether the objectives are being achieved. Teachers are also urged to discuss this problem with each student. What data will it take to tell the *student* whether he is achieving his objectives?

Looking at testing in this way removes the unfortunate possibilities that "tests" may be looked upon as motivating devices, weapons for punishing students, threats to keep students doing something they see no sense in doing, or ways to know how to "reward" students. In a program of personal evaluation, none of these ways to "use" tests is appropriate.

A test is, and is only, a way to tell whether an objective is being reached or a skill is being mastered or a hypothesis can be accepted. Testing is almost constant, and the student is at least as much involved in selecting and undertaking the test as is the teacher. Almost always, testing, so conceived, will be a satisfying experience to the student.

Part Three

Evaluation
and the Larger Organization

*I*T'S *a lovely dream we've been having, but how will it stand the light of day? It's all very well to portray an almost-private world of one teacher and a group of learners, a pressure-free world in which the only need is to facilitate learning and teaching by opening up communication, encouraging self-evaluation and sensitizing evaluation to the full range of objectives. But can this little world really be that free of outside pressures? Won't this pretty little scheme break down under the added demands of producing the records and the information needed by the system as a whole—all the added load of meeting college entrance requirements, for instance? Can these added demands actually be kept "off the back" of the teaching-learning process?*

The answer to that last question is yes. *In a very large degree teachers can be freed to teach and learners can be freed to learn if* we go about the whole thing in a different way. *The systematic data-collection and record-keeping which every educational system needs can be accomplished with amazingly small interference. What is more, the data collected can be very superior to those we now generally gather—reaching across a much broader spectrum of valued objectives—and the records produced can be much more intelligible and significant to all who use them.*

Furthermore, in the very process, the data and the records can easily be mobilized into genuine feedback to guide decisions about curriculum development and school organization. This comes close to being a brand-new gain for we have not had a system able to get the big, significant questions into the open and channel the data to the people who need them. It can be done.

These are large claims. We make them because several members of the Yearbook Committee have gone right into a school system and done the job. Time has been short and the development is by no means complete. Yet we believe they have already demonstrated that the approach is feasible: that a school can gather superior data, channel these into a workable feedback system, do it with less routine labor than we now put into testing and measuring and record keeping—and at the same time take the distorting pressures off learning and teaching.

The next two chapters are largely the story of the tryout to date. Even though the story is not finished yet, we hope our account will show that it is possible to break the old pattern and put something better in its place.

6

A Cooperative Evaluation Program

Frances R. Link and Paul B. Diederich

AS HAS been said, some members of the Yearbook Committee tried out a new cooperative evaluation program in the three junior high schools of one school district. The program was designed ultimately to replace course grades and report cards with measures of both status and growth with respect to the major objectives of these schools. In the two years which have elapsed, the schools have been able to establish only the essential features of the program and to secure measures of only a limited number of objectives. Yet enough has been done to illustrate how the new program will work. In the report which follows, a few missing pieces have been supplied from experimental studies in other schools, but all of the procedures reported have been tried out somewhere.

Enough experience has been accumulated to show that these procedures are not only feasible; they also take less time and effort than are usually devoted to testing, grading and record keeping in secondary schools and they cause less heartache. At first they may take more time, since it takes time to learn how to do anything new, even when the new procedure is simpler than the old; but over the long haul these procedures are practically guaranteed to reduce measuring and record keeping to a properly subordinate role. Teachers will be free to devote their minds to teaching and students to learning—except at a few scheduled times during each year's work in each field.

Parents and some educators may regard this as altogether too little. One of the few propositions on which almost all teachers agree is, "We ought to be doing more about evaluation!"

We agree that teachers probably ought to be doing more about evaluation because the chances are that neither they nor anyone else in the school system is doing anything at all about it—in the sense that we shall discuss and illustrate in this chapter. Nothing mysterious or esoteric is meant by this statement; nor does it stretch the ordinary meaning of "evaluation" in any way. Just answer this question: How much does the average student in an average class grow in one year toward any objective that teachers regard as important? The question is not meant to convey, "How much does he grow in terms of standardized test scores?" Take any kind of scale or unit of growth that can be explained; take any kind of measurement procedure that is appropriate. How much growth on this scale is average? superior? alarming? How much growth can be expected from various types of students? What does a department or team of teachers know about the relative amount of growth per year of the main subgroups of the school population toward each of its three or four most important objectives?

Many teachers and administrators can give at least superficial answers to these questions. For example, it may be possible to say that an average fifth grader reads at the fifth grade level; an average sixth grader reads at the sixth grade level; and about a sixth of the children in each grade are more than two years above or below their grade level in reading. So far so good; this is probably the most important of all school objectives and the one on which the most solid work has been done by experts. Where ordinarily a teaching team or department has to devise its own measures, here it can buy them ready-made. But what does the teacher really know about the growth that such measures reveal? What in particular have the students learned about reading in grades five and six? What are they good at? What gives them the most trouble? What are the teachers doing about it? To what extent does it work for various types of students? Has a different method ever been tried? Can the school show results of any kind—numerical or otherwise—that would convince any reasonable, informed person that the present procedure is working better than the earlier procedure?

Does anyone know at what point in the school system the independent reading of self-chosen books takes an alarming turn downward? It is during or at the end of grade 8. Why? For one thing, at this point (puberty), children have to make the transition from juvenile to adult books, and a surprising number cannot do this successfully. Why not? What kinds of difficulties are they having in learning to cope with adult books—other than those which teachers create by starting with Scott, Eliot and Dickens when they ought to be starting with something more nearly like Clarence Day? What are pupils' real difficulties with books that are no longer written down to their level? Vocabulary is one obvious barrier, but what else? Do curriculum developers really know anything at all about this, or are they only guessing? What is being done to find out?

For example, to what extent are students learning to cope with nonliteral statements? Have teachers ever asked them to choose three or four such statements from a list and explain what the statements mean? "In skating over thin ice, our safety is our speed." We once read 110 explanations of this sentence by thirteen-year-olds, and not one of them tumbled to the fact that it might refer to a conversation in which the "thin ice" was something implausible that someone tried to cover up or to get out of by passing over it quickly. They all thought it referred to quite literal skating over the ice on a pond. The literal-mindedness of this age-group is astounding. To what extent is it a factor in their inability to make sense of adult books, and what are some of the other factors? What are reading supervisors and teachers doing about them in grades five and six? Has any teacher or any department ever tried three or four different ways of overcoming any of these difficulties and found that some of them yielded a higher percentage of successes than others—especially with identifiable types of students?

This is what we mean by the evaluation that each department ought to be doing four, five or six times a year as a check on its progress. We agree that teachers ought to be doing more about such evaluation because it is a fair guess that neither they nor anyone else in the school is doing anything about it in a systematic way. In other words, teachers are going through the motions of teaching, but they only rarely try to find out whether students are learning the things they need to learn; whether they are learning them well enough to avoid the danger points that lie just ahead (the real ones, not bugaboos like "The high school teacher will flunk you if you do not know what a demonstrative adjective is!"); and most teachers are not bothering to find out whether some ways of overcoming the real and important difficulties of their students work better than do other ways—either in general or for identifiable types of students. Teachers take time to pass judgment on anything and everything that students hand in; they seem to have time to fill up a class record book with long rows of hieroglyphics that are not worth the time and effort devoted to them; they have time to mark sense cards for the computer which become reports to parents; but they do not have time to find out whether or to what extent or in what respects their teaching does students any good.

Time? As a matter of fact, that is a teacher word. The reason most teachers and supervisors are not doing as much about evaluation as they should is that they have not systematically considered new approaches. That is what this chapter is about. We propose to show by the example of one stout-hearted school district how this job of evaluation can be done, how little time it takes, how many silly and useless substitutes for evaluation can be cleared out of the way to make room for it, and how much fun and excitement such evaluation can add to teaching.

Other Reasons for Cooperative Evaluation

If teachers or supervisors need other evidence to convince the superintendent or the board or the doubters on the staff, here are some of the strongest professional reasons for a cooperative evaluation program:

1. If a teacher has a teaching problem and does not know it, such a program is practically certain to make the problem known. The difficulty may be ascribed to all sorts of fanciful causes, but the evaluative procedures used by the department will sooner or later bring the problem to light. Maybe that is what most teachers fear, but the overriding consideration must be the growth and welfare of the students.

Be of good heart, however. The teaching problems brought to light by a cooperative evaluation program *never* indicate that teachers are not up to the job. There is no valid way in which such a conclusion could be established by such a program. What is more likely to come to light is that teachers are doing something wrong or not doing something right about some easily corrected part of the program. This can happen to anyone, and a school principal and colleagues will think all the more highly of the teacher for finding it out. For example, maybe a teacher is teaching vocabulary in a way that simply does not work; or maybe he thinks that identification of figures of speech (by name) will help the students with their grave problem of learning to cope with non-literal statements, but the evaluative procedures show that it is ineffective.

2. If a teacher knows that he is having a teaching problem, evaluation provides a whole kit of tried-and-true methods of finding out just what the problem is, what factors or elements are related to it, and their relative importance or urgency.

3. Once the teacher sees the teaching problem and its elements and antecedents, evaluation can suggest any number of methods of finding an answer or several answers and of determining their relative effectiveness—either in general or for identifiable types of students. For example, he may have at his command three different ways of treating the problem: three things that he knows how to handle, or three different sets of materials. After trying them out systematically and testing them, treatment A proves more effective with the North Enders; treatment B proves more effective with the South Enders; and treatment C, while highly respectable, proves to be no good at all for anybody.

4. Once the teacher has found a feasible, appropriate and adequate answer to the teaching problem, evaluation can prove to the teacher's satisfaction and that of his colleagues, students and parents that this is

indeed a satisfactory solution. For example, maybe last February the students stood at the bottom of the department in the skill Mr. D was trying to improve; now they stand in the middle, which is as high as their known abilities warrant. If need be (to settle an argument), evaluation can even prove that Mr. D's solution is so many points better—on the average—than the one favored by Mr. X.

A good political reason for instituting a cooperative, systematic evaluation program may be illustrated by the following anecdote.

5. We once visited a high school of some renown at the behest of the principal, supposedly to help the English teachers with their evaluation problems. But the principal failed to warn us about the department head —partly because we would not have come and partly because *she* was their main evaluation problem. She was a lady of formidable appearance, scholarship, and fluency, and undoubtedly of great teaching skill.

About ten minutes after the meeting had started, she sailed in and blew us clean out of the water. All this testing and evaluation, she declared, was only a fad that had never done anyone any good. In teaching, the only things that mattered were inspiration, scholarship and high standards. Once you had them, you did not need to know anything or do anything about testing. Without them, no amount of testing would do any good. Testing, evaluation, probing, prying, fact-gathering, naming things, recalling names and dates—all this was mere busy work: a suitable occupation for people with the souls of clerks. Scholars had more important things to attend to.

After delivering this broadside, she left the meeting, obviously intending to boycott it. The principal quietly declared a coffee break and asked the others to return in fifteen minutes. While they were out, he told us:

That's all very well for her to say, but somebody has to follow in her wake and pick up the pieces. Do you know what she does? In every one of her tests, she flunks at least 50 percent of her students—sometimes 75 percent. She is capable of picking on any one statement in a whole paper that she does not like, calling the child an imbecile, and flunking him. All for one ill-advised expression that she often misinterprets! Next day I may have twenty to thirty parents sitting in my office complaining to high heaven but afraid to say anything to the teacher lest she give their child "the works" in the next test. I can do little but comfort them because she really is a good, inspirational teacher; she has been here a long time; and she has more power and influence in this town than I have. What can we do about her?

An insoluble problem? If the reader thinks so, he underestimates our powers. We have that lady's number. We have met her in various guises over the past thirty years and we know how to deal with her. We might dislike her but we would not try to oust her. There she could beat us hands down, and even the principal recognizes that she is a good teacher. We would do nothing to curtail her freedom to teach in any way she likes. In her own classes she could give any sort of test she pleased and grade it by her unrealistic standards. She might be called on the carpet for unethical or unprofessional conduct until she learned to mend her ways and mind her expressions, but that would be done not by the principal but by the Evaluation Committee—a committee of her peers, made up of department heads.

The trick that would trim her claws and take away her power to torture the helpless students in her classes would be that nothing that she wrote on any of her own tests (including the grade) would enter the record of any student. Her own tests would be regarded as "instructional evaluation," intended to guide and reinforce her own teaching and nothing more. If she wanted the effects of her admittedly good teaching to enter the records of her students, she would have to submit them to the regular departmental examinations, made out and scored by a committee of the most experienced and trusted teachers.

All these papers would be identified only by code numbers so that there would be nothing to indicate which had been written by her students and which had been written by those of other teachers. If she proved to be good at it (as she undoubtedly would), she would be allowed and even required to do her share of the scoring, but her scores would never stand unchallenged.

Every paper she scored would also be scored by someone else, and if the two scores differed by more than a certain amount, the paper would automatically be passed along to a small committee of the most trusted readers for a final arbitration. Thus there would be nothing that she could do to flunk a student on her own initiative. Once her students found this out (as they would immediately), they would be able to take whatever abuse she resorted to in class with a good deal less suffering. They would know that it would never enter their records or impair their chances of getting into college. "This is all talk," they might say. "Disagreeable talk, even unpardonable talk—for a teacher—but it breaks no bones."

Although this is an extreme sample, it is unfortunately not rare. This lady undeniably exists and causes untold suffering in countless American high schools. No individual and especially no teacher should ever have that amount of unchecked power over other human beings who are in as vulnerable a position as students, but what can one do about her? Try to oust her and you are licked from the start. Call her on the carpet and she sneers at you and defies you. She is convinced that she is in the right, and that she is upholding the standards of civilization in a barbarous age. Enough of her contemporaries agree with her so that she gets away with it. What can supervisors do?

When people go to a doctor, they expect him to be able to prescribe something that will work. When school people go to an expert on educational measurement, they are not so sure. But for once we know precisely what to do. Here is the prescription. Institute a cooperative evaluation program of the sort to be described in this chapter. There are plenty of other reasons for it, but one of the strongest of the lot emotionally is that it will put this lady in her place. And oddly enough, it will let her go on doing the one thing she really knows how to do. She knows how to teach. The one thing she most disastrously does *not* know how to do is evaluate—and that source of power will be taken out of her hands.

In this and the next chapter we shall tell and show how to institute such a program, what kinds of things are done from month to month, what kinds of instruments and procedures are used, what kinds of reports are issued for various purposes, and some illustrative results. Although there is no one right way of doing it, we intend to tell about one way— the one we have been developing—and let the readers work out any variations they like or adaptations they need.

An Experiment in Evaluation

Site of the Experimental Program. This cooperative evaluation program was tried out in an old-suburban district (close to the inner city) with better than average resources in the way of money, brains, and disposition to change. It is especially blessed with enlightened and progressive leadership. Like any small, independent school district, it can run its own show without the elephantiasis and political pressures that impede experimentation in large cities. The parents are, in general, proud of their schools and inclined to support them.

The three junior high schools were chosen to initiate the program for several reasons. First, in this period of intense competition to get into colleges of high prestige, the senior high school feels too restricted by either real or imaginary college pressures to initiate change in evaluation. Second, since there were three junior high schools, they presented an opportunity to tackle the problem of organizing a cooperative evaluation program on a district-wide basis rather than in a single school.

Of these three schools, two have about 700 students each; the third has about 500. The student-teacher ratio is about 25 students per teacher if all school personnel are counted as teachers. There is a bit of overcrowding here and there but nothing disabling like double sessions, and a new junior high is in the planning stage. The amount of team teaching and large-group and small-group instruction is about average for a progressive district, but nothing previous to the cooperative evaluation program had been done in any systematic way about flexible scheduling. Schedule modifications were arranged informally by the teachers involved. We will describe how the beginnings of flexible scheduling grew out of the evaluation program.

Some of their programs are quite advanced. For example, these three schools were among the first to adopt descriptive linguistics in place of traditional grammar, and this program has been going on so long that there is no longer any controversy about it. In fact, it was the new cooperative evaluation program that raised the first serious questions about it that have been raised in years. All the other new curricular materials (in mathematics, physics, chemistry, biology, modern languages, etc.) are so familiar to these teachers that they can pick and choose among them and are no longer limited to any one school of thought.

Teachers have been involved in curriculum development and in-service programs with evaluation consultants. In other words, this is basically a healthy educational situation—as it ought to be if any real break with the individualistic tradition of school evaluation is to have a chance to succeed. In any experiment as drastic as this, the cards must first be stacked in its favor. After it finds out how to do things, such an innovation can then compete against traditional systems in less favorable circumstances.

The Initial Proposal. The actual proposal to initiate this program, which was presented to the administration and faculty and later adopted by the Board of Education, was only a page in length. This proposal suggested the organization of a district-wide *Evaluation Committee* to direct the program and the appointment of *advisers* to small groups of students (usually between 20 and 30) to receive reports on all measures "for the record," to file them in the record folders of these students, and to transmit copies to parents at least three times a year with interpretive comments whenever they were needed.

These are the only two organizational changes that are absolutely needed in order to bring the new program into being; the details can be filled in as the program develops. This excessively brief proposal, however, proved inadequate, and many other details of what we had in mind had to be discussed with the administration, faculty, and board before permission to go ahead was granted.

In this chapter we shall not hesitate to reproduce documents (or tests, record-forms, etc.) in their original form even though they were later found to be defective—if the mistake throws light on any problem of evaluation. But the reproduction of this single-page proposal would be only a waste of space. Its substance is included within the more extended proposal below, which more nearly represents the points actually discussed with the administration and faculty, and also represents the sort of proposal that other schools may want to consider.

Proposal for a Cooperative Evaluation Program

Purpose. The ultimate purpose of this program is to replace course grades and report cards with measures of both status and growth with respect to all major objectives of the schools that will participate. By "major objectives" we mean the four, five, or six most widely recognized objectives of each field of study—those that teachers are able and willing to measure in one way or another at this stage—not the long lists of 100 or more objectives that they often submit as claims that are never substantiated. In addition to these objectives of each field, we expect to assign to each department primary responsibility for initiating the collection of evidence on at least one objective of schoolwide concern that is not now adequately measured (because what is everyone's responsibility is the responsibility of no one in particular).

For example, we expect the guidance counselors and the assistant principals in charge of discipline to assume responsibility for the collection of data on interests and values and on learning how to get along with other people (sociometric ratings, records of behavior problems, etc.) as well as for the measures of aptitudes (both scholastic and vocational) that they already collect. We expect math and science people to spearhead the collection of data on critical thinking and scientific attitudes. The social studies will be primarily responsible for evidence of awareness of social problems, attitudes, and democratic behavior. English and the library will secure and interpret records of independent reading and study. As they come into the program, the fine and applied arts will try to develop measures or records of performance concerning appreciations and practical competence. As they also become involved, our vocational courses will bring together data on work habits, wherever collected, and physical education will assume primary responsibility for records of health and physical development.

These assignments of objectives of general concern to particular departments should not distract attention from the fact that the primary goals to be evaluated by each department are the primary goals of instruction in that department. In English, for example, these will be chiefly the various facets of reading and writing. (Speaking and listening will receive attention later.) Reading will include reading skill as a tool in all subjects, reading interests, and the various elements of literary competence that make it possible for students to develop a lifelong interest in the reading of reputable literary works—not exclusively what are now regarded as "the classics."

Report Cards. Until a great deal of evidence of this sort is secured routinely—usually by cooperative action of teaching teams and departments rather than by individual teachers—and is reported adequately and understandably by departments to advisers and by advisers to parents, we intend to keep on sending out report cards as usual. We contemplate no further change in the present form of these report cards until they are finally abandoned. This will occur only when parents are receiving so much better and fuller information from the new reports on actual measures than they are now getting from the unchecked judgments recorded on report cards that they will begin to ask, "Why do we need these report cards?"

Our present estimate is that this will happen in about five years, and that the volume of evidence then secured on the recognized objectives of the various fields of study will be so impressive that no college or accrediting agency will interpose any objection. Of course, it may take longer than that, but by the end of the second or third year parents should already be receiving a great deal of authenticated evidence supplementary to the grades recorded on report cards. Since the new evidence will be secured and reported cooperatively rather than individually, the division of labor as well as the fun and excitement of securing actual evidence of growth in this novel manner should make it possible for teachers to endure a double burden of reporting during the transitional period. In the end they will benefit greatly, since they will no longer have to turn in subjective and over-general reports of progress every six or eight weeks on all 120 to 150 students in their classes. Instead, the department will routinely report the results of all measures "for the record" in multiple copies, and each adviser will transmit one copy of each report to the parents of the student concerned in his advisory group of 20 to 30 students, sometimes with interpretive comments written on the back by the student or by himself or by both.

At present, it seems to us that students are fantastically over-evaluated. They receive marks on practically everything they do in school and practically every time they turn around. Most of these marks are only repetitions of the mistakes their teachers made in sizing up these students during their first month in class. Still, at the end of each marking period, all these marks are given various weights and added together, then divided by some obscurely determined number to strike an "average," which becomes the basis for the grade. Although this process usually has no rational or mathematical foundation, both teachers and students probably suffer more from it than from any other aspect of school work. It is thought to be necessary because, if daily marks were not recorded in the class record book, nobody would do any work.

One hundred years ago every practical schoolman was equally convinced that the only way to teach a boy Latin was to beat him. But when the beating stopped and better incentives were found, the boys learned better than ever. We are convinced that the same thing will happen in the case of our present superstition with regard to daily marks. Departmental measures "for the record" at much longer intervals will probably prove to be a much more effective substitute. Except on a few scheduled occasions per year in each field, teachers will then be free to devote their whole minds to teaching and students their whole minds to learning.

Evaluation Committee. The Evaluation Committee will be the directing committee of this whole enterprise. It will consist of heads of the departments and special services (such as Library and Guidance) that will be involved in the initial phases of the new program. It will be headed by the Coordinator of Secondary Education and assisted by an outside consultant on measurement. Guidance is here meant to include not only counselors but also assistant principals with special responsibility for discipline. Principals are *ex officio* members of the Evaluation Committee and are invited and urged to attend its meetings whenever they have time to do so. We believe that they will find these meetings the most exciting and rewarding in-service education they have ever witnessed—all the more effective because it will be self-induced rather than poured on from outside. That is, it will be generated by arguments among equals, all of high standing, as to proper means of measuring growth toward major goals of instruction and by their discussion of the results of such measures.

During the first year we intend to involve chiefly guidance (including the assistant principals), English (together with the library), and social studies. Our principal concern will be *the organization and work of the Evaluation Committee itself:* agreement upon certain departmental measures of major goals of instruction, scheduling these at times that will not conflict with other commitments, preparing and reporting the measures within each department in each school, and reporting results back to the Evaluation Committee. Starting with just three fields will leave the committee of convenient size (normally 18 to 20 people representing all three schools), and the objectives to be considered will be few enough to manage in the time available without confusion. We request only four meetings of the Evaluation Committee per year but each time for a full morning, with substitutes or teacher aides hired to cover classes. A clean break with the individualistic tradition of school evaluation cannot be made by tired people who always have to meet after school.

The detailed work goes on behind the scenes as committee members meet with their departments in their own schools to prepare, review, revise, administer, score and study the results of the measures for which they are responsible.

Questions that these groups are unable to decide for themselves are cleared with the chairman of the Evaluation Committee, who also (on request) attends meetings of the groups that run into trouble. It is worthy of note that, although some department heads report shortcomings in the measures devised by their groups, no one reports failure to prepare or administer a measure by the scheduled date. These are formal commitments on which reports are expected at the next meeting of the Evaluation Committee, and it would seriously embarrass a department head to confess that his group had failed to meet its obligations. Compare this record with the usual results of exhortation. The control is democratic, but this program gets things done.

Advisers. During the second year we expect to add science, mathematics, and foreign languages to the subjects represented on the Evaluation Committee. If the principal measures needed in the first three fields are being collected routinely, it may be possible to reduce their representation on the committee—even though the department head in each school must still approve all measures "for the record" and reports of such measures to advisers.

The principal concern of the second year will be the role of the adviser, since by this time enough new evidence will be flowing in to make it necessary for all (or nearly all) students to have an adviser. He will receive, scan and file reports from all departments on all measures for the record and transmit one copy of each report to the parents of the student concerned in his advisory group of 20 to 30 students. The adviser will not be expected to attempt even limited therapy (or scolding or discipline) or the academic and vocational guidance provided by school counselors. His principal function is to know how each student in his advisory group is getting along in all courses and activities. He will find out not by word-of-mouth (although this will happen, too, in teaching teams) but by official, detailed reports on each measure "for the record" that will be prepared, approved, and sent out routinely by the department of origin *only* to the advisers of the students concerned, *not* directly to parents. Ultimately only the adviser will report directly to parents and only to the parents of the 20 to 30 students in his advisory group. Quite naturally, the evidence he receives will include some items that he will want to discuss with some of his advisees—either to congratulate the student or to find out what went wrong. It may also include items that he will occasionally want to discuss with parents—sometimes immediately by telephone when something particularly nice happens or something that causes him grave concern.

In this initial phase of the new evaluation program, advisers are usually members of teaching teams in which most of the new "measures of record" have been tried out. As time goes on, this restriction will probably not be feasible. Instead, students will be given some time at the beginning of the year to get acquainted with their teachers and will then be asked (during an assembly program dealing with the role of the adviser) to fill out a card indicating their first, second and third choices among these teachers as their adviser for the year. Schools that have used this system report that, by utilizing second choices in about a fourth of the cases, they are able to distribute the advisory load as evenly as it ought to be distributed. No one has less than fifteen nor more than thirty-five students, and most advisers have between twenty and thirty. The third choice on the card is only a cushion: students who get their second choice feel happy that it was not their third.

There are three reasons for this method. First, students should have a voice in choosing their adviser because an adviser is first of all a friend, and one cannot assign friends. Second, the adviser should be a teacher (or coach or librarian) with whom the student will have some regular contact, because it is very difficult to follow and understand his development without such contact. This rules out the adviser of the previous year unless the student remains in his classes. Third, no teacher should be excluded from the advisory role even though he seems ill adapted to it. This role is one that can transform teachers, and when a seemingly unlikely person is freely chosen by even a small group of students, he rises to the occasion. Besides, if some teachers are excluded, others will have advisory groups too large to handle effectively.

Reports from Departments to the Adviser on Measures for the Record. Probably the major subject of discussion and experimentation during this second year will be the form that reports on measures for the record should take. The general principle is that any measure important enough to enter the record of a student is also important enough to explain so clearly and adequately that advisers, students, parents, counselors, and admissions officers at the next higher level of education can understand it. This can usually be done in a single page that can be duplicated in enough copies for the teacher of origin to retain one copy, to give one to each student tested, and to send two to his adviser: one to be filed in the record folder, the other to be sent to parents (along with reports from other fields, possibly at intervals of three months). Sometimes a fifth copy is made for the guidance counselor.

These reports usually include a statement of the objectives measured;

a description of the measuring device or procedure, sometimes with sample items; the reliability and standard error of the scores if these have been computed; distributions of scores (sometimes in graphic form) for the groups tested; if there were comparable earlier measures, similar distributions of growth scores; and some indication of the position of the student in these distributions: an arrow, a numerical score, or a letter referring to some described qualitative category. This last will vary for each student, but it requires only a touch of the pen; hence it can be entered by hand in four or five mimeographed copies without the expense and delay of printing these reports on carbon-backed forms.

Record Folders Kept by Advisers. These are plain manila folders of either regular or legal size. Inside we place eight "dividers" of light cardboard with half-inch tabs projecting at the top, labeled as follows:

1. NAME. Current material. Reports are filed in this slot until one copy is sent to parents; the other copy is then filed in one of the other slots

2. ACADEMIC RECORD. Biographical data. Official records of courses and activities taken, grades received, other schools attended, home background, etc.

3. GUIDANCE. Interests, values, aptitudes, records of social behavior

4. MATHEMATICS AND SCIENCE. Critical thinking, scientific attitudes

5. SOCIAL STUDIES. Awareness of social problems, attitudes, democratic behavior

6. ENGLISH, FOREIGN LANGUAGES, LIBRARY. Independent reading and study

7. FINE AND APPLIED ARTS. Creativity, appreciations, practical competence

8. VOCATIONAL EDUCATION. Work habits

9. PHYSICAL EDUCATION. Records of health and physical development.

The subheads after each of these main headings refer to the "objectives of schoolwide concern" for which special responsibility is assigned to or assumed by the various departments and services. The main headings show that closely related fields have been combined within a single slot to keep the folders from getting too bulky. The eight "dividers" are not glued or stapled or held in place in any way; they are simply confined by the stout covers of the manila folder; and their 10" by 12" size makes them stand out above the sheets they separate. They are numbered, so that if they get out of place, they can easily be reassembled in the right order.

Major Objectives of Instruction Measured "for the Record." The objectives officially recognized by each department—those that it will attempt to measure in one way or another—will eventually be printed on these dividers. They are not so printed at the present time because these departments are still in the throes of trying to decide what objectives they will include in their program of measurement "for the record." These will not be coextensive with the whole list of objectives actually sought at one time or another by various members of the department. A number of these will be variable and shifting as members develop or lose interest in various activities—sometimes in response to specific needs of new groups of students, sometimes in response to their own professional development. The variable and shifting objectives will usually be treated in each teacher's own program of "instructional evaluation," which is intended solely for the guidance and reinforcement of his teaching, which does not enter the permanent records of students, and which is not under the jurisdiction or control of the Evaluation Committee.

In his own classes, a teacher may give whatever tests, performance tasks or other measures he likes and may grade or interpret them in any way he pleases *if* he does not intend to report the results to advisers for inclusion in the record folders of the students measured. This restriction saves him the trouble of consulting with his department head or evaluation representative every time he wants to give a test or grade a set of papers. It also protects advisers against the possibility of having to scan and file a great mass of evidence of dubious value in the record folders.

Difference Between "Instructional Evaluation" and "Measurement for the Record." Hence a good many of the objectives now being debated by our various departments may eventually be relegated to the domain of "instructional evaluation," and only the objectives for which rather solid departmental measures have been developed will remain to be printed on the dividers. This is not to say that any objective that is hard to measure will quietly drop out of sight. Our own record to date proves that. During the past two years we have developed measures of many important but hard-to-measure objectives that nobody dreamed of measuring before, but now these are solidly incorporated in our program of measurement "for the record."

What makes the difference is not whether an objective is hard to measure. If everyone in the department regards it as a major goal of instruction, it will go down in the official list whether we now know how to measure it or not. But what gets into this list is not what *anyone* in the department regards as a major goal of instruction but what *everyone* (or almost everyone) regards as a major goal. These are relatively few in number: commonly not more than four, five or six distinct major goals per department—although any one goal may have many subheads on which separate scores or ratings are obtained. For example, our Evaluation Committee agreed to start with just six goals: writing competence, independent reading, critical thinking, interests, work habits, and acceptance of and by peers. The other objectives are treated as major goals by some but not by others, or as major goals for a few types of students but not for all. These are the goals that are usually treated as a part of "instructional evaluation," which is not subject to review by the Evaluation Committee.

Why not put everything under "instructional evaluation," then, so as to avoid responsibility for carefully controlled evaluation? Because, if you do not get a goal into the record, what you have taught your students and what they have learned from it will not show up in their records at all. In the terms now employed (which are somewhat taboo among us), "They won't get credit for it." Suppose a teacher has taken three months to teach his college-bound seniors how to analyze and interpret the classic form of the novel. Yet this teacher cannot agree with any other member of the department on how to test this ability, so he simply whips off a test of his own and grades it as he likes. Presto! The whole thing has vanished. There will be nothing in the record to indicate that the students have ever been taught the classic form of the novel.

It is obviously to the teacher's advantage, then, and to that of his students to get everything of major importance that has been taught them into the record. In fact, if teachers do not insist upon it, students will. That is why we have to face continual pressure from both teachers and students to get items taught and learned into the record—not to evade responsibility for measurement by keeping them out. True, most students object to tests, performance tasks, etc., on general principles, but given a choice between such tests and no recognition that they have ever studied a given subject, they prefer the tests.

Requirements for Getting Measures into the Record. Basically, what gets into the record is what the Evaluation Committee approves, and its standards or criteria may differ from school to school and from one period of development to another. The first requirement, however, is always that *a measure must be approved by the department head or representative on the Evaluation Committee* before reports on its results can be sent to advisers for inclusion in the record folders. At yearly intervals the whole departmental measurement program will be formally reviewed by the Evaluation Committee (or a subcommittee thereof) and one or two measures previously approved by the department head may be disallowed —but not retroactively.

The department will only be asked not to use such measures again for one of several possible reasons. Perhaps the evidence duplicates evidence that can be secured (and is being secured) more naturally and with less trouble in some other department. Possibly it is so highly correlated with some other measure now secured in this very department that it constitutes duplication. Perhaps more evidence is being collected by the department on this objective than is actually needed; hence this measure should yield its place to one on some other objective that is now inadequately measured. Or perhaps the evidence is simply not good enough to carry the implicit guarantee of authenticity by the school; and if the department still wants this evidence, substantial revision is needed. Any of these reasons (and more) can block continuance of a departmental measure one year after its first use, but even that first use must be approved by someone with responsibility for measurement (normally the department head) or the advisers will not accept it.

How does one secure that approval? The first requirement is very simple, but if faithfully adhered to, it can work a revolution in school evaluation.

No measure may enter the permanent record of a student unless it represents the independent judgment of more than a single individual. Such measures have consequences too serious to be subject to the unchecked judgment (or whim, idiosyncrasy, and sometimes the ignorance or prejudice) of a solitary individual. At the very least, a test prepared by one teacher must be reviewed and checked (as to both content and scoring) by one other teacher before it can be approved for inclusion in the record. If it is an objective measure, only an independent check of the content and scoring key may be necessary; but if subjective judgments or ratings are required, the papers or other products may have to be judged independently by the second teacher without knowledge of the prior ratings or the identity of students; and products on which the ratings differ by more than a certain amount may have to be referred to a third teacher who is qualified to judge. (See the following chapter for this procedure.)

As a matter of fact, most departmental measures are prepared, reviewed, revised, administered, scored and reported by cooperative action of the whole department—partly to guard against one another's mistakes, partly to make the job easy and interesting by a division of labor. There are not enough departmental measures in any one year to make such cooperation impossible; the format of these measures does not vary a great deal from grade to grade; and many of the departmental measures are given in exactly the same form across a span of three grades in order to measure growth. (The details of this last procedure will be given in the following chapter.) Cooperative action by teams or departments is almost the normal procedure in measurement for the record. Sometimes, however, a test must be produced and checked by just a pair of teachers because so few students are affected; others may be produced by committees of three, four or five. But unless at least one person can act as a real check on the judgment of another, the measure will not get into the record.

Other Requirements. Beyond the basic requirements of approval by someone with responsibility for measurement (and ultimately by the

Evaluation Committee) and cooperative production and checking of measures lies the whole territory of measurement sophistication or know-how. The basic requirement here is simply that the measure be "good" by the standards usually accepted by testmakers. The most important of these are validity, reliability, and freedom from bias.

Validity means that the measure must get at the behavior in question, not something else that may be mistaken for it or substituted for it. For example, ability to analyze and interpret a literary work must not be counterfeited by ability to recall and reproduce—to "parrot back"—the teacher's analysis and interpretation. For that reason, a departmental examination on a suitable literary work that all teachers were forbidden to discuss, and that students had to read on their own before the examination, would ordinarily be preferred to an examination on a literary work that had been directly taught. The work directly taught may be regarded as the vehicle for instruction; that set for the examination as the vehicle for evaluation. For example, students may learn how to analyze a classic Greek drama through the *Medea* of Euripides, which has been taught in class, but the parallel work set for the examination might be *The Trojan Women* by the same author, which no teacher has been permitted to discuss.

Reliability. A measure must also be *reliable* in that two measures of the same objective taken at about the same time must yield approximately the same results. There are quick and easy ways (taking three to five minutes and requiring no computation that would puzzle an eighth grader)[1] to determine the amount of agreement between two measures and even the estimated amount of agreement from the "internal consistency" of any one measure. If a measure of a given objective is not sufficiently reliable to enter the record permanently after the first test, the reliability may be increased to a satisfactory level by including other measures of the same objective in subsequent tests that are spaced throughout the year. In fact, this is the normal procedure in departmental examinations.

Each examination is likely to test several different objectives in order to get at all aspects of the work covered up to the examination. But in the short time available for these examinations (or rather, the short exposure that students can stand and teachers can score), the reliability of the part-score on any one objective is unlikely to be high enough to enter the record—permanently. (Note how this was said. Certainly the students will want to know both their total scores and part-scores immediately; hence they must be reported provisionally—but with a warning that the part-scores are not yet sufficiently stable to be taken very seri-

[1] See Appendix B. p. 260-77 for some "Pinhead Statistics."

ously.) If the same objective, however, is tested in three or four examinations in the course of the year, the reliability of the cumulative total for each objective across the series of examinations is likely to reach a satisfactory level. In fact, there is a very easy way to determine in advance just how much more testing of a given objective is needed to reach a satisfactory level of reliability if one knows the reliability attained on the first test—or up to any given point. This procedure will be discussed in the next section, since it brings out a very important point about how much measurement is enough. (Usually less than one might think.)

First, however, let us say that—on the advice of our consultant on measurement—we have decided to accept .8 as a satisfactory level of reliability for a practical judgment in the ordinary course of school work. The traditional requirement is .9—and certainly this level or better is highly desirable in controlled experiments—but we regard this requirement as unrealistic if a department intends to measure several different objectives that are hard to measure and not confine itself to knowledge and simple skills. Sometimes we have to put up with less, but when we have reached the level of .8, we feel no compulsion to provide additional measures of the same objective. It will not change the relative position of enough students to make the additional time and effort worthwhile.

Compare this knowledgeable attitude toward the practical requirements of measurement with the squirrel-like activity of teachers who keep on adding test after test, paper after paper, and mark after mark— all directed toward the same objective—without any conception of how many measures are enough. The truth is that one reaches a point of diminishing returns very quickly in this measurement business. Most of the important traits or abilities we try to measure in education are fairly stable; they change only slowly over considerable periods of time; so that after a limited number of carefully designed measures we reach a cumulative total that is not likely to change very much or in very many cases by adding more measures. It is like the annual measurement of the height of our children that we parents often mark on the wall behind the door on their birthdays. Even though children grow a lot and at somewhat different rates, we know that height is quite a stable measure, and that there is no point in measuring height every day of the year. Yet this, in effect, is exactly what teachers do when they keep on putting down mark after mark on a skill or behavior pattern that is slow to change.

We know too much at this stage of the game to waste all that time and effort on compulsive measurement—adding more and more measures when anyone can figure out in two or three minutes with the simplest possible computation how much additional measurement is needed to reach a satisfactory level of reliability—beyond which not much significant change is to be expected. If we wrote it in mathematical notation, the formula might scare teachers who are inclined to faint whenever they catch sight of a number, but let us write it out in words to show how very simple it is to find out how much measurement is enough, once you know the reliability you achieved in the first subtest. You "lengthen this test X times" when:

$$X = \frac{(\text{Desired reliability}) \times (1-\text{obtained reliability})}{(\text{Obtained reliability}) \times (1-\text{desired reliability})}$$

This formula is so simple and symmetrical that one can hardly forget it. Suppose you want a reliability of .8 and hit a reliability of .5 in the first subtest—possibly a 10-minute section of the first departmental examination. Let us substitute these numbers in the formula:

$$X = \frac{.8 \times (1 - .5)}{.5 \times (1 - .8)} = \frac{.8 \times .5}{.5 \times .2} = \frac{.40}{.10} = 4 \text{ (times longer)}$$

Do not tell us that teachers cannot understand this; we shall not believe it. Of course they may not understand the mathematical reasons why this is so, but this is the sort of thing they ought to accept on authority. After all, they probably do not understand what happens inside a television set, but they know how to turn it on. This is the formula the professionals use, and they know both theoretically and empirically that it works. All teachers need to understand is how to turn it on: that is, how to substitute numbers in it. The rest is simple arithmetic.

But its result is startling. You hit a reliability of .5 with just one 10-minute section in the first departmental examination. The formula tells the staff members that they need just four times as much material of the same sort to raise this reliability to the level they want—a reliability of .8 for the cumulative total for the year. This is simple; they will probably have at least four departmental examinations anyway, spaced evenly throughout the year, and the formula tells them that they will need just a 10-minute section of the same sort in each of them (40 minutes in all) to boost reliability to .8. After that, additional measures will not change the position of enough students to worry about.

Avoidance of Bias. The requirement of cooperative production and checking of measures for the record is one way to avoid the distorting effect of *bias*. Another is to have written answers or other products given code numbers and then rated independently by two different teachers without knowledge of the identity of the students. Otherwise the judgment of the product is too likely to be confused with a prior judgment of the general goodness of the producer. One critic writes, "Is this depersonalized evaluation any more likely to be right than a judgment made with full knowledge of the student, the progress he has made, his background and circumstances, the effort he has put forth, and the like?" Yes, a judgment of a product made without knowledge of the identity of the producer is almost certainly more accurate—more nearly what it purports to be—than a judgment made with full knowledge of the producer. In the latter, one's prior judgment of the net worth of this individual as a person tends to color one's judgment of the degree of skill, understanding, etc., exhibited in his products.

This distorting effect of prior knowledge is sometimes called "halo effect" but the more general term is "bias." For example, in one study, teachers in twelve school districts judged monthly test papers for various aspects of writing ability. The papers were known to be from grades 9 and 10 but there was no indication on any paper of the grade represented, the curriculum or special group (such as regular or honors), the sex of the writer, or even the school in which the paper was written.

The teachers protested vigorously that it was impossible for them to judge the merit of a paper unless they knew at least the grade (year in school) and whether it came from a regular or honors section. They said they might rate a paper 4 if it came from a regular section but no higher than 2 if it came from an honors section. Honors sections should expect to be graded by higher standards.

The consultant listened politely and said that this presented an opportunity to find out what kinds of information about the writers were essential to an accurate judgment of their writing. He proposed to supply such information one item at a time in subsequent sets of papers and to study the effect of each item on the reliability of the ratings.

Hence one set of papers was stamped either "Boy" or "Girl"—referring to the sex of the writer. Another set was stamped either 9 or 10, representing the grade from which it came. Another set was stamped either "Regular" or "Honors" to indicate the sort of group in which it was produced—and so on.

What these teachers did not know was that half of this information was true and half was false. The papers had been written on carbon-back forms so that there were three identical copies of each paper. One of these was stamped "Boy," another "Girl." In the next set one copy was stamped "Regular," another "Honors"— and so on. All such copies were sent out to the twelve school districts in a random order to see what the results would be.

The only bit of information that made any difference at all was "Regular" vs. "Honors," and the difference was in the opposite direction from the one predicted by the teachers. The copies stamped "Honors" were rated significantly *higher* than the other copies of the very same papers that were stamped "Regular." The explanation is that we find what we expect to find. If we think a paper came from an honors section, we expect it to be pretty good—and so it proves. But if we think it came from a regular section, we expect it to be only so-so—and so it proves. Since none of the bits of information did any good (i.e., led to a greater agreement among the readers) and since this one did obvious harm, the group decided to supply no information whatsoever about the writer in the future.

Other Effects of "Depersonalization." The double grading of unidentified papers has many other salutary effects besides the avoidance of bias. These can be illustrated chiefly from college experience, where such grading in important examinations is almost the rule, while in high school it is rarely attempted.

1. *"Depersonalization" helps separate judgment of product from judgment of producers.* Teachers who blithely pass judgment on everything handed in by their students, including examinations, with full knowledge of the identity of the student, obviously do so in disregard of the admonition of the greatest teacher of all, "Judge not lest ye be judged!"

Although there are ways of explaining away this admonition, the more we learn about teaching, the more we are disposed to accept its importance. Evaluation, whenever possible, should avoid judgments of persons and concentrate on judgments of products. In the marriage feast of Cana, the statement is quoted with approval, "This man has saved the best wine until the last!"

Although this point may seem fanciful, it really does feel better morally to separate the judgment of a product from our judgment of the producer. Many students for whom we have the greatest respect and liking get the equivalent of D's and F's in this sort of unidentified appraisal. It helps them to know that, whatever the outcome, it will not alter our regard for them as persons. To a real teacher, the worth of any student must be infinite. But some of his tools for living need sharpening, and he will not resent this information if he is assured of our genuine and unalterable acceptance of him as a person.

2. *"Depersonalization" sets appropriate goals for different levels of ability.* This point may be illustrated by the testimony of a venerable teacher of German at Harvard:

> The two grades achieved in this course for which I have always had the highest respect were two D's finally achieved by Swedish twins in my Radcliffe course. They were lovely girls, but solid concrete from the neck up, and for some months I despaired of getting them up to the level of passing. But I have never seen anyone work harder—and that made me work harder, too. In their final examination (graded as usual by two other members of the department who did not know the students) they both got D's. They passed! I am not ashamed to say that I embraced both of them warmly to congratulate them, and even at my advanced age—then 65—we joined hands and danced around in a circle.

On the other hand, I have seen many grades of B that left me cold with anger. The student should have made an A. I would call him in and ask him, "What happened? With your gifts, and with a four-year scholarship at stake, you cannot afford to fool around with B's. Why didn't you make an A?"

Thus some get kissed for passing; others get bawled out for making B's. The instructor could not simply award these grades, they had to come from other members of the department without knowledge of the identity of the students; otherwise there would have been no triumph in the first case or anger in the second. Thus students of different levels of ability can set their hearts on different goals. (In early grades the Swedish twins might be given A's for trying hard, but that sort of thing becomes unthinkable at higher levels.)

3. *"Depersonalization" practically eliminates arguments over grades.* In this era of fierce competition to get into the "best" colleges, some students will contest almost every grade—from that on a homework assignment to that on the final examination. Some argue, some bluster, some wheedle, some even break down and cry. In some cases we have to deal with parents as well. Now we can say to them, "I don't know who gave you that grade, but it is already entered in the departmental records and I have no power to alter it. There is no point in arguing. Let me get your paper, go over it with you, and show you where you went wrong. There are three more such examinations to come. If you work hard at your weak points, I am sure that you can raise your score. You have it in you."

This puts the teacher and the student on the same side of the fence. Both want to make the grade as high as possible, but this can be done only by solid achievement, not by arbitrary fiat, after the teacher is worn down by argument. Arguments do no good; hence they almost disappear. And students no longer say "Look what *you* did to me!" but "Look what *they* did to me!"—a significant and salutary change.

4. *"Depersonalization" reduces the emotionality of evaluation.* It was pointed out in Chapter 2 that all serious evaluation is highly charged with emotion for the recipient. It is hard to see how this can ever be avoided. Rudolf Serkin, the great pianist, recently admitted that after sixty years of successful experience on the concert stage, he still has butterflies in the stomach on the day of a concert. Still, college people who conduct examinations that are graded anonymously by two different staff members testify that students are less nervous about such examinations than about examinations that are graded by their own teacher, who has full knowledge of their shortcomings. In the latter case, the losers often rationalize their failure by making themselves believe that

the teacher "had it in for them." Yet if the two people who grade the examination do not know them from Adam, there is obviously "nothing personal" about the grade. They do not feel despised and rejected. Instead, they tend to treat the grade as impersonal information about themselves that can help them improve.

5. *The teacher also gets feedback on the effects of his teaching.* If he awards all the grades himself, knowing whom he is grading, the teacher can make the grades come out in any way he likes. If he is honest, some of his "adjustments" of grades must embarrass him. If a good student does very badly, he often says, "Too bad! He had an off day. I'll have to reduce his grade to a 'B.' " But the same paper written by a "bad" student might easily get a D or an F. Since the teacher knows that the outcome has been manipulated, he can feel neither pride when average grades improve nor alarm when they decline. But if the papers are graded anonymously and independently along with those from other classes, the teacher can take real pride in an average improvement and try to find out what went wrong when there is an average decline. Hence such grades can lead to the improvement of teaching, while self-awarded grades only confirm what the teacher thinks he already knows about his students. In the broader sense, when papers are graded anonymously the teacher and pupil are freed to raise the kinds of expanding questions which evaluation feedback suggests.

Summary of Requirements for Approval of Measures for the Record. This final section has been devoted entirely to requirements for the approval of "measures for the record." It was stated earlier that these measures must be clearly related to major goals of instruction. Beyond that, there are basically only three requirements: (a) The measure must be approved by someone with responsibility for measurement—usually the department head—before advisers will accept it, and ultimately it must be approved by the Evaluation Committee or a subcommittee thereof. (b) The measure must represent the independent judgment of more than a single individual, and usually it is produced and checked by cooperative action of a whole department or team rather than by individual teachers. (c) The measure must be "good" by the standards accepted by testmakers, of which the most important are validity, reliability, and freedom from bias. Of these standards, it is reliability that most often works out in a direction contrary to what teachers expect. If the reliability is computed, and if a projection is made of the additional measurement needed to reach a satisfactory level of reliability—here set at .8—this usually reduces the number of measures or the testing time that teachers think they need. Moreover, if the reliability of the initial measure is low, there is no need for despair. One simply adds other measures of the same objective until the cumulative total reaches a satisfactory level of reliability.

The numerous advantages of double grading of unidentified papers (or other products) have been explained at great length, chiefly because this highly desirable practice, while common in many colleges, is seldom attempted in high school. If teachers would only try it, they would find that it takes less time and causes less embarrassment than they think. See the next chapter for details of a double-grading procedure.

The Third Year: More Subjects; Summaries and Transcripts

We have devoted all these pages to our prospectus for the first two years (interspersed with occasional references to what actually happened) because that is as far as we have gone. Between our appointment to the Yearbook Committee and the writing of this report we had only two years in which to work. Hence we have treated these two years in detail even in this prospectus, and further details will be added as we get on to the actual history of what was done.

What lies beyond is imaginary, but we can at least report what we had in the prospectus for the third year. First, the fine and applied arts, vocational education, and physical education and sports were to have representatives on the Evaluation Committee and were to have special responsibility for the "objectives of general concern" previously specified. Second, the principal matter for experimentation and discussion during this year was to be the format of summaries or transcripts of the data in the record folders for transmission to the senior high school. By this time some students would be in the third year of this new evaluation program and would be entering senior high the following year; hence the need for summaries or transcripts would be urgent.

Of course, we could simply send on the record folders with the original reports on all measures for the record, since not enough of these were developed during the initial phases of this program to become too bulky to handle. Still, we doubted that very many people in the senior high school would have time to read them and form defensible conclusions about them. We also realized that in a year or two more the number of such reports would be so large that no one would attempt to digest them.

Hence it seemed desirable during this third year to make at least a beginning toward ordering and summarizing the records in some fashion that the mind could grasp in a reasonable length of time. Since that task will only be begun six months after the writing of this report, we must confess to no actual knowledge of how it will be done. In the final chapter of the Yearbook, however, we shall attempt some extrapolation of how the high school record of a student may look to the college admissions officer of 1970 or 1975. It will certainly be nothing like "English: B, B, B, A." That is far too simple, too uncontrolled, and too general.

Instead there will be data on how well the student can read, what sorts of books he reads on his own, and various aspects of literary competence. In writing, there will be data on eight distinguishable aspects of writing competence, familiarity with descriptive linguistics, ability to apply it, and possibly some test of ability to detect common student errors in writing. In speaking there may be nothing at all, since this is a hard objective to measure and not a crucial one with us, since our students (who nearly all come from favored backgrounds) speak fluently, correctly and effectively. There may be a test of listening comprehension. All this, mind you, in a single field—English. For a more complete account of measures being tried out in this field, see the following chapter.

We did not have space or time enough to give equally detailed accounts of the measurement programs of the other subjects (most of which are not as far along as English). Nevertheless for these subjects also the record will consist not of a single overall grade for each year but of data on status and growth with respect to the major objectives of each field. All this will yield a profile of achievement in each field rather than a single grade. Unless we can develop some simple way of showing this profile at a glance, college admissions officers will groan over it and wish they had the old-fashioned simplicity of grades—even though they know that course grades are about as trustworthy as the prognostications of a fortune-teller. Yet we are quite confident that, given actual data, we can invent ways of making it understandable in the short time that college admissions officers can devote to it.

Letters from Teachers to Advisers (and vice versa). As we looked back over this rather formidable apparatus, it occurred to us that there ought to be an "escape hatch" at some point that would permit those occasional flashes of insight on the part of either teachers or advisers to get into the record without too much red tape. We remembered those letters that we had to write at one dreadful period to the parents of all 120 students in our classes as a substitute for marks. They were abandoned because they took far more time than they were worth and because the parents complained that they were too vague to tell them anything they wanted to know. Yet in each batch of 120 letters we wrote, there might be as many as ten to twelve that contained some flash of insight—one that would not find a place in the formal measurement program here outlined. In general, the other letters could be interchanged among students without anyone's noticing the difference. There are many anecdotes of this period: for example, of the wife, a teacher, who could not think of anything to write, and of the husband, a journalist, who undertook to write the letters without knowing anything at all about the students. The first effect of this novel procedure was that many parents telephoned the principal to tell him how much more illuminating these letters were than the first set!

Then it occurred to us that the ten or twelve letters out of 120 that showed real insight were the only ones that should have been written. How could we make a place for them in the present program? Once we had formulated the question, the answer was obvious: If any teacher notices something about the development or problems of any student that is not getting into the measures of record, let him tell about it in a brief letter or memo to the adviser. If the adviser finds out anything about a student that will help a certain teacher to deal with him, let him do the same. There is no obligation to write such memos at all, and if they are written about more than 10 percent of the students, let the sender consider whether he is actuated more by a need for self-expression than by concern for the well-being of his students. If this teacher gets to be a nuisance, advisers will complain, and the department head or evaluation representative will ask him to pipe down. Otherwise, we felt, there ought to be no red tape about such letters or memos at all. If a teacher or adviser feels a genuine urge to write one, let him do so without asking anyone's approval. After all, there is a built-in check here: if the communication seems silly, the person at the other end need pay no attention to it. Only in a few cases will copies be made for parents. Such letters are intended only to help a teacher or adviser to deal better with the needs and problems of a particular student.

Such a communication as the following might then reach the adviser:

> Walter is truly a scholar and a gentleman—too much of the latter for his own good. There is a really sadistic girl in his class (grade 8) who is pestering the daylights out of him. He takes it with angelic meekness. I am hopefully awaiting the day when he loses patience and slugs her. I'll let you know if it happens.

There is obviously a place in any school that cares about its students for this sort of communication, but the measurement program thus far outlined has no place for it. Very well; let it be added. The only restriction is that no one should try to think of an observation like this on all 120 students in his classes. If he notices anything like this (or much more academic but crucial) and feels an urge to tell the adviser about it, let him do so. Only these spontaneous communications will reach advisers without prior approval. They may provide that bit of looseness in the system that will make it more comfortable and livable.

How Does Evaluation Feed Back into the Curriculum?

Departmental Autopsies. After each measure of record is administered and scored, the department head or evaluation representative has a clerk, aide, or student assistant prepare distributions of scores on each objective for the groups tested, and these results are discussed at the next weekly meeting of the department or team. It is rarely necessary or desirable to compare classes taught by one teacher with those taught by another, since everyone knows that some classes are brighter, better prepared, and more highly motivated than other classes. Their higher scores can lead to no defensible conclusions about the strengths or weaknesses of the instructional program.

Instead, results are presented for significant subgroups of the school population, for different curricula, for groups that have been trying out different methods or materials, and so on. Groups that have made better scores than one usually expects from their level of ability (even when their scores are low) will be scrutinized with special care. How in the world did they do it? Sometimes their teacher is able to offer a pretty shrewd guess. Other teachers who have tried something similar in the past with no such luck will question him closely to find out what made the difference. If his explanation sounds convincing, these others may decide to modify their previous treatment in the light of his experience and try it out again in one of their present classes.

They may also suggest putting some new element into the next measure of this ability to bring out this effect more sharply. If the next results are almost uniformly favorable to the new procedure, then the department will have learned something about one of its teaching problems, and the teacher who started this train of events will get deserved recognition. The departmental meetings following these measures will also take on new life and interest, for the teachers will have something of real import to discuss with one another.

There is just one commandment: *Always* look for some favorable result and try to discover what accounts for it. Once we start looking at the unfavorable results, we may possibly discover what went wrong, but we will also stop our new evaluation program dead in its tracks. If the results are ever used in any way that will publicly embarrass or humiliate a teacher, all teachers will revolt against it. A better policy is to look only for things that work. As these procedures are adopted, they will automatically drive out the mistakes.

A dramatic example of feedback which led to curriculum change occurred recently in the area of the social studies. Members of our Evaluation Committee had heard how an item analysis made by teachers of three social studies departments of the *Topical Tests in American*

History (Cooperative Tests) had revealed certain facts. This analysis showed that students could handle historical data which dealt with broad concepts, but failed to understand historical time and failed to have knowledge of geography. Also social studies teachers had gained new insights as they examined more closely their testing procedures. Teacher-made tests were revised to meet the stated departmental objectives. The selection of content and methods of teaching became more precise as teachers began to use the diagnostic data.

Reports to the Evaluation Committee. During the past two years of experimental development, brief reports have been presented at each meeting of the Evaluation Committee on all new measures tried out since the last meeting. While this has been extremely desirable and stimulating, obviously as the program expands to cover all major objectives of instruction in every department, such reports will no longer be feasible.

Something brand new will always find a place on the agenda, but as a regular procedure each department should expect to prepare and submit to the Evaluation Committee a formal, written report on its evaluation program only once a year. Normally these reports will be prepared by the evaluation representative during the summer (at full pay per day) and submitted by him to his department for approval by its members upon their return to school in the fall.

This furnishes a natural occasion for a thoughtful review of what the department has learned about its program during the previous year and for a discussion of anything that needs to be added or changed during the present year. When the report is approved by the department, it will be transmitted to the Evaluation Committee and scheduled for a formal review at some time during the year. At some future time, these reviews may multiply to an extent that will make it necessary to divide them among subcommittees, but each subcommittee should always include some representatives of fields unrelated to the field under review. We do not want each discipline to become a tight little enclave, always reviewed by representatives of its own kind.

Naturally the content of these reports will vary enormously from one field to another depending on the complexity of its evaluation problems, its sophistication in measurement, its interest, and other factors. As a rough outline, however, each report will ordinarily describe the measures of record used for each major objective recognized by the department and the procedures by which they were prepared, reviewed, revised, administered, scored and reported. Each report will present distributions of scores for the groups tested and for significant subgroups of the school population, and similar distributions of growth scores. Whenever feasible, the report will present the reliability and standard error of scores on each measure and of cumulative totals across measures for the year. Whenever important differences have been discovered, the significance of these differences will be appropriately computed. But above all else, the reports will include whatever has been discovered about the strengths and weaknesses of the instructional program, the conclusions drawn, the supporting evidence, the recommendations for action, and some indication of the extent to which this action has been initiated.

It is not the business of the Evaluation Committee to approve or disapprove any action taken or contemplated by any department with regard to its instructional program. The Evaluation Committee would be rightly concerned, however, if the measurement program of any department led to *no* conclusions or recommendations, or if the conclusions were not in line with the evidence, or if any changes proposed were in serious conflict with the evidence. The Evaluation Committee needs to assure itself that the measurement program of each department is as soundly conceived and executed as the present state of the art permits, that the conclusions drawn from its results are defensible, that these conclusions lead to some sort of action, and that the action is in line with the evidence. Sometimes the only safe conclusion is that more evidence is needed, but this should be regarded as a last resort. If a measurement program never leads to anything but a demand for more measurement, it is a waste of time.

Instruments, Procedures, and Some Results

Academic Interests. Let us start with a measure of interests in twelve fields of study, since interests are the mainspring of learning and the years in junior high are a good time to explore and develop such interests. For this purpose the guidance counselors used the *Interest Index* developed in the Eight-Year Study (1933-41) and recently revised by John W. French of Educational Testing Service. It is now a list of 192 activities, 16 in each of the following fields:

English	Foreign languages
Social studies	Mathematics
Biology	Physical sciences
Secretarial	Business
Home economics	Shop
Art	Music.

Students indicate whether they like, are indifferent to, or dislike each activity, and these responses are scored as 2, 1, or 0 in order to get a single score representing the relative amount of interest they express in each field. This instrument is one of the few that French found to be useful in comparative prediction.[2] Gerald Halpern of Educational Testing Service reported that the reliability of these 16-item scales clusters at .91 (by internal consistency) and at .86 (by test-retest correlations after an interval of three weeks). Only four of the 192 items were more highly correlated with a related field than with the field they were supposed to represent, and only 8 percent of the correlations between fields exceeded .50 (and these were between fields that are logically related).[3]

Our first use of this instrument in grades 7 and 8, however, yielded little but frustration. The scoring took a long time and cost over one dollar per student. The scores written on the answer sheets were not labeled and had to be identified by a code on a cover sheet. Scores representing related fields were not grouped together. Worst of all, raw scores on this instrument have little meaning and have to be interpreted by separate norms for boys and for girls, which were not available until we found a table that would serve this purpose in Halpern's report. For example, one boy had the same numerical score (21) in English and social studies, but this score indicated a high degree of interest in English for a boy and only an average interest in social studies. For a girl it would have been average in both cases. He also had a higher numerical score (15) in business than in home economics (11), but that proved to be a low score for boys in business and about average for boys in home economics; while for girls the home economics score of 11 would have been abysmally low—two standard deviations below average.

This must already seem impossibly complicated, and we would not have reported our experience with this instrument had we not found a way for each student to score his own answer sheet in five minutes and to interpret each score as high, middle, or low (H, M, or L) by reference to norms for boys and for girls that were printed right on the answer sheet. This illustrates the point that a published instrument that proves unsatisfactory need not be abandoned. If the idea seems good, one can secure permission to revise the instrument for experimental use in a way that obviates the difficulties of using it in the original form.

[2] John W. French. *Manual for Experimental Comparative Prediction Batteries, High School and College Level.* Princeton, New Jersey: Educational Testing Service, 1964.
[3] Gerald Halpern. *Scale Properties of the Interest Index.* College Entrance Examination Board Research and Development Reports 65-6, No. 5. Princeton, New Jersey: Educational Testing Service. 1965.

First, we reprinted the activities in a different order so that the items representing each field would all lie in two widely separated lines across the answer sheet, and the numbers written in these two lines (either 2, 1, or 0 for each item) could be added together in one's head, since the highest possible sum would be 32 and the average about 18. The following is the first half of our revised page 1 with one item representing each of the twelve fields in the order listed previously:

Page 1

A Write stories.

B Analyze, compare, and criticize the platforms of political parties.

C Put eggs into an incubator and open one every day to see how the chick develops.

D Have a job in a business office or store as training for a regular job.

E Learn how to cook well (in camp or at home).

F Make posters.

G Speak a foreign language.

H Learn how mathematics is used in figuring life insurance rates, taxes, etc.

I Study rock formations and learn how they developed.

J Visit stores, factories, offices, and other places of business to find out how their work is carried on.

K Make things of wood, metal, etc.

L Sing in a glee club, chorus, or choir.

The revised answer sheet is reproduced in **Figure 1.**

We made the self-scoring of answer sheets practically foolproof by issuing "scoring aids" that were a third of a page (3⅔ inches) from top to bottom and had the following directions printed on them:

SCORING AID FOR THE INTEREST INDEX,
SELF-SCORING FORM, EDUCATIONAL TESTING SERVICE

Use this sheet to help you count the sum for each subject on the Answer Sheet. The first sum called for in the right-hand column is "A+M." This means the total of the numbers you have written in lines A and M in the boxes at the left. Place the top edge of this sheet just below line A. The bottom edge of this sheet will then lie just above line M. Add together (in your head) all the numbers you see just above the top edge and just below the bottom edge of this sheet. Write the total of these numbers in the blank after A+M.

The next sum called for is "B+N." Move this sheet down one line so that the top edge is just below line B, the bottom edge just above line N. Again, add together all the numbers you see just above the top edge and just below the bottom edge. Write this total in the blank after B+N. Keep on doing this, moving the sheet down one line at a time, until you reach the bottom of the Answer Sheet. Write down all twelve sums that are called for before you start to label them L, M, or H (low, middle, or high) by reference to the table for boys or for girls

INTEREST INDEX, SELF-SCORING FORM, EDUCATIONAL TESTING SERVICE

Name_____ Grade_____ Date_____
Teacher_____Adviser_____
In the box corresponding to each item (below at the left), write
2—if you *like* the activity or think you would like it;
1—if you don't know or don't care one way or the other;
0—if you *dislike* the activity or think you would dislike it.

Page

	1	2	3	4	5	6	7	8
A								
B								
C								
D								
E								
F								
G								
H								
I								
J								
K								
L								
M								
N								
O								
P								
Q								
R								
S								
T								
U								
V								
W								
X								

Do this after filling all the boxes:

A+M _____ Eng _____ G+S _____ Lang _____

B+N _____ Soc _____ H+T _____ Math _____

C+O _____ Bio _____ I+U _____ Phy _____

D+P _____ Sec _____ J+V _____ Bus _____

E+Q _____ Home _____ K+W _____ Shop _____

F+R _____ Art _____ L+X _____ Mus _____

Directions: In the blank after the sum of two letters (such as A+M), write the sum of the numbers written in those two lines at the left. In the blank after the abbreviation of a subject, write L, M, or H (high) depending on the number nearest your sum in the table for Boys or Girls.

Boys	L	M	H	Boys	L	M	H
Eng	7	15	23	Lang	5	15	25
Soc	10	19	28	Math	11	20	29
Bio	10	19	28	Phy	14	22	30
Sec	10	17	24	Bus	12	19	26
Home	6	13	20	Shop	14	22	30
Art	7	15	23	Mus	6	15	24
Girls	L	M	H	Girls	L	M	H
Eng	13	21	29	Lang	13	22	31
Soc	10	19	28	Math	5	14	23
Bio	9	18	27	Phy	4	13	22
Sec	12	20	28	Bus	10	17	24
Home	18	25	32	Shop	3	11	19
Art	12	20	28	Mus	10	18	26

Figure 1. Interest Index

The tables for boys and girls just referred to and printed at the lower right of the answer sheet were based on the means and standard deviations for college-bound students in grade 11 in five cities as reported by Halpern (*loc. cit.*). The "low" point is one standard deviation below the mean; the "high" point one standard deviation above. Since we ask students to use the number nearest their sum, the dividing lines are half a standard deviation from the mean. Hence about 30 percent of the scores of the comparison group would be labeled L (low), about 40 percent M (middle), and about 30 percent H (high). We did not have room to say what to do if a sum was exactly halfway between two of these numbers, but teachers added the instruction that these sums should be labeled M with a plus or minus to show that it was high borderline or low.

These provisional norms will soon be replaced by norms for our own students in grades 7-8-9, but meanwhile it is not a bad idea to take grade 11 as an anchor year and note how the interests expressed in each grade approach or exceed this standard. We used the figures for college-bound students because practically all our students are certain that they will go to college. It would be cruel and pointless to try to convince some of them that they are mistaken, but if their academic interests do not measure up to those of genuinely college-bound students in grade 11, some may wonder whether college (especially a liberal arts college) is what they really want.

Here are some minor improvements. To reduce monotony we cut out the "To" at the beginning of each item and started with the simple verb as it appears on page 152. We discarded the term "Find out how distances to inaccessible places are measured, such as from the earth to the sun" (since it had a higher correlation with physics than with math, which it was supposed to represent) and substituted "Learn how mathematics is used in surveying and map-making." Three other ambivalent items were not changed because they had appropriate meanings for the group affected. We changed "Engineering" to "Shop" as a label for one field since the latter fits the listed activities better. "Secretarial" and "Business" seem to overlap, and they do, but they are the business courses designed to appeal to girls and boys respectively and most often elected by them. They are highly correlated, but so are these interests. Both may be taken as a measure of immediate interest in getting a job. When there is a difference, business refers to management and sales, secretarial to work in an office.

Do these scores really reveal interests? Apparently they do. French reports in his *Manual* that this instrument was "particularly good for differential prediction of college-major grades and satisfaction." In the Eight-Year Study it was found that a strong high school program in a given field such as art was reflected in high and increasing interest scores in that field. Students testify that the picture of their academic interests that they get out of this instrument (when their scores are interpreted as high, middle, or low by reference to norms for boys or girls) is true on the whole—with possibly one or two exceptions that they can explain. (For example, a boy whose principal interest is music but who likes only one or two activities in this field will get a low score, but such cases are rare.) Students also testify that this instrument is informative: it gives them a profile of their relative interests in these twelve fields that they never saw so clearly before. The most convincing evidence to a teacher who is trying to decide whether or not to use this instrument is to take it himself. Even though these are the activities of high school students, the teacher will usually find that his scores give a true picture of his own interests.

Can students fake an interest in a given subject? Of course they can, and they might do so if the instrument was administered by the teacher of that subject with evident concern for the interest expressed in his field. But this instrument is administered by guidance counselors with no vested interest in any subject, and the purpose is obviously to help students organize what they know about their interests in order to make a wiser choice of electives. In this situation there is no point in falsifying interests.

Book Cards. Another measure of interests is a record of independent reading of self-chosen books on 3″ x 5″ "book cards" like that shown in Figure 2.

```
Name................................................ ............Grade.........Date......................
Author, title.............................................................................................  ..........
Type.............Rating  1  2  3  4  5      Difficulty   E   M   H
Comment:



— — — — — — — — — — — — — — — — — — — — — — — — — — — —
```

Figure 2. Record of Independent Reading

These cards are filled out in the library, independent reading rooms, and English classes as soon as possible after a student has finished a book or has decided to give it up. The blank after "Type" is filled with a number corresponding to one of the following types of books:

Fiction	*Nonfiction*
1. Story about boys and girls	16. Book of information
2. Story about animals, nature	17. Sports, games, outdoor life
3. Story about school life	18. Hobbies, practical arts
4. Fantasy, magic	19. Vocations
5. Sports, hunting, outdoor life	20. Travel, exploration
6. Adventure (western, sea, war)	21. Biography, autobiography
7. Success story	22. History
8. Humorous story	23. Social science
9. Detective-mystery-spy	24. Science, natural history
10. Science fiction	25. Philosophy, religion
11. Love and romance	26. Music, art, architecture
12. Historical novel	27. Essays, criticism
13. Tragic, satiric, problem novel	28. Plays
14. Unclassified novel	29. Poems
15. Book of short stories	30. Unclassified nonfiction.

All students have a copy of this list, and it is prominently displayed wherever they make out "book cards." The number of the type of book may eventually be written on the title page of all books for independent reading available in school. Meanwhile, students must decide for themselves what type it is, and some of their decisions are revealing. For example, if an eighth grade boy calls a book an adventure story while an eighth grade girl calls the same book a love story, the difference reveals their stages of development, and both decisions are valid. These types are arranged roughly in order of maturity so that a crude measure of increasing maturity of reading interests (especially in large groups) may be obtained simply by averaging the recorded type-numbers from 1 to 15 for fiction and from 16 to 30 for nonfiction.

After the heading "Rating" the student encircles a number from 1 to 5 to indicate how he liked the book in comparison with others that he has read. After "Difficulty" he encircles E, M, or H to indicate whether it was easy, medium, or hard to read. This information is of particular interest to slow readers, especially when it is given by another slow reader.

The rest of the card (including the back if necessary) is for a candid comment for the benefit of other students who are looking for something to read. Since they see other students using these cards, looking for a book that someone they know has recommended with genuine enthusiasm, their comments are frank and often devastating. They are obviously directed toward their classmates—not the teacher. Although a teacher or librarian may question a student about an adverse reaction to find out in more detail what he objected to, there must be no reprisal or these cards would soon lose the value they have for other students.

Since these cards take only a minute or two to fill out, and since the students themselves make use of the cards filled out by other students, they do not resent this task as they resented the former full-length book reports. When a teacher or librarian is preparing for a conference with a student on his independent reading, these cards are invaluable as an indication of where he stands and of the type and level of book that one can safely recommend. For a discussion of the most important results of keeping such a record, see the following chapter.

Values. Although we discussed ways of finding out the values that students express in words and action, we have not yet attempted any systematic study of this domain. It is next on our agenda, however, and we hope to try out a very simple device that our consultant on measurement developed in three neighboring school systems and two colleges. It is a valid indicator of personal-social values prevailing in large groups but not of the values of any individual; hence the responses to this instrument are not signed.

It consists of a single sheet of paper divided by a line across the middle of the page. At the top it says, "Tell about something a person did that made you like him better." Below the middle line it says, "Now tell about something a person did that made you like him less." The incidents reported are tallied under the following headings, which emerged from a study of 2,045 incidents reported by students in grades 4, 7, 10, 13:

Positive	*Negative*
10 INCLUSION	15 EXCLUSION
11 Recognition, tolerance	16 Intrusion
12 Yields precedence	17 Intolerance
13 Introduces, puts at ease	18 Favoritism
14 Loyal, sticks together	19 Unfaithful, leaves friends
20 HELP, KINDNESS	25 AGGRESSION (a. physical)
21 Gifts, loans	26 (b. non-physical: e.g., blame)
22 Counsel, teaching	27 Cruelty to animals
23 Assumes blame, helps out of trouble	28 Cruel practical jokes
24 Helps in peril, sickness	29 Refuses to help, interferes
30 HONESTY, SINCERITY	35 STEALING, CHEATING, TAKING PROPERTY
31 Trustworthy	36 Ruins property
32 Meets obligations, keeps promises, returns favors	37 Evades obligations, breaks promises, does not return favors
33 Accepts responsibility	38 Takes advantage of others
34 Trusts others	39 Unfairness
40 VERBAL POSITIVE	45 VERBAL NEGATIVE
41 Polite, friendly, apologizes	46 Inconsiderate, rude, talks too much
42 Understanding, appreciative	47 Lying, slander, gossip, betrayal
43 Tells truth, is frank	48 Brag, stuck-up, show-off

Positive *(Continued)*

44 Respects confidences

50 CONFORMITY

51 Obeys rules or people

52 Respects, sticks up for people

53 Respects rights, standards

54 Good sportsmanship

60 LIKABLE QUALITIES

61 Change in desirable direction

62 Talent or achievement

63 Similar tastes, views

64 Sense of humor, cheerful

Negative *(Continued)*

49 Profanity, indecency

55 NONCONFORMITY

56 Disobeys, breaks rules

57 Wants own way, self-centered

58 Bad sportsmanship

59 Drinks, gambles

65 UNDESIRABLE QUALITIES

66 Childish, can't take a joke

67 Boy or girl crazy, makes passes

68 Nosey, prying

69 Bossy, arrogant, bad-tempered, jealous, complaining.

The headings in capital letters are used to classify all incidents that do not fall more specifically under one of the four subheads of each. For example, if an incident lies in the area of "Help, Kindness" but does not fall into any of the four subheads of this category, it is classified under this main heading (given the number 20) which means "All other kinds of help, kindness." This convention accounts in part for the fact that in the original study 92 percent of the incidents classified independently by two investigators were assigned to the same categories.

In this study we had data on the age, sex, type of environment, social class, social adjustment and acceptance, frequency of church attendance, liking for church attendance, and verbal intelligence of the respondents; but the only background variables that made any significant difference were age and sex. Interest in inclusion declines with increasing age, but girls are more interested in it than boys, who report more incidents concerned with help-kindness. Honesty-sincerity and likable qualities appear more frequently at higher age levels as do verbal positive qualities, which are of greater interest to girls. Interest in aggression decreases sharply with age and is mentioned most frequently by boys, as is stealing-cheating. Verbal negative incidents appear more frequently at higher age levels and also nonconformity, mentioned most frequently by boys. These were the only significant differences (not explained by artifacts) that we found out of 156 that we computed.

In general, the picture of the values of American children that emerged from this study was appallingly uniform and conventional. Nothing made any difference except the basic forces of age and sex. If a school expects to make any significant change in the personal-social values of its students, it must use something stronger than casual discussion. But if it is successful, it is likely that an instrument of this sort would reveal the change—especially if it were adapted to the type of change expected. For example, one might say: "Tell about something a person did that made you respect him because it showed that he was a good citizen."

Sociometric Ratings. We adapted the old technique of sociometric ratings to the junior high school level by duplicating a set of nine "Descriptions of Classmates":

1. I don't know this student well enough to check any column but this.
2. This student is one whom I admire and look up to.
3. This student is honest and truthful.
4. This student is courteous, tactful and pleasant.
5. This student can often explain things that others do not understand.
6. This student is good company and fun to be with.
7. This student would make a good leader for our group.
8. If I were a leader, I would want this student to be in my group.
9. This student is one of my best friends.

These descriptions were selected by counselors from a long list of descriptions obtained from students (see Figure 3); others may be added or substituted. For example, "one of my best friends" is the least reliable of the favorable descriptions (averaging .81 after six weeks) and is used so infrequently that it will probably be replaced with a less extreme description.

Students placed these headings over a list of their classmates with nine columns after the names, and they put checks in the columns corresponding to the descriptions that they would apply to these students. If they checked column 1, the "unknown" column, they would not check any other column for that student; otherwise they might give anywhere from zero to eight checks to each student. This rating was repeated after six weeks and after three months with no intervening discussion and proved to be unusually stable or reliable. Correlations between the number of checks received in single columns on these occasions averaged .88 after six weeks and .78 after three months. The most important score was the sum total of checks received in all favorable columns (2-9), since it was the most inclusive measure of acceptance by others. Its reliability was .95 for boys and .93 for girls in one school and above .90 in the others.

The second most important score was the total number of checks that each student *gave* to all the rest of his classmates in columns 2-9, since this was a measure of his acceptance of others. We gave no hint at any time that we would count the number of checks each student *gave*, since this could easily be faked. The reliability of this score was more variable: .89 for boys, .67 for girls in one school; .69 for boys and .93 for girls in another. The third most important score was the number of checks given or received in column 1, the "unknown" column, as a measure of nonacceptance. The average reliability of this score

Sample Sociometric Form

School District of_____

Student's Name_____   Date_____

Section 47

School_____

This edge should be farthest away from you and under the list of "descriptions".

	1	2	3	4	5	6	7	8	9
Jeffrey A.									
Jamie B.									
Saul E.									
Reynold G.									
David G.									
Gary G.									
Carl K.									
Hal R.									
Neil S.									
Leopold S.									
Lawrence S.									
Paul S.									
Norman W.									
Michael W.									
Carol C.									
Margie F.									
Toby F.									
Kathy F.									
Catherine G.									
Bonnie G.									
Mindy H.									
Annette L.									
Adrieene M.									
Ruth Ann N.									
Barbara S.									
Jill S.									
Sheri S.									

Figure 3. Sample Sociometric Form

was .71, somewhat lower than the others, because students differed from one occasion to another in where to draw this line and because certain students gained prominence at different times; but the reliability is still high enough to be useful, especially if the measure is repeated.

In one sense, then, this measure was highly successful in that we could get reliable scores on social acceptance in little time with little effort. It caused no trouble, for we warned students in advance that we would not tell any student how he came out, because then we would have to tell others, and sooner or later someone would get hurt. We explained that teachers needed these scores in order to form congenial working groups, but the scores would be treated as confidential information.

In another sense, however, this measure was unsuccessful because the teachers could not see any real use for it. They said that they already knew which students were popular and which were unpopular, and the scores showed that they were right—although some confessed that they never dreamed that there would be such wide differences in scores, or that so many would be checked in the "unknown" column. Still, they did not see that they could do anything about the state of affairs revealed by this instrument.

This was shocking to the few who began teaching in the 'thirties when acceptance of and by others was an important value, and when we would worry and scheme for months over students with low sociometric ratings if they were hostile or unhappy. These ratings also showed us how quickly students of different ethnic and religious groups became integrated in the friendly atmosphere of our schools.

The intellectual atmosphere of the 'sixties seems to have eclipsed our earlier interest in the personal relationships of our students. We hope such interest will return, and that this instrument may help to revive it. One junior high school counselor related how the sociometric data led her to an early interview with a seventh grader, when she discovered the child had been checked as "unknown" by everyone in her section. The counselor assumed that the student was new to the district. When she discovered that the student had been with most of the group throughout elementary school, the counselor was alerted to a problem soon enough to do something about it.

Behavior Problems. When students were sent to the office of the assistant principal for misbehavior, they were asked to fill out a page with the following questions while they were waiting:

RECORD OF BEHAVIOR PROBLEMS

Objective: Learning to get along with other students and with teachers.

Name.. Grade............... Date...........................

Teacher who sent you.. Adviser.....................................

What happened? (If others were involved, you need not mention names.)

What were you really trying to do? Was this something you wanted to do, or were you trying to do something else—only something went wrong?

What, if anything, was wrong about this? What harm was done? To whom?

To what extent were you to blame?

Is there anything we could do to help you put things right?

What, if anything, should the school do about this?

What, if anything will you agree to do about it?

What should the others do who were partly to blame?

Any other comments?

Teacher's comments:

Some may regard this as a negative approach, but remember that the negative thing had already happened: the student had been sent to the office. As he sits there expecting to get "chewed out," it settles him down, gives him perspective, and helps him to regard the incident as his own problem (not the teacher's problem or the principal's problem) if he analyzes what happened from his own point of view. The last item on the page, "Teacher's comments," is fair warning that the teacher who sent him to the office will see what he has written and challenge inaccurate statements.

This record form yielded so many insights into the causes of misbehavior and offered such good leads into a discussion of these problems with the student and sometimes with his parents that the assistant principals who first tried it out said to the Evaluation Committee, "We don't care whether you approve this thing or not. It is so helpful to us that we'll use it anyway." As indicated earlier in this chapter, they had a right to do so as part of their "instructional evaluation." Yet when the Evaluation Committee heard some of the students' responses to this form, they were happy to approve it.

Incidentally, this record also brought to light a few teachers who sent students to the office far too frequently for petty offenses or for violations of unreasonable rules. Of course, the principals knew this before, but the sheer number of these forms accumulated by certain teachers made impressive evidence to discuss with them. What was done about each case of misbehavior could be recorded at the bottom or on the back of this form. After the teacher had seen it and added his comments (or at least his initials), the form was sent to the adviser of the student concerned. If the case became chronic, the forms were sent to the counselor for more intensive follow-up with the student and parents. The most important outcome of this procedure is what happens to the student. It is our goal to have the pupil develop insight about his behavior as it affects his relationship with others.

Incomplete and Unsatisfactory Work. A similar form was devised for use whenever an important assignment (usually one made a week or more before it was due) was not completed satisfactorily and on time. "Unsatisfactory" meant completely unacceptable—not deficient in some minor respect. The first form we tried out was altogether too long, and most questions were answered "no" or left blank, but here is the form:

Record of Incomplete and Unsatisfactory Work

Objective: Learning to get work done satisfactorily and on time.

Name.. Grade.............. Date..............................

Teacher................................... Subject..................................... Adviser..............................

What work was incomplete or unsatisfactory?

Why?

Was there anything you did not understand about this assignment?

Did you have trouble getting the necessary material?

Did something else interfere? If so, what?

Did you put off this work because it seemed dull or unimportant? Too hard?

How might the assignment have been changed to make it more interesting or worthwhile?

What did you do instead of doing this assignment?

About how much time have you spent thus far on this assignment?

When will it be done, or done over?

Is there anything a teacher, a student or others could do to help you?

What changes in attitude, work habits, hours of study, etc., do you need to make in order to stay on top of your school work?

Any other comments?

Teacher's comments:

We tried out all these questions to find out which of them yielded pay dirt, but the answers of students with serious problems in this area were so laconic and evasive that we reduced the questions to three:

What work was incomplete or unsatisfactory?

Why?

When will it be done or done over?

The teacher can then indicate whether the work was received and accepted on the date indicated. The answers to the "why" question were seldom illuminating or convincing; they sounded as though the student did not want to mention the real reason and put down a conventional answer instead, such as "I did not have the book." Why not? In this instance, the book was the regular textbook and the student had a week to work on the assignment. Evidently he put it off until the night before the assignment was due and then forgot to bring home his textbook. Why? Such answers can serve only as leads into a discussion of the real reasons with the student.

There can be no question as to the importance of this objective:

students must learn to get their work done. This record can at least reveal the students who habitually fail to complete important assignments satisfactorily and on time in many different courses year after year. The adviser is in the best position to observe how these danger signals are piling up in the record folder of any given student, since only the adviser will assemble these records from all courses that the student is taking. The adviser can then discuss the problem with the student and, if necessary, with his parents. Operationally this procedure identifies the underachiever. When three or four teachers send records of incomplete work to the counselor for the same child, the counselor is alerted to a learning problem before it becomes chronic.

The Problem-student Syndrome. Taken together, four of these measures can reveal deep-seated problems that should probably be brought to the attention of the guidance counselor. What is the matter with a student who reveals a low level of interest in almost all activities carried on in school, who shows in the sociometric device that he does not like or trust his classmates and is not liked or trusted by them, who continually gets into trouble, and who habitually fails to get his work done? Without long psychiatric treatment, it would be hard to get a more comprehensive description of a disturbed student than this.

Some students will require such treatment, but others can be helped by a concerted effort initiated and followed up by the guidance counselor. As we help these students to come to grips with their problems, these indices begin to move up, and we can take real pride when the general level of the school in these indices is healthy. We hope the day will soon come when high schools again take as much interest in such indices as these as they now take in College Board scores.

Evaluation and the Humanities

English. The next chapter will discuss in detail three instruments (in addition to the "book cards") that shed most light on the strengths and weaknesses of our program in English. We called these instruments the Test Essay, the Shadow Test, and the Pesky Errors Test. Minor devices and techniques of measurement are described briefly. Music and visual arts have not yet become involved in this program but will do so next year, and some of the more unusual instruments projected for these fields will be discussed in the following pages. Evaluation in the humanities focuses on five types of objectives represented by the following series of verbs:

1. Produce, perform, practice, participate, create, construct, compose
Examples: Sing, play an instrument, invent tunes, improvise, transpose, read

music. Draw, paint, work in clay, etc. Dance, take part in theatrical productions. Do some creative writing.

2. Respond, perceive, listen, understand, interpret, appreciate

Examples: Respond to literary works with understanding and appreciation. Understand artist's purpose, means used, relation of parts to whole. Listen to music with understanding; perceive and respond to aesthetic elements in visual arts.

3. Know about, recall, recognize, relate, classify, identify, talk about

Examples: Know about authors, composers, artists, performers, periods, styles, important works, instruments, media, devices, terms, etc. Classify examples of these in appropriate categories. Recognize important works, characters, quotations, references, allusions, etc.

4. Seek, enjoy, esteem, value (interests, attitudes, habits)

Examples: Seek literary, musical and artistic experiences (through amateur performance, reading, concerts, exhibits, lectures, etc.). Express increasingly mature views about literature, music, art, artists, etc.

5. Judge, prefer, discriminate, evaluate, criticize (taste)

Examples: Express preferences for works of increasing complexity and importance. Form reasoned critical judgments of significance and quality of art works. Recognize differences between good and poor works, performances, etc. Respect good work in the arts (whether one likes it or not); outgrow and discard the bad.

In general, production or performance is not difficult for experienced judges to rate reliably when they see students' work or listen to their performance. But the junior high school is the point at which most students drop out of music and visual arts and only the talented continue. Hence there is no way to tell what the majority can or cannot do in these fields, or what factors in ability or perception differentiate those who will continue from those who will drop out. One device for a survey of what all students can do in music is presented in the following section, and it is easy to prepare a similar checklist backed up by performance tests for visual arts.

Music: Performance. A device we have projected for use in the near future is a questionnaire or checklist of what students can do in music at this stage, backed up by testing a sample of students on one or two tasks each to find out whether they can really do some of the harder things they have checked. If they know that they may be tested, few students will intentionally falsify what they can do, though some may be mistaken. A check of perhaps a random tenth of the students will then indicate the extent to which their replies may be taken at face value. A small number of typical items are reproduced below.

Survey of Musical Ability

Directions: Check all of the following that you can do. The list goes from easy to hard. You may be asked to do some of the harder things you check. Your score will be the number of the hardest task that you can do—not perfectly, but as well as is expected of students of your age.

1. You will hear a tape recording of a well-known song such as "Old Black Joe" and get a copy of the words. Can you sing it along with the recording?

2. You will hear a recording of a simple song that you have not heard before and get a copy of the words. After hearing it once, can you sing it along with the recording?

3. You will get a sheet of music with the opening bars of three well-known songs, without words. Below each of these the names of three songs will be listed. Can you read music well enough to recognize songs you know from the notes alone and pick out their names from the list?

4. The same sheet of music will have one line of notes of a song that you have not heard before. Certain points in this line will be lettered A, B, C, D, E. You will hear a recording that will stop at one of these points. Can you mark the point at which the recording stopped?

5. The next line of notes of the same song will be lettered in the same way. At one of these points the recording will not do what the notes say. Can you mark the point at which the recording differed from the notes?

6. The next line of notes will be a familiar melody with words in two-part harmony, and you will hear a recording in which both parts are sung. Can you sing along with the part that is not the melody?

7. The next line of notes will be the next line of the same song with words in two-part harmony, but the recording will have only the melody. Can you sing the other part from the notes without hearing it in the recording?

8. The next line of notes will be a simple melody with words that you have not heard before. The recording will play only the first bar. Can you sing the rest of this line (melody only) by sight-reading the notes?

9. Can you sight-read a short, simple piece on a musical instrument that you have studied?

10. Can you sight-read a part other than the melody on this instrument?

Any number of questions like these may be asked, but these will do as a sample. Remember that the subsequent testing will be feasible because only a random tenth of the students will be tested individually, and each will be asked to do only one or two of the harder tasks he has checked. The quality of performance will not be rated; the teacher will decide only whether he can or cannot do the tasks that he has checked.

Music: Listening. This will be a test based on short passages of tape-recorded music averaging about a minute in length. At the end there will be one or two complete selections lasting four or five minutes. Such questions as the following will be asked:

1. Did you like this excerpt better than the last?............ less?............ about the same?...............

2. What type of music was it? (march, waltz, symphony, concerto, opera, choral work, folk song, song from a musical comedy, etc.)

3. Who or what was playing or singing? (tenor, baritone, violin, orchestra, etc.)

4. What section of the orchestra (or what voice) carried the main melody?

5. What other instruments or voices could you hear?

6. Were there three beats per measure (as in a waltz) or four (as in a march)?

7. Was the key major or minor?

8. Was any part (or phrase) of this melody repeated? If so, how many times?

9. Did you recognize the work from which this excerpt came? If so, which of the following was it? (three choices)

(Questions on the longer selection)

10. Four musical phrases will be played. Indicate whether each phrase occurred or did not occur in the long selection you have just heard. (To get at attention span and musical memory.)

11. Which of the following is the name of this musical form?

12. Check any of the following that you heard in this selection. (Variations, counterpoint, solo, duet, cadence, modulation, etc.)

(Questions on quality of performance)

Some excerpts may be played twice: once by professionals and once by amateurs, or once on a fine piano and again on a piano that is out of tune. Which was the better performance? First.............. Second.............. No difference.............. The same excerpts will be played again. Check any faults that you hear.

	First	Second
Wrong notes	——	——
Out of tune	——	——
Poor tone quality	——	——
Some started or stopped later than others	——	——
Some parts drowned out more important parts	——	——

(Uneven rhythm, exaggerated emphasis, sliding into notes, etc.).

Visual Arts: Perception. The test in visual arts corresponding to the foregoing test of listening to music will be based on a booklet of small reproductions—some in color, some black-and-white—with eight reproductions on two facing pages. A task that gets at ability to perceive aesthetic elements in these works with minimal reliance on words is to pick out pairs of reproductions that are alike in some way. Such questions as the following may be asked:

1. Which two are most alike in the type of subject they represent?

2. Which two were originally parts of the same picture?

3. Which two are a preliminary sketch and a final form of the same work?

4. Which two were done by the same artist in the same style?
5. Which two works by different artists are most nearly alike in style?
6. Which two make the greatest use of pure, unmixed colors?
7. Which two give the greatest illusion of depth?
8. Which two are most nearly alike in handling the effects of sunlight?
9. Which two show the greatest knowledge of anatomy?
10. In which two are the figures standing most firmly on the ground?
11. Which two were done before the rules of perspective were understood?
12. Which two disregard the rules of perspective for some artistic purpose?

Any number of such questions can be formulated with reference to any given set of eight reproductions. One set may be reproductions of the work of students of about the same age as that of the respondents. Another set may be reproductions of very good and very poor works, each pair treating the same sort of subject with about the same degree of realism. These two sets may be used to get at critical judgments and reasons for such judgments.

The preparation of the booklet of reproductions will require the assistance of a research grant, but the cost should be moderate because many plates may be borrowed from museums and art magazines. An alternative is to get four projectors and project four different slides at once in different corners of a large screen. Then questions may be asked in the form, "Which slide does A? Which does B?" For example, which was originally an oil painting on canvas? which was a fresco? in which are the main lines of the composition an S-curve? in which are they a triangle? which was the earliest of these works? which was the latest? which was painted by Michelangelo? by Rembrandt? by El Greco?

Remember that the instruments projected for music and visual arts have not yet been tried out, and there is no guarantee that they will work. It is likely that many more questions will have to be formulated and tried out before we find those that are easy enough for students of this age to handle and still have some relationship to continuance or dropout. The difficulty of such questions will depend largely on the context (the set of reproductions) in which each pair is placed. For example, while it might be difficult for a young student to pick out two similar paintings by Picasso in a gallery of modern works, it would be easy to see that they were two works by the same artist in the same style if the others were from the Renaissance.

Some particular stumbling blocks of young students may be discovered and eliminated. In an earlier form of this test, the younger students were unable to see that the head and shoulders of Adam (by Michelangelo) and the full figure of Adam were from the same painting —although they spotted some less obvious resemblances. We surmised that the nudity of the full figure kept them from looking at it closely enough to see the resemblance. For this and other reasons we avoid the use of completely naked figures in these tests.

Instruments in Other Fields. In addition to the instruments discussed in this chapter and the next, we expected to report on instruments used in social studies—the only other field for which data had been analyzed at the time of writing this report. But the recent publication by the National Council for the Social Studies of a whole volume on *Evaluation in Social Studies*, edited by Harry D. Berg, went so far beyond anything we had to report that we decided to use only guidance, English, music, and visual arts as our examples. These may be enough to illustrate the wide variety of instruments and procedures through which data on hard-to-measure objectives may be secured. Further illustrations will be presented in the next chapter.

Subject-matter Examinations. We have not provided any illustrations of ordinary subject-matter examinations because they would look too familiar. The cooperative production, review and revision of such examinations by a department or teaching team, however, is not familiar to most high school teachers.

Such a cooperative process can be a frustrating experience—especially if the teachers think that the only way to do it cooperatively is to get together every day and talk until the questions somehow get written. Perhaps a more efficient procedure is suggested by the following reminiscences of a college examiner:

In my nine years as examiner in humanities I rediscovered the universal law (as has every other examiner) that no one ever likes anyone else's question or topic. There is a corollary that arguing over an examination is thirsty business and should never be attempted except at a party in the evening at the home of the examiner after suitable refreshments have been provided. One has to be careful that some staff members do not pass from the mellow into the bellicose stage, where argument is unprofitable; hence it is prudent to serve no more than two drinks at the start with promise of more to follow when the business is completed.

Then one can take a look at the previous examination at this stage in the course and at significant figures on student performance brought out by item-analysis. The examiner usually leads off by telling what he thought was most successful in the previous examination and what parts did not work well and should either be dropped or improved. If he has something new to propose, such as a new section or type of question to get at some previously unmeasured objective of the course, he may introduce it at this time—since this is the time of night when the host has every right to make a short speech. If he expects strong resistance, however, he may keep his proposal like an ace up his sleeve until the staff bogs down in an argument over some section of the examination that has never worked well. Then the general relief at the prospect of getting rid of an unpopular section of the examination may combine with the attraction of a new idea to win acceptance.

This bit of strategy illustrates the point that, although the examiner must be permissive and allow everyone to speak his mind, he has to keep a firm hand on the reins or the discussion will get nowhere. Before the meeting begins he must have a pretty clear idea of the outline of an examination that he will accept, and he must steer the discussion toward it. If he doesn't, the group will complain of a lack of leadership. On the other hand, if he is unwilling to compromise when his ideas are firmly opposed, the group will regard him as stubborn, inflexible and overbearing. It helps if he knows the group well enough to call on the right people to answer objections for him, and if he learns how to slide around objections that are not worth an argument. Most of all, he has to get the group on his side. They must respect his competence and judgment, but that is not enough. It sounds corny, but they must know that he loves them and is always willing to listen and to help.

If all goes well, it will not be long before the group agrees upon the main outline of the examination. Then they divide up the work of preparing the questions. Tom may volunteer to do the questions on Hawthorne, Dick on Melville, and Wilma on Twain. It is not hard to get volunteers because they know that each one will have to do part of the work, and if they don't make a bid for an author and work that they like, they may get stuck with one they dislike. One naturally turns to certain people for certain parts of the examination because that is their specialty, but sometimes there are surprises. Although Dick usually does the questions on Melville, he may say, "If you don't mind, this time I'd like to take a shot at the questions on Henry James. I've never been satisfied with our questions on James, and it will clear my mind if I try to prepare a new set. Naturally I'll want all of you to take a long, hard look at my questions. I know that Ed would like a chance to do the questions on Melville, and it is high time for somebody to have a fresh look at him."

After the parts of the examination have been assigned, there will be some discussion of the proportion of questions to be devoted to recall, recognition, interpretation, analysis, criticism, etc., and which selections will lend themselves particularly well to one or another of these types of questions. If some new staff members do not understand how to write these types of questions or the distinctions between them, questions from past examinations may be dug out to illustrate them. The examiner will also help them privately if they have trouble framing the types of questions that they have undertaken to write.

Most of the questions will probably be written in multiple-choice form because that is the most definite way of asking a question about a point of interpretation or analysis. If you merely ask, "What is the author getting at in paragraph two?" and students have to write out their answers, there is no way for them to guess what sort of answer you have in mind. They usually play it safe by paraphrasing what the author said, and they are either purposely or unconsciously so vague that it is hard to tell whether or not they got the point.

But if you ask, "What is the author getting at in paragraph two: A, B, C, or D?" they have to make a definite choice. Your teaching experience will suggest the kinds of poor answers that the less able students give in class so that the wrong answers will not be too obviously wrong. Each represents a type of misinterpretation that you have often heard. Critics of multiple-choice questions assert that, if you frame an acceptable answer for students and they do not have to think it out and put it in their own words, even an idiot should be able to recognize which answer is supposed to be the best. They should look at the results of such examinations. The idiots fare very badly.

Besides, if students do not have to puzzle over their wording of each answer —often a subtle point that even the teacher finds it hard to express unambiguously—you can get in about ten times as many questions as students would be able to answer in their own words. The sheer number of such questions is important. Even a good student may stumble in his interpretation of a work that does not appeal to him, and he may not get the point of certain types of questions. To be fair to all students in a large course, you have to cover many works and present a wide variety of questions, preferably composed by different teachers and reviewed by others, so that no single point of view dominates the examination.

If I had to pick out a single fault of a typical high school examination that I would condemn above all others, I would say that it usually represents the opinions and preferences of a single teacher, unchecked by the criticism of his colleagues. Hence it requires an ability to diagnose the teacher that is hard on a student of independent mind. On the other hand, we do not want to fall into the common fallacy that a passage means whatever a student thinks it means—and who are we to judge? The answer is that we are teachers, and if we are qualified to teach literature, we and our colleagues should be able to see that some interpretations of a given passage are better than others. If we present one good interpretation and three others that are clearly wrong and ask students to mark the best answer, we are not stifling creativity or originality. These are valuable qualities that should be tested—but not in every single question that we ask.

Although we prefer objective questions, we never hestitate to use either short written answers or long essays if they are the only ways we can think of to get at certain objectives of the course. I must, however, record one objection to essays that often turns up in reviewing the results. The essay solution to an examining problem may merely put off the trouble of making up one's mind about what kinds of responses are desired until the time comes to grade these responses. Then, although the professed aim may have been to get at something lofty like creativity and imagination, it may turn out that none of the answers can reasonably be regarded as either creative or imaginative.

In retrospect it seems incredible that the staff hoped to get creative or imaginative responses in dealing rapidly with unexpected questions or topics in the context of a crucial examination, in which students cannot afford to take chances. Still, there is the stack of papers, and the automatic response of teachers to a stack of papers is to grade them. Since the desired behavior did not appear, the tendency of a staff is to grade the papers on some other basis, such as the correctness or incorrectness of each student's account of what the author said. It is part of the examiner's job to put a stop to this sort of thing. If the papers do not reveal anything about the objective that prompted the inclusion of this question, the only honest thing to do is to throw the papers away.

After some discussion of the types of questions that are to be prepared, the examiner may close the business part of the meeting by announcing that all assignments are due Monday the fourteenth. If he does not receive any set of questions by the close of that day, the examiner will call on the delinquent author with a sharp tomahawk on Tuesday the fifteenth. After the chorus of groans has subsided, the revelry begins.

Long before the deadline the examiner will call on some of his procrastinators and ask how they are getting along. If they have not started and have no urgent business elsewhere, he may sit down with them, talk over the kinds of questions they have to write, and help them to write four or five that may serve as examples. The great point is to get them started.

Teachers are usually conscientious about completing assignments that they have publicly agreed to undertake, but not all of them will get their work done by the due date. Then a few brisk sessions with the tomahawk are called for, and nearly all the laggards will straggle in with their questions by the end of the week. In rare instances the assignment may have to be taken over by another staff member, or the examiner himself may have to do the task. Unless there is a good excuse, the one who did not carry out his assignment may be in serious trouble—not only with the examiner but also with other members of the staff. They know that his dereliction makes it necessary for someone else to do the work under heavy pressure just before the deadline. When his reappointment is being considered, some questions are likely to be raised.

After all sets of questions have been received in first draft, the examiner edits them to remove obvious errors and has photocopies of them made for all staff members. They are asked to answer every question, to voice their objections to questions that they would reject, and to write in any changes that would make a question sharper or more acceptable. The examiner transmits the answers, objections and suggestions to the author of each section and asks for a revision by a certain date. At that time he usually goes over the revision privately with each author to see whether all valid objections have been satisfied. He may agree with the author that certain objections should be ignored and others held in abeyance until someone thinks of a better way to get at the desired behavior. In the present state of the art of examining, we cannot expect perfection, but it is our duty to students to come as close to it as we can. Out of his wider experience with examination questions, the examiner may be able to suggest a way of meeting an objection that had not occurred to the author.

It is seldom necessary or wise to hold a second staff meeting to consider the revised examination, since it would generate as many objections as the first draft. Nearly all revisions are either accepted or amended in these individual conferences with staff members. It must be understood, however, that the examiner reserves the right to make a few editorial changes in the final copy in the interest of consistency, balance, clarity and good form. If his changes violate the intent of any question, he will hear about it afterwards.

It is unnecessary to take up the further steps of reproducing the examination, proctoring it, scoring the answer sheets, grading the written answers, doing an item-analysis, and issuing reports. These are routine matters that are easily handled by an experienced staff.

Results of Cooperative Evaluation

We have stressed the need to focus on the teachers in the processes involved in cooperative evaluation, because teachers have the greatest stake in evaluation and have power to initiate changes. At the first meeting of our Cooperative Evaluation Committee, a teacher asked, "Is it your intent to replace course grades with the system of evaluation you described?" Another question directed to us was, "Will our teaching be judged by the results of the tests and instruments we decide to administer?"

A frank discussion of these questions revealed the loneliness and anxiety which teachers feel at crucial times of evaluation. We explained that the old system would continue until the new program had accumulated enough data to replace it. Principals and counselors expressed more firmly their feelings of dissatisfaction with single course grades as inadequate and untrustworthy measures of educational development, while those concerned with the development of the curriculum would give little or no value to "marks" in attempting to appraise the success of the educational process. These frank expressions were clues that our Cooperative Evaluation Committee had a real purpose.

Administrators, counselors, librarians and teachers wanted something better than the prevailing type of evaluation. Teachers were concerned and became committed to the work of the committee when they were assured that we were proposing that measurement is something that is done at a few strategic times in the course of each year's work. We would try to gather only enough "evidence of record" on departmental objectives and a few major school-wide objectives. It was not our objective to evaluate teachers.

However, we were committed to find ways to improve instruction and the curriculum through precise methods of cooperative evaluation. If our measurement or evaluation program did not feed back knowledge of strengths, weaknesses, and ways of improving the curriculum it would be a waste of time. We were convinced that this would not be the case. We have described some of the feedback which led to new insights on the part of social studies teachers, counselors and librarians. The following chapter will give details in the area of English.

How evaluation feeds back into the larger questions of curriculum development and educational policy. As teams of teachers and departments work together on curriculum development and evaluation, it is our experience that their findings influence many significant decisions

T. W. Junior High School Class Roster: Seventh Grade Section 7D

PERIOD	1	2	3	4	5	6	7	8
MONDAY	Social Studies	Language Arts	Music	Language Arts	Science		Math	Elective A
TUESDAY	Social Studies	Language Arts	Home Economics &	Industrial Art	Science	FLEXIBLE PERIOD	Math	Elective A
WEDNESDAY	Social Studies	Language Arts	Art	Physical Education	Science		Math	Elective A
THURSDAY	Social Studies	Language Arts	Independent Reading	Language Arts	Science		Math	Elective A
FRIDAY	Social Studies	Language Arts	Physical Education	Independent Reading	Science		Math	Elective A

Figure 4. Class Roster: Seventh Grade

concerning the organization and scheduling of pupils, the assignments of staff, and the policies which control budgeting, staffing, and selection of instructional materials. Specifically, in the junior high schools where we instituted the Cooperative Evaluation Program, the schools have in the space of two years made several organizational changes as described in the following paragraphs.

T. W. Junior High School Class Roster: Eighth Grade Section 8R

PERIOD	1	2	3	4	5	6	7	8
MONDAY	Math	Social Studies	Elective A	Science	Independent Reading	Music		Language Arts
TUESDAY	Math	Social Studies	Elective A	Science	Home Economics &	Industrial Art	Physical Education	
WEDNESDAY	Math	Social Studies	Elective A	Science	Independent Reading	Typing		
THURSDAY	Math	Social Studies	Elective A	Science	Independent Reading	Art	Physical Education	
FRIDAY	Math	Social Studies	Elective A	Science	Independent Reading	Typing	Language Arts	Independent Reading

Figure 5. Class Roster: Eighth Grade

T. W. Junior High School   Class Roster: Ninth Grade   Section 9F

PERIOD	1	2	3	4	5	6	7	8
MONDAY	Elective A	Elective B	English	— FLEXIBLE PERIODS — HUMANITIES Social Studies	Art Music	Independent Reading	Math	Science
TUESDAY	Elective A	Elective B	English	HUMANITIES Social Studies	Art Music	Physical Education	Math	Science
WEDNESDAY	Elective A	Elective B	English	HUMANITIES Social Studies	Art Music	Independent Reading	Math	Science
THURSDAY	Elective A	Elective B	English	HUMANITIES Social Studies	Art Music	Physical Education	Math	Science
FRIDAY	Elective A	Elective B	English	HUMANITIES Social Studies	Art Music	Independent Reading	Math	Science

Figure 6. Class Roster: Ninth Grade

In one junior high school, we decided that if we really valued independent reading, we had to provide school time for this activity. Students respond to what we say we value to a large extent in relation to the amount of school time we are willing to devote to it. This provided the rationale and the means to break through the traditional schedule. All 7th and 9th grade pupils will have at least two 40-minute periods a week scheduled for independent reading. All 8th grade pupils will have five periods of independent study, two of which must be for independent reading. The change may seem minor. It represents only an initial breakthrough.

Figures 4, 5 and 6 are actual 7th, 8th and 9th grade schedules which will be operative in a junior high school.

Teachers were anxious to know what a typical teacher schedule would look like. Figure 7 (see p. 176) gives one example.

Orientation to this more flexible schedule and other innovative features in the curriculum took place at the first faculty meeting in the fall. A report by a seventh grade team of teachers was featured at this meeting. This team described how the flexible period in the seventh grade schedule had been programmed. Teachers in this team developed curricular activities in a summer workshop to provide for large group, small group and individualized instruction for every seventh grader in the school. Twelve teachers are on the seventh grade team.

Then we had to set up independent reading rooms and stock them with paperbacks related to all subjects and interest areas. The English staff and curriculum coordinator developed the following guidelines for

PERIOD	1	2	3	4	5	6	7	8
MONDAY	Prep.	8-1	7th Gr. Flex.Pds	7-4	7-6	←	7-1	7-4
TUESDAY	←			↓		→		Prep.
WEDNESDAY	←			Prep.		→		7-4
THURSDAY	Prep.			Prep.	↓	←		
FRIDAY	7-6	↓	↓	7-4	Prep.	Prep.	↓	↓

Figure 7. Representative Teacher's Schedule: Language Arts

instructional activities and supervisory responsibilities related to independent reading.

Goals of the Independent Reading Program

1. To develop criteria for the selection of independent reading.

2. To teach students how to discuss books on an informal or conversational level as opposed to the formal, analytical approach to required reading.

3. To provide an opportunity for each student to explore and enjoy reading without consideration to grading; to stimulate an interest in reading as an end in itself; and to demonstrate that the school values this by providing time for independent reading.

4. To develop the reading habit as a means of learning.

Suggested Guidelines for Student Discussion Groups

1. Discussions led by students may take such forms as the following:

a. How a particular book was a new kind of experience—specifically, what different feelings, attitudes or knowledge did the book convey?

b. Convincing another student of the values of a book, revealing only enough of the book to spark interest on the part of a potential reader.

2. Discussions may be organized around themes or types of books: mysteries, travel, biography, etc.

Responsibilities of English Teachers

The English teacher should devote some class time to these discussions. Size of discussion groups will depend upon the number of students who are prepared to discuss and to listen in on discussions: possibly from five to twelve students.

Students may choose their own discussion chairman; perhaps this responsibility should rotate within the group as the discussion points change. From time to time teachers also should chair the discussion groups, particularly in the beginning. Teachers will circulate among the groups and offer assistance where possible, and become a part of the discussions. The teacher should consciously teach the skills of group discussion, conversation and dialogue by models and analyses of group process.

Guidelines for the Supervising Teacher in the Independent Reading Classroom

The most important point to impress upon the students is that reading is the only activity approved during this period. The students may read books they have brought from home, chosen at the school library, or chosen in the Independent Reading Room itself.

Students who choose books from the libraries provided in the independent reading rooms should be reminded to sign out and sign in any books they are borrowing or returning. Cards will be provided with the books. Students should be encouraged to "swap" books which are a part of personal collections. Students should be encouraged to collect books and to become discriminating about the books they choose to buy.

Theme Conferences. The goal of writing competence led to the employment of teacher aides to help English teachers grade papers. We discovered early in the program that just more writing was not enough; teachers and teacher aides needed time to talk with students about their compositions. We speculated that the theme conference would probably do more to improve writing skill than any other single approach.

Teacher aides who could commit themselves to work twelve hours a week in school were employed to conduct most of these conferences. These "teacher assistants" are paid $4.00 an hour. Needless to say, the budget has been affected, the nature of staffing has changed and the instructional emphasis has been modified. Best of all the students have improved in writing skill.

GUIDELINES FOR THEME CONFERENCES

Why hold individual conferences?

Personal contact; develops rapport; someone cares about me and my writing; one-to-one relationship

Convinces student of importance of writing, that writing is something that can be improved

Explain personally what may have been hazy in symbols used to grade papers

Reinforces with the student the progress of his writing regardless of grades

Student sees who is grading his themes.

Kinds of conference

Single paper with special problems; rewrites; follow-ups

Single paper as yet ungraded; student sees teacher's process of grading. Student is able to question as process proceeds

Conference on progress to date—with self-evaluation

Conference as writing is taking place.

Guidelines for conducting the conference

Keep conference on the subject; keep it short

Have a specific piece of writing to use as guide

Use reading aloud—good writing reads like good conversation

Beware of "This is what I *meant.* . . ." Make the point, "This is what you actually *said!*"

Try not to lecture; ask questions; get reactions

Concentrate on what cannot be indicated by symbols and comments on paper

Discuss purpose, content, organization and diction (explain wrong words)

Explain why the student got the assigned grade.

The decision to develop a humanities curriculum at grades 9 and 12 is an outgrowth of a number of factors including the evaluative comments made by students. Could the pupils be scheduled to provide for such a curriculum? This is always a first question raised by administration and teachers. The ninth grade schedule has a three-period block of time for literature, history and the arts. The school principal was supportive and anxious to develop a schedule to accommodate individualized instruction, independent reading, large-group instruction and a "new" humanities curriculum.

Why the humanities approach? In our discussions with students we have often heard them evaluate favorably what the school has to offer, but then add the comment, "But nobody pulls anything together for us!" The humanities curriculum promises to build on and pull together the concepts developed earlier in the curriculum as well as providing for new experiences with literature, history, and the arts. This curriculum will focus on the study of man and the ways he has expressed, formed and preserved the social, moral and aesthetic ideas he has valued. Such a curriculum promises to demolish the fences which have kept the curriculum separate, and sometimes unspirited.

Such a humanities curriculum must have as its major objective the experience of raising creative questions and making better use of answers, if the student is to become a responsible member of the community.

How Evaluation Facilitates Teaching, Learning and Self-evaluation

Teaching and learning were facilitated in two of our schools in the project by intensive child study and curricular modification. Each school organized seventh grade teaching teams. One school emphasized the teacher's role as the faculty adviser. Four teachers who taught the same groups of pupils met daily (a scheduled period) to discuss the learning progress of their pupils. A folder on each child was kept containing the kind of evidence for the record previously described in this chapter. Parent conferences and student conferences were held during this period, also. An amazing outcome of the work of the faculty advisers team was the absence of student failures at the end of the year. For the first time in the long history of this school, not one student in the slower sections had to go to summer school to repeat a course.

In the other junior high school the seventh grade team was mainly interested in flexible scheduling and curricular modifications to meet the needs of their seventh graders. The regrouping of pupils for remedial, accelerated, large group or individualized instruction in each field led to the disappearance of the block schedule. The group or section designation and the stigma attached to being in the slow group which has caused so much heartache for pupils, parents and administrators has disappeared. The positive impact of this team approach was clearly reinforced when the school principal said he would never go back to the old schedule and when a letter of commendation upon the new program was sent to the school board by the parents association.

When teachers begin to feel the support which a cooperative evaluation system offers, the nature and atmosphere of instructional evaluation changes. One practice being adopted by more and more of our teachers has had the effect of making the student more responsible for his learning. Pupils are given the opportunity to take certain important tests several times until mastery of the concepts is achieved. This is not punishment. The student may choose to take an examination and arrange the time to take it. He may take the test as many times as he chooses; however, after the second trial, the student usually requests, or the teacher requests, a conference. An analysis of the learning problem comes through the insights of both teacher and student as they seek the source of difficulty. The student, if he is willing to take the trouble, knows there is always a second chance.

A rather direct approach brought the following self-evaluation statement from a tenth grade student as he responded to a composition assignment:

SELF-EVALUATION AND WRITING COMPETENCE

Over the school years writing composition has always been a difficult thing for me to do. My difficulties are mainly using commas, quotation marks, and general punctuation. Also it is difficult for me to choose a topic unless the subject is one that I particularly enjoy. In spite of my difficulties once I start a composition I usually enjoy finishing writing it.

The writing I do today is pleasing to me because, I can think far more clearly than I could before I took this course. Also, I had a tendency to tense-up when I was told I had to write a composition. I am pleased to say that I can spot my errors much faster than I could before I started this course, and many of my writing problems have begun to leave me.

Occasionally my parents read my compositions. Their opinion of what I write is usually that I can use some improvement.

Run-on sentences, punctuation, awkward sentences, and word usage caused me the most trouble when I began this course. I enrolled in this course because my English teacher suggested it.

My writing is different now that I have begun this course. I write with far greater ease. I can locate my errors far more easily. And I find that I have truly begun to really enjoy writing.

As teachers and pupils are given the time and the opportunity to identify their real problems, to engage in cooperative evaluation, and place adequate value on facts matched by the desire and ability to find out what they mean and where they might lead, we will produce a climate of unlimited good in our schools. We can hope to extend the learners' awareness of the need to come to terms with himself. The biggest single need in evaluation is not improved methods of testing, but for human beings to know who they really are and what their possibilities are for creative growth.

7

Cooperative Evaluation in English

Paul B. Diederich and Frances R. Link

E NGLISH has been chosen to illustrate how a department analyzes its measurement problems and organizes its forces to secure reliable evidence of status and growth with respect to major goals of instruction. It must be understood to include the library, since the librarians work with us to assess reading habits and interests.

The problems of measurement in this field are complex. An enlightened English department can give very little weight to the retention of factual knowledge. We have to devise reliable, non-threatening, helpful ways of measuring reading habits and interests, literary understanding and appreciation, reading skills, writing ability and its components, ability to learn by listening to large-group presentations, ability to participate effectively in small-group discussions, and the like.

As if these were not enough, we are now trying to study what we call "evaluative competence": the evaluative skills, attitudes and criteria of our students. At one end of the continuum this competence is related to what has been called "self-evaluation" in earlier chapters: the ability of a student to size up his own performance, growth and potential in the tasks English opens up for him. At the other end, it is related to "critical thinking."

Our point of entry into this unmapped territory is to provide regular opportunities for students to react both appreciatively and critically to the writing of other students, to the kinds of questions they raise about literary works, to their interpretations of these works, and to their handling of ideas in small-group discussions. As students clarify the criteria they use in judging the products, questions, interpretations, arguments, etc., of others, we provide stages by which they may apply these same criteria to themselves.

Guiding Questions

Our consultant on measurement convinced us that we ought to start our Cooperative Evaluation Program by bringing into the open the most disturbing questions that lurk in any of our minds. Such questions may relate to the value of what we are doing, the possibility of getting anywhere with the means we are using, and even the validity of many assumptions that we did not realize we had been taking for granted without evidence. Examples of such assumptions are the need for five class meetings per week, the desirability of working with groups of 25 to 30 students, and the importance of criticism and revision in learning to write. After some prodding by the consultant and resistance on our part, we drew up the following set of questions:

Question 1. *Why does independent reading of self-chosen books take a sharp turn downward after grade 8?*

In study after study, it has been found that the reading of self-chosen books reaches a peak in grade 8 and declines thereafter with each increment in age and education until, in a recent Gallup poll, 77 percent of the adults questioned said that they had not read a book in the past year. In a comparable sample in West Germany, only 33 percent said they had not read a book. True, the paperback revolution has increased the number of books *sold* per capita five-fold since 1940, but the bulk of this book-buying and book-reading among adults is still done by a minority—lonely women, for example, and persons who travel a great deal—and it is concentrated in large metropolitan areas.

English teachers cannot take these figures as evidence of their own superiority to the common herd, or as an interesting fact about society that does not concern them, or as proof that reading on one's own is not very important after all. Instead, such findings are tantamount to a declaration of professional bankruptcy, and we might as well sell our stocks of *Silas Marner* and *Ivanhoe* at public auction. It is a matter of common observation that the mind does not keep on growing (in very many cases) unless it is nourished by books. If students graduate from high school without the habit of reading books firmly established, intellectually they are as good as dead.

Book Cards

We thought that our "culturally advantaged" community might be immune to this general decline, but our first year's collection of "book cards" showed the contrary: ninth graders reported reading on their own about two-thirds as many books as eighth graders. The "book cards" make the task of reporting both easy and helpful: they are

3″ x 5″ cards with spaces for title, author, and type of book; a candid comment for the benefit of other students who are looking for something to read; and the student's name, grade, and the date.

The students are given time in class and in the library to fill out these cards, and they can see that other students make use of them when they are at a loss as to what to read next. Thanks to these cards, the full-length "book report" as a record of independent reading is now outmoded in our schools, although students who are so inclined may still write an occasional paper expressing some reaction to a book, but not a summary of the plot.

Some of our teachers ventured the opinion that ninth graders actually read on their own as many books as eighth graders but are more reluctant to report them. But since this same decline of independent reading has been found at this point in nearly every American high school that has studied this problem, this explanation of our findings seemed a flimsy rationalization.

Homework

Many other explanations for this decline in independent reading have been offered. Movies, radio and television have successively been blamed, yet there is no evidence of any sudden upsurge of interest in these media in grade 9. There is probably some increase in social activity, but hardly enough at this point to interfere with reading. A more likely culprit is *homework*. Since grade 9 is still regarded as the end of childhood and the beginning of the high school "grind," this may be the first point at which teachers feel virtuous about assigning as much homework as the traffic will bear. Although students do not get the homework done, it is always there to do, and they put it aside to read a book of their choice only with a guilty conscience.

This possibility suggests a study of the effect on independent reading of the type of schedule that is characteristic of the vanguard high schools of the 'sixties: one large-group presentation and two small-group discussions per week in most subjects plus a long period (11:30-1:30) every day for *study*, when no classes may meet but when all teachers must be in their rooms to assist students with their assignments and independent study projects.

Figure 1 (p. 184) gives an illustrative schedule of this sort and Figure 2 (p. 185) gives a floor plan showing how two adjoining classrooms can be remodeled inexpensively to provide space for large-group and small-group instruction, independent study, and conferences. This new program puts homework into the school day in centers that have all

Continued on p. 186

	8:30– 9:55	10:00– 11:25	11:30– 1:25	1:30– 2:55	3:00– 5:00
Grades 7, 10:	SOLIDS	*Fluids*	Study	Play	Special and
Grades 8, 11:	*Fluids*	Play	and	SOLIDS	Adult Education,
Grades 9, 12:	Play	SOLIDS	Lunch	*Fluids*	Varsity Sports

Solids: Science, mathematics, social studies, English

Fluids: Science lab, home ec., business ed., shop, art, music, independent reading, foreign language or remedial English

Study: No class meetings; all teachers in classrooms to help with assignments. Band, orchestra, chorus, and play rehearsals permitted. Lunch 30 min.

Play: Intramural sports, modern dance, hikes, etc. (showers and dressing)

Monday schedule: large-group presentations: science and social studies in time scheduled as solids; English and the arts in time scheduled as fluids. Study and play as on other days. Separate large-group presentations for fast and slow groups when necessary.

Most subjects have 40-minute small-group meetings either Tuesday-Wednesday or Thursday-Friday. Those that require double periods (science lab, home ec., shop, art) meet once a week Tuesday through Friday. Most teachers will teach four 40-minute periods Tuesday through Friday (or two double periods) and share responsibility for one or two large-group presentations on Monday. All must be available during the study period to help students with assignments and independent work. Any half-hour during this period may be taken for lunch.

This schedule permits college-bound students to take five academic subjects. Most of these have one large-group and two small-group meetings per week and average two additional periods in study on school time. Mathematics and foreign languages do not have large-group meetings but make heavy demands on study time. In addition, all students have time for two double periods per week in "labs and arts." All may elect two single periods per week of independent reading (no homework, but varied occasionally by viewing films or listening to records through earphones). In the study period, rehearsals have priority over everything else, since this is the only time within the school day for meetings of activities that must draw talent from all grades.

Figure 1. An Illustrative High School Schedule

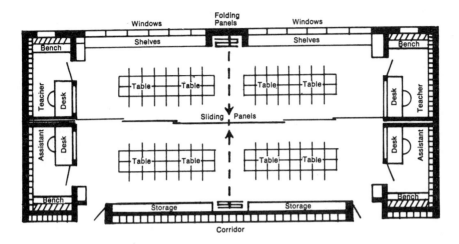

Teachers need not wait for a new building before they can reorganize for large-group and small-group instruction. All the space they need is right before their eyes, and the cost of remodeling it in this manner is within the resources of the average community. Two classrooms of ordinary size (24′ x 30′) can be thrown together by taking out the partition between them and replacing it with soundproof folding panels (each 4′ wide) hung from a swivel head in the middle of the top of each panel. These swivel heads run across a track in the ceiling and meet in the middle of the room (as shown by the dotted lines and arrows). The last eight feet at the ends of these classrooms can be made into soundproof offices for the two teachers and their two part-time assistants. Between each pair of offices there is space for sliding soundproof panels (each 8′ wide) that divide the window side of the room from the corridor side during small-group discussions. Each small-group room is then 12′ x 22′ and accommodates 16 students. When all panels are retracted, the total space (24′ x 44′) is suitable for large-group presentations to 64 students if they are seated around the tables. If the tables are folded up and put into the storage cabinets and are replaced by folding chairs, the room will easily hold 120 students. When soundproof dividers are placed on the table-tops (extending 18″ beyond the sides as shown in the diagram), the tables can be used for individual study. If two groups need to talk while the rest study silently, the panels can easily be arranged to make this possible. Conferences with one to four students can be held in each of the four offices without disturbing those in the room. The office wall in front of each desk has a large window to give each teacher and assistant a clear view of the room. The space under the bench in each office is wide enough for five file drawers side by side. The back of each office can have bookshelves from floor to ceiling.

Figure 2. Remodeling Two Classrooms for Large-group
and Small-group Instruction

Continued from p. 183
the necessary materials and equipment as well as competent assistance. The program keeps teachers from assigning an excessive amount of homework because they see students less frequently—but still as frequently as college teachers.

Independent Reading Rooms

There may also be one or two periods per week in independent reading rooms in which students are not permitted to do anything but read books of their own choice. These periods, of course, are only long enough to "hook" the student. He then checks out the book he has started and often finishes it before his next period of independent reading.

Many high schools that have established independent reading rooms as a regular, required part of the English program report that their average student now reads a book a week. It must be understood, however, that these independent reading rooms are definitely *not* the sort of thing that is often done in self-contained classrooms in which the teacher somehow gets hold of a three-foot or six-foot shelf of books and devotes an occasional period to independent reading while he calls one student after another to his desk for a short conference.

For one thing, the independent reading rooms usually start with a stock of 1200 books (mainly paperbacks), frequently exchange parts of their collection with other book rooms, and add 100 or more titles per year. For another, they are supervised by part-time semiprofessional assistants, who come in for the morning or afternoon at the present rate of about $2.50 per hour. The cost of maintaining and supervising these independent reading rooms is approximately one-fourth the cost of the same number of student hours of instruction.

Independent reading rooms also differ from the school library in that they contain only books that may be read for pleasure (no reference works); work on assignments for other classes is forbidden; and students are required to spend one or two periods per week in them on a regular schedule. They provide comfortable chairs and very few tables. They try not to look like the monumental reading room of a library.

Book Buying

These independent reading programs are often accompanied by the sale of paperback books in or near the cafeteria during the hours that students are permitted to go to lunch. Book outlets provide the books on credit, restrict their offerings to books approved by a committee of librarians, teachers and parents, and charge only for the number of books sold. The school makes a profit of five to ten cents per book, which helps replenish the stock of the independent reading rooms—although students may also be charged a book fee of something like two dollars per semester for the use of these rooms.

One group of high schools in and around Rochester reported sales of over 50,000 paperbacks last year. These students are now spending almost as much on books as on high-fidelity phonograph records. The effect of book-buying on book-reading deserves investigation. One never finds a confirmed book-reader among adults who does not take pride in his own collection of books, and who does not add to it regularly. It is likely that this habit must be established before graduation from high school if it is ever to be established on a sincere foundation—leaving out of account the successful adults who buy carload lots of books as interior decoration.

Transition to Adult Reading

Another hypothesis that we must look into is that we can practically guarantee to get the average student up to the level of enjoying the series of adventure stories that are popular in early adolescence, but to get beyond this point a student has to make the leap from juvenile to adult reading: from books that are deliberately written down to an audience to books written for adults. This may be more of a leap than we imagine, and possibly everyone whose true verbal aptitude is below the national average (as it stands at present) is foredoomed to failure. At any rate, if typical passages from typical adult books meant what the average student says they mean in reading comprehension tests, there would be no point in reading such books. They would be sheer nonsense.

Hence another point that needs investigation is the nature of the difficulties that early adolescents (particularly ninth graders) find in adult books. A large fraction of these difficulties might be accounted for simply by vocabulary, and this source of difficulty might be obviated by programmed instruction. Other difficulties such as sentence length and complexity, interrupted time sequences, the "point of view" from which a story is told, the replacement of "good guys" and "bad guys" with more complex characters, unfamiliar settings, and the special problems of metaphor, irony and symbolism might then be made the focus of direct instruction.

Whether instruction can do anything about the depth of experience, ideas and emotion required for the understanding of the greatest works remains to be seen, but there are plenty of adult books of no taxing amount of profundity or complexity to bridge the gap between juvenile and adult reading. Possibly our insensitivity to the "sound barrier" between these points in reading development has led us to choose the wrong books. We have been using authors like Scott, Dickens, and Eliot to introduce students to adult reading when maybe we should have used authors like Agatha Christie, Rex Stout, Carter Dickson, P. G. Wodehouse, Clarence Day, and James Thurber. Possibly—for average and below-average readers—we ought to use something like the *Reader's Digest Condensed Books*. Whatever the trouble may be, we can no longer ignore the fact that we lose a very large proportion of our book-readers beginning in grade 9, and the first business of our measurement program must be to find out what causes this decline and what can be done about it.

The General Anthology

A related issue that may concern us is the very format in which literature is presented to students in grade 9 and above. The chief vehicle now in use is a general anthology: a big book that often measures seven by ten inches, is two inches thick, weighs two pounds, has about 1,100 double-column pages, is lavishly illustrated, and has an extensive critical apparatus of section introductions, biographical sketches of the authors, footnotes, and questions for discussion. It is hard to imagine anything less like a book that anyone would ordinarily pick up and read for enjoyment.

If we think of the process of developing the habit of reading adult books on one's own in the behaviorist framework of simple conditioning, we ought to spare no effort to secure attractive specimens of exactly the sort that we want students to like. We ought to arrange them in an easy gradation of difficulty from the juvenile books that these students already like, to introduce each new work with delicate regard to the new reading problems that it presents and to make sure that the students overcome these problems and experience satisfaction. When they finish such a book, they ought to be in the frame of mind that would lead them, if they had fifty cents, to go out and buy another book like it.

On the other hand, the general anthology is the most readily available source of the light, easy reading that the less capable readers need as a bridge to adult reading, and it is usually accompanied by a teacher's guide that tells the inexperienced teacher what can be done with each selection and anything he may need to know about it. While an older teacher may feel almost insulted by the down-to-earth, step-by-step instructions in these guides, he must recognize that about half the faces in the department are new each year, and he must wonder what these people would do with a literary work without such assistance. When teachers are given a free hand, their most common fault is to choose the works they remember with pleasure from their last English course in college or graduate school and to teach these in the ninth grade in the same way that they were taught at the higher level. After a series of disasters with these choices of inexperienced teachers, the older hands in the department are usually willing to settle for the anthology.

Perhaps this dilemma is now being resolved by the publishers themselves. They are bringing out more and more paperbacks (or easily portable books in hard-cover editions) that have about the same proportion of easy, appetizing fare for the less capable readers and the same kinds of assistance for inexperienced teachers as the large general anthologies. Once they provide books that look like books, that bridge the gap between juvenile and adult reading by easy stages, and that furnish guides to interpretation and teaching, the problem of conditioning students to like books and to continue reading them will be within reach of a solution. It is true that there is more to the teaching of literature than this, but this is an indispensable first step.

Question 2. *If the independent reading rooms are as effective as claimed, why not fire all English teachers and use nothing but independent reading?*

Our answer to this question is: Because these rooms have shown more clearly than ever before the need for and purposes of literary instruction. In the reading rooms, we are continually backing away from the difficulties of reading adult books. If a student tries *Moby Dick* and cannot understand it, we may suggest *Two Years Before the Mast*. If this also proves too difficult, we may turn to *Captains Courageous*. This may also fail to grip the student, and we cannot resort to *Treasure Island* because the student has already read it in class. Where do we turn next?

Possibly the student has already solved his problem by thumbing through the book cards filed by his friends and noting the books they have recommended with particular fervor. Through these cards he may discover the redoubtable Captain Horatio Hornblower, and after a cautious trial of his adventures, he may find that this is exactly the sort of book he likes. He may plow through a whole series of these works, thereby adding to his skill in reading and his acquaintance with the patterns, rhythms, and order of English sentences—the basis of improvement in his own writing. But he is still at the level of enjoying the series of adventure stories that are popular in early adolescence. How does he make the leap from this point to the enjoyment of books written for adults?

Obviously there has to be some point in the English program in which we do not back away from the difficulties inherent in adult reading. We take up a number of adult books of varied types, carefully graded in difficulty, and require students to read them. From the questions they raise in small-group discussions, the complaints they make, and the responses of other students to these questions and complaints as well as to other questions of our own, we find out what their difficulties are and not only how to resolve them but also how to enhance their skill in meeting similar difficulties in the books they will read later. We may even set examinations on these works that will reveal to both the teacher and the students what they understand and still fail to understand in the common core of required reading.

This may be regarded as the ski-lift to the top of the mountain. From that point they may practice and enjoy what they have learned in somewhat easier books that they select and read on their own. This is the payoff, the consolidation of gains, and the establishment of reading habits and interests. Yet in itself, it never got anyone to the top of the mountain except a few geniuses like Ben Franklin and Abe Lincoln—poor boys who were able to cope with the works of genius without any help. The common or garden variety of student still requires the help of a teacher.

Examinations on Books Not Discussed in Class

The measurement problem here is to discover the most common difficulties that students experience in learning to read and enjoy adult books, and their progress in overcoming these difficulties. One measuring device appropriate for grades 9-12 is to assign one or two literary works of appropriate difficulty per year that are to be read "for examination only"—which means that all teachers are forbidden to discuss them. They may be allowed one period to answer any direct questions that students ask about these works, but they are not to add any questions of their own or supply gratuitous information. The examination is usually made out by a small committee of the most experienced teachers and is reviewed and criticized by others. The department head or departmental examiner will see to it that the revision of the first draft satisfies as many legitimate objections as possible.

The examination may consist of both multiple-choice questions and questions that require written answers. The latter are to be graded independently by two members of the department without knowledge of the identity of the writers. This task requires prior agreement upon rules for grading the answers and some practice in applying these rules to a set of sample papers before the teachers begin grading in earnest. The departmental examiner makes an item-analysis of the results and communicates his findings as to both strengths and weaknesses to all members of his department. Possibly one such examination per year may be given across a span of two or three grades in order to assess progress. At a later stage, a harder form of this examination on a more difficult work may be given to the better readers in a span of two or three grades, while an easier form on a less difficult work may be given to average and below-average readers. There may be one section that is common to both forms in order to establish their relative difficulty. Students who could not read a whole book on their own may be given an article or a short story.

The point of these departmental examinations on literary works that have not been discussed in class is that they get at the ability to tackle such a work on one's own. Too often the examinations made out by teachers on works they have taught require chiefly the ability to remember and parrot back what the teacher and the editor have said about the work. They may also overemphasize factual details that have no bearing on literary competence. For example, one teacher reported that his last examination in college on *Moby Dick* had only two questions: (a) List and describe the ships encountered by the *Pequod* in its last voyage. (b) List and describe the various species of whales.

The professor who set these questions probably congratulated himself on his ingenuity in devising an examination that only a few students could pass, that could be scored with nearly perfect reliability, and that would reveal which students had read the work with minute attention and a photographic memory. What never entered his mind was the possibility and desirability of finding out to what extent the students were able to understand and appreciate the literary qualities of a work of this stature. He had probably failed to notice these qualities himself.

Student Responses to Pairs of Passages

Another measuring device is to circulate in advance several provocative *pairs of passages* from literary works of different levels of difficulty and ask students to choose a pair on which they would be willing to answer some questions. On the testing day, one may surprise them by asking them to write the most interesting question they can think of about each passage they have chosen: a question that would show whether a person really understood the passage and appreciated it. Then one may ask them to answer their own questions as well as they can without resorting to a library—just on the basis of the evidence at hand. One may also ask them to discuss any likenesses or differences they noticed between the passages they chose, and possibly to indicate which passage they preferred, or regarded as better writing, and why.

Then one may ask any other questions pertinent to this particular pair of passages: for example, which was probably written first, what sort of work each passage came from, what traits of character were exhibited, whether the author was speaking as himself or assuming a certain role or character, the literary devices used in these passages, their literary merits or how the difference in their points of view might be explained or reconciled.

At some later point one may circulate a list of the questions the students asked about each passage and have them rate these questions as (A) interesting, (B) average, (C) dull, trivial or based on misunderstanding. After some discussion of questions that were rated differently by different students, one may ask them to choose the more interesting questions and answer as many as they can. Sample answers to the more popular questions may then be duplicated and circulated for discussion and rating on something like the same scale.

Evaluative Competence

This approach to the measurement of literary understanding is obviously based on the idea that it is the questions a reader asks himself and the quality of his answers to these questions that most clearly indicate his literary competence. This device also furnishes an approach to the measurement of the "evaluative competence" of students that was mentioned at the beginning of this chapter. After they have rated the questions and answers of others and have discussed those on which the ratings differed, they may be asked to rate their own questions and answers on the same scale, and to give the kinds of reasons for each rating that were accepted by the group as good reasons in the course of the discussion.

After this mind-set has been established by responses to several sets of mimeographed questions and answers, one may carry over the same practice to the kinds of questions that are raised and the kinds of answers that are given in small-group discussions. One must not do it continuously or the discussion will be stopped dead in its tracks, but occasionally either the teacher or a student may say, "Jim, how would you rate your question on our three-point scale?" Jim may admit sheepishly that he would rate it C: trivial, dull or misguided; or he may defend his question as having more in it than meets the eye, or as leading up to a more important question. Then the others will challenge him to clarify the point he had in mind, or another student may say, "I think we might get further by turning Jim's question around: why didn't the author say what Jim thought he said?"

Teaching and Practice Needed

This sort of practice should not be tried once or twice and then abandoned on the ground that the students were not very good judges of the worth of their own questions and answers, or of those of other students. Naturally they are not very good judges at the outset. They need to be taught how to raise questions relevant to a particular literary work, and they need practice—practice in which the good judgments they make will be accepted by the group, and the bad judgments they make will be challenged. Ultimately they must look upon their small-group discussions from the viewpoint of the teacher: this is a good question that will enhance the group's understanding of the work they are discussing; that is a silly question that should either be disregarded or given some unexpected turn that will make it meaningful.

The same may be said about the answers that are given and the arguments by which they are defended: this one leads to better understanding of the work; that one leads away from it and had better be cut short or the students will forget what the author had to say and concentrate instead on what *they* have to say about an issue that has only a flimsy connection with the *subject* of the work—not with the author's ideas about that subject. It is natural for students to think that their own ideas are more interesting than those of the author, but it is part of their literary training to find out that they can learn something from the author's ideas, while their own reactions may lead only to endless discussion of the same little stock of ideas they started with.

In summary, we have now explored the measurement problems arising from the fact that independent reading declines in grade 9 and above for a number of possible reasons. The reason that most intimately concerns the instructional program, however, is that students at this point have to make the transition from juvenile to adult reading. Such adult reading is extremely difficult for the majority of youngsters to understand and to appreciate so thoroughly that they will read adult books on their own. Hence we believe we must use appropriate and interesting measurement procedures to find out what their difficulties are and also their progress in overcoming these difficulties. The very knowledge that they are growing in their ability to like more mature and sophisticated works will keep many of the youngsters going until this crucial transition has been made. This may be a turning point in their whole intellectual development. On one side of this chasm stand the book-readers whose minds will keep on growing in adult life. On the other side stand the nonreaders, the readers of trivia, and even the occasional subscribers to book-clubs who will wonder throughout their lives what "culture" is all about. Unless such persons are very lucky, their minds will gradually atrophy until they have almost no ideas of general interest. All they will be able to contribute to a conversation will be a series of anecdotes about their relatives.

Hence the first duty of measurement at this point is to study the bridge between one side of this chasm and the other. Obviously this cannot be done merely by giving standardized reading comprehension tests and reporting whether the school stands above or below the national "norm." The national norm in this case is a national disgrace. We must do far better than this before we can develop a nation of book-readers.

Writing

Now let us turn to the second most important goal of English instruction, the development of writing ability. Here we have framed two "guiding questions" along different lines from those we examined in the case of reading:

Question 3. *What accounts for the large amount of growth in writing ability that is discernible from one grade to the next?*

Question 4. *Why is the quality of writing still so unsatisfactory in the end?*

The first of these questions is surprising when we contrast it with our concern over the decline of independent reading in grade 9 and above. There is no such decline in writing ability. Instead, every high school that has studied this problem with the procedures outlined below has found a significant and convincing increase in the quality of writing from one grade to the next right through to the end of senior high school. The only trouble is that the general level of attainment at the end of this long period of growth is still unsatisfactory—not merely by the hypercritical standards of English scholars but by the ordinary common-sense standards of the man in the street. We shall examine some representative specimens of this writing to see whether the usual complaints about it are well founded.

Test Papers Across Several Grades

First, however, let us get at the fact of growth. This can be demonstrated in any high school in a single weekend by having all students in a span of three or four grades write a short paper on the same topic in their English classes on Friday. Each student numbers his own paper with any number of six digits (such as 224,399 or 001,432) and writes no other identification on his paper. He copies his number on a slip of paper and adds his name, grade, curriculum or special group, teacher, and section.

These name-slips are locked up by the principal until the grading is finished so that no teacher can find out what grade or curriculum any paper represents.

If there are eight English teachers, each gets *a random eighth of the papers written in each class* that day. He must arrange them in the numerical order of the paper-numbers before leaving the room in which they are distributed. This puts them in a random order and ensures that there will not be one clump of obviously immature papers (all from the same tenth grade class) followed by another clump of more mature papers (all from the same twelfth grade class). Although the teacher would have no way of knowing which grade or class they represented, clumps of papers of obviously different levels of maturity would provide an extraneous clue to their presumed merit. Arranging them in the order of their paper-numbers breaks up these clumps, and then the teacher must judge each paper entirely on its merits—with nothing to indicate whether it "ought" to receive a high, middle, or low grade.

In the first trials of this measurement procedure, each reader sorts his papers into just three piles:

High: top quarter in general merit, marked H

Middle: middle half in general merit, marked M

Low: lowest quarter in general merit, marked L.

Teachers who have never tried to sort unidentified papers from several grades solely on the basis of the quality of writing may fear that they will be unable to do it. They are used to all sorts of extraneous clues in grading papers (such as their estimate of how hard the student has tried and how much encouragement or pressure he needs), and without these clues they fear that their inability to tell whether writing is good or bad may be exposed. Yet once they try it, they find that this is the easiest grading problem they have ever tackled.

The differences among the papers they receive will be much more obvious than among the papers they get from any one class. They need make only three gross distinctions in merit—high, middle, or low—and they have to decide only whether this paper is better than that, considered simply as a piece of writing; not whether this paper represents a better *effort* than that, considering the background and circumstances of the writers. They do not have to indicate or correct errors or write any comment on these papers; in fact, they are forbidden to do so, for these papers may have to be rated at some future time for some other purpose, and we do not want anything written on the papers that will distort the judgment of the later reader. The mark (H, M, or L) is written only in the top right-hand corner of page 1, where it can easily be cut off.

Analysis of Results

The teachers return the papers, marked in this fashion, to the department head on Monday morning. With the help of a few clerks or student assistants, he has all the papers and name-slips arranged in numerical order. If two or more students have chosen the same paper-number, it is easy at this point to tell which student wrote each paper by matching the handwriting on the name-slip with the handwriting of the paper. The grade (H, M, or L) written on the paper is transferred to the corresponding name-slip, and the name-slips are sorted out by grade and curriculum to find the percentage of high, middle, and low grades assigned to each group.

The following is a typical result for one senior high school of 1,065 students:

Grade	Nonacademic (476)			Academic (589)		
	10 (145)	11 (167)	12 (164)	10 (238)	11 (190)	12 (161)
High	5%	8%	9%	22%	41%	53%
Middle	34%	53%	63%	65%	52%	42%
Low	61%	39%	28%	13%	7%	5%
Average	326	397	455	475	606	650

The averages reported in the last line need not concern us, for they represent a rather complicated scoring procedure (in which 500 was the theoretical average) that we have since discarded as unnecessary and misleading. Yet these averages do bring out the point that the nonacademics (general and vocational students) leave off in grade 12 slightly below the point at which the academics (college preparatory and business students) begin in grade 10. The gain in each case is impressive: 129 points (in 24 months) for the nonacademics, 175 points for the academics. While the academics tend to move from the middle to the high bracket, the nonacademics tend to move from the low to the middle bracket. Since their papers were mixed together in a random order, the competition was such that the nonacademics could not achieve many high grades at any time, nor the academics many low grades. But the decline in the percentage of low grades received by the nonacademics (from 61% in grade 10 to 28% in grade 12) was just as heartening evidence of growth as anything achieved by the academics. These verbally disadvantaged students do not become really good writers, but fewer than half as many wrote papers that would disgrace the school in grade 12 as in grade 10.

Whenever we discuss these findings, someone always asks whether the apparent improvement may be attributed solely to dropout of the less able students. That is why we included the number of students in each group in parentheses. As these figures reveal, this school did not have a very serious dropout problem, but there was some drop-down of the less able academics into the vocational and general curricula. On the other hand, the apparent gain from one grade to the next was almost certainly less than the true gain, due to the unreliability of the grading. This factor must always reduce the apparent difference between grades—never increase it. One can see why if one considers the extreme case in which all marks are assigned at random. Then, in a school as large as this, the averages for all six groups would be almost identical; hence any element of chance that enters into the grading tends to make the groups seem more nearly equal than they really are. Evidently this factor more than offsets any spurious gains due to dropout or drop-down, for we find gains of the same order of magnitude in junior high schools in which there is no dropout problem at all. We have not yet tried this measurement procedure in grades 4-5-6, but friends tell us that gains at this level are equally impressive.

Components of Writing Ability

As teachers come to take this general growth for granted, they will want to find out *in what respects* the writing improves. This calls for the rating of test papers on several distinguishable aspects of writing competence. Although there have been many armchair analyses of the components of writing ability, the only empirical study of factors that account for differences in the grades of qualified readers is *Factors in Judgments of Writing Ability* by Paul B. Diederich, John W. French and Sydell T. Carlton of Educational Testing Service. The original report of this study, published in 1961, is now out of print, but the following summary of its methods and findings will serve well enough for our present purpose.

The study was a "factor analysis" of grades on 300 college freshman compositions given by 53 distinguished readers in six different fields: 10 college English teachers, 9 social science teachers, 8 natural science teachers, 10 writers and editors, 9 lawyers, and 7 business executives. The factor analysis picked out five clusters of readers who agreed with one another and disagreed with other clusters to a greater extent than could happen by chance. The distinctive emphasis of each cluster was revealed by a tabulation of their comments under 55 headings. In all, 11,018 comments on 3,557 papers were tabulated and reduced to percentages of comments written by each reader so that readers who wrote the most comments would not unduly influence the interpretation.

The largest cluster (16 readers) was most influenced by the *ideas* expressed: their richness, soundness, clarity, development, and relevance to the topic and the writer's purpose. The next largest (13 readers) was most influenced by *mechanics:* the number of errors in usage, punctuation, and spelling. Seven of the ten English teachers stood high on this factor. The third (9 readers) showed the highest interest in *organization* and analysis. Four of the seven business executives stood high on this factor. The fourth (9 readers) stood highest in comments on *wording* and phrasing. The fifth (7 readers) emphasized style, originality, individuality, interest, sincerity—the personal qualities of the writing, which we decided to call "flavor." The four readers who stood highest on this factor were all writers or editors.

Ratings on These Factors

When ratings on these factors and their main components were secured in three large high schools over a period of one year and subjected to another factor analysis, the principal new finding was that, under the pressure of time and the teaching tradition, these five factors had collapsed into two: a general factor and a distinct mechanics factor. The ratings that had the highest "loadings" on the general factor were, however, four of the five original factors: *ideas, organization, wording,* and *flavor.* These four factors had merged into one because at this stage (while teachers were just learning to make these distinctions) they were highly correlated with one another: if one was rated high, the other three tended to be rated high also.

The main components of *mechanics* were similarly correlated with one another, but mechanics was not highly correlated with the general factor. While this finding would temporarily have justified a single rating on "general merit" and another on mechanics (and thus fortified the ancient distinction between "content" and mechanics), the decision was made to continue asking for separate ratings on the four main components of each, hoping that in time some would emerge again as separate factors. Since these ratings were now applied to handwritten papers, the mechanics factor was broadened to include "handwriting, neatness." This factor had been ruled out of the original study by the fact that the 53 readers saw only typed copies of the 300 papers, but it emerged as a separate factor in a study by Remondino in Italy.

Definitions of Ratings

In a subsequent workshop, the English department heads of several high schools analyzed a large number of papers that had been rated high, middle, and low on these eight qualities and wrote brief descriptions of their common characteristics. Their definitions of ratings on the first four factors are reproduced below in order to give a concrete idea of the qualities in student writing that make a difference in the grades of qualified readers. The four aspects of mechanics (usage, punctuation, spelling, and handwriting) are too obvious to justify inclusion in this report.

GENERAL MERIT

1. Ideas

High. The student has given some thought to the topic and has written what he really thinks. He discusses each main point long enough to show clearly what he means. He supports each main point with arguments, examples, or details; he gives the reader some reason for believing it. His points are clearly related to the topic and to the main idea or impression he is trying to get across. No necessary points are overlooked and there is no padding.

Middle. The paper gives the impression that the student does not really believe what he is writing or does not fully understand what it means. He tries to guess what the teacher wants and writes what he thinks will get by. He does not explain his points very clearly or make them come alive to the reader. He writes what he thinks will sound good, not what he believes or knows.

Low. It is either hard to tell what points the student is trying to make or else they are so silly that he would have realized that they made no sense if he had only stopped to think. He is only trying to get something down on paper. He does not explain his points; he only writes them and then goes on to something else, or he repeats them in slightly different words. He does not bother to check his facts, and much of what he writes is obviously untrue. No one believes this sort of writing—not even the student who wrote it.

2. Organization

High. The paper starts at a good point, has a sense of movement, gets somewhere, and then stops. The paper has a plan that the reader can follow; he is never in doubt as to where he is or where he is going. Sometimes there is a little twist near the end that makes the paper come out in a way that the reader does not expect, but it seems quite logical. Main points are treated at greatest length or with greatest emphasis, others in proportion to their importance.

Middle. The organization of this paper is standardized and conventional. There is usually a one-paragraph introduction, three main points each treated in one paragraph, and a conclusion that often seems tacked on or forced. Some trivial points may be treated in greater detail than important points, and there is usually some deadwood that might better be cut out.

Low. This paper starts anywhere and never gets anywhere. The main points are not clearly separated from one another, and they come in a random order— as though the student had not given any thought to what he intended to say before he started to write. The paper seems to start in one direction, then another, then another, until the reader is lost.

3. Wording

High. The writer uses a sprinkling of uncommon words or of familiar words in an uncommon setting. He shows an interest in words and in putting them together in slightly unusual ways. Some of his experiments with words may not quite come off, but this is such a promising trait in a young writer that a few mistakes may be forgiven. For the most part he uses words correctly, but he also uses them with imagination.

Middle. The writer is addicted to tired old phrases and hackneyed expressions. If you left a blank in one of his sentences, almost anyone could guess what word he would use at that point. He does not stop to think how to say something; he just says it in the same way as everyone else. A writer may also get a middle rating on this quality if he overdoes his experiments with uncommon words: if he always uses a big word when a little word would serve his purpose better.

Low. The writer uses words so carelessly or inexactly that he gets far too many wrong. These are not intentional experiments with words in which failure may be forgiven; they represent groping for words and using them without regard to their fitness. A paper written entirely in a childish vocabulary may also get a low rating, even if no word is clearly wrong.

4. Flavor

High. The writing sounds like a person, not a committee. The writer seems quite sincere and candid, and he writes about something he knows—often from personal experience. You could not mistake this writing for the writing of anyone else. Although the writer may play different roles in different papers, he does not put on airs. He is brave enough to reveal himself just as he is.

Middle. The writer usually tries to appear better or wiser than he really is. He tends to write lofty sentiments and broad generalities. He does not put in the little homely details that show that he knows what he is talking about. His writing tries to sound impressive. Sometimes it is impersonal and correct but colorless, without personal feeling or imagination.

Low. The writer reveals himself well enough but without meaning to. His thoughts and feelings are those of an uneducated person who does not realize how bad they sound. His way of expressing himself differs from standard English, but it is not his personal style; it is the way uneducated people talk in his neighborhood. Sometimes the unconscious revelation is so touching that we are tempted to rate it high on flavor, but it deserves a high rating only if the effect is intentional.

Rating the Test Papers

Raters of the test papers record their ratings on 2¾″ by 4¼″ slips of paper duplicated as shown in Figure 3 (p. 201) and cut into eight slips per page. Raters encircle the number representing the scale position of the paper on each quality and write the sum of the encircled numbers at the bottom. Some departments also record subtotals on the first four

Topic_____	Reader_____		Paper____ _____		
	Low		Middle		High
Ideas	2	4	6	8	10
Organization	2	4	6	8	10
Wording	1	2	3	4	5
Flavor	1	2	3	4	5
Usage	1	2	3	4	5
Punctuation	1	2	3	4	5
Spelling	1	2	3	4	5
Handwriting	1	2	3	4	5

Sum of ratings_____

Figure 3. Rating Slip

qualities and the last four. Note that *ideas* and *organization* are given double weight by doubling the numbers representing each scale position. This practice has no basis in research, but many high school teachers like to emphasize the importance of these two qualities in this way.

The lowest rating (usually represented by 1) normally designates the bottom 5 percent of the grades tested; 2 the low fifth; 3 the middle half; 4 the high fifth; and 5 the top 5 percent. The midpoints of the 2 and 4 ratings are about one standard deviation from the mean (1.04 to be exact); those of the 1 and 5 ratings are about two standard deviations away (1.96). Although there is nothing sacred about these proportions, agreement between raters is higher when they think in terms of 5%, 20%, 50%, 20%, 5% than when they think in terms of 10%, 20%, 40%, 20%, 10%. As a rough rule-of-thumb, the smallest visible difference between grade-intervals in rating compositions is a standard deviation.

Since writing is not a uniform product, we need more than one sample of each student's writing to work up to a reliable score (one that will not change very much with additional measures). We have found that four test papers per year, written in class in November, January, March, and May, usually yield cumulative total ratings with a reliability of about .8 if each paper gets two independent ratings by the procedures outlined below. That, at least, is the tentative conclusion of two large studies in which eight test papers per year were rated in this fashion over a period of three years. The reliability thus attained was necessary for research but higher than is necessary for a practical judgment in the ordinary course of school work. The smaller number of test papers also makes this procedure more acceptable to English teachers.

The usual procedure is to have all students in a span of three grades write a paper on the same topic in their English class on the scheduled dates. A list of twenty to thirty topics suitable for short, impromptu papers written in class has been discussed, rated and agreed upon in advance, but the topic chosen from this list for any given date is announced by the department head only on the morning of the testing day. The teachers write this topic on the blackboard and read aloud any "stimulus material" that goes with it. It has not been found necessary to provide one topic for the morning and a different topic for the afternoon because the average ratings of morning and afternoon classes are almost identical when the same topic is used. Each student numbers his own paper with any number of six digits and makes out a "name-slip" in the fashion previously described. If there are to be eight readers, each teacher divides the papers from his first class into eight random piles. At the end of each succeeding class period, he adds equal numbers of papers to each pile until, at the end of the day, each pile contains a random eighth of the papers from each of his classes.

He cross-stacks these piles and takes them to the room of the department head, who has eight chairs (or boxes) ready to receive them. Each teacher puts one of his piles of papers on each chair, and when the last teacher has done so, each chair contains a random eighth of the papers written in every English class that day. Each teacher then picks up all the papers from one chair and arranges them in the numerical order of the paper-numbers before leaving the room. These are the papers he is to rate. It is also desirable for each teacher to choose a different "rater number" of three digits for each test so that neither the students nor the teachers will know who rated any given paper. But the department head must know, for a reason to be explained later; hence each teacher should leave with him a card with his name, his "rater number," and the date.

Time Needed for Each Rating

Each teacher will ordinarily have between 120 and 160 papers to rate, and he should understand that he must not average more than five minutes per paper even in the first set he ever rates. After a little practice, teachers usually average between two and three minutes per paper. Agonizing over the papers only confuses them and lowers reliability. In fact, the breakthrough in reader reliability that permitted the College Board to use essays in a nationwide examination after a lapse of twenty years was achieved mainly by forcing the readers to work rapidly (an average of forty seconds per paper—but these papers were very short, and only a single rating was given).

Remember that these are not homework papers that may need to be corrected and annotated for instructional purposes. These are test papers, and their only purpose is the measurement of competence in writing.

Furthermore, they must be rated by a second reader, and we do not want any marks or comments that may influence his judgment. Even the second reader must not write anything on them, for a sample of these papers may be mixed in with another batch on the same topic written several years hence to find out whether some new program is achieving better results than the old. Hence we do not want them to be marked up in any way that would indicate that they had ever been read before.

This fact in itself will reduce the time ordinarily devoted to grading papers. As soon as teachers get used to the idea, it will be further reduced by the knowledge that any serious injustice to the student will probably be balanced out by the ratings of the second reader. One does not have to believe that he will be a better judge but only that he will have a different set of prejudices. Hence any mistake one makes in one direction is likely to be offset by a mistake on his part in some other direction. This comes about because only subtotals on "general merit" and mechanics are likely to enter the record, and sometimes only totals on all eight qualities that are rated. For its own purposes, the department may study average ratings on some one quality such as *wording*, but these averages will be far more reliable than the rating of any one student, and they will not adversely affect the standing of any student.

Finally, if there is any wild discrepancy between the two ratings of any given paper, it will probably be brought to the attention of a small committee of the most experienced teachers, and this committee will substitute its own rating for whichever of the two previous ratings it regards as aberrant. At first this prospect will make the less secure teachers apprehensive, but after they get used to it and find out that all teachers have some of their ratings rejected, and nothing unpleasant is done about it, it will give them confidence and enable them to rate the papers more rapidly. What really slows up a conscientious teacher is the idea that he is wholly responsible for seeing to it that justice is done to every student in a record that may have serious consequences. But if he knows that any serious error on his part is almost certain to be caught and rectified by the older hands in the department, he can launch out boldly and record his ratings at the rapid pace that is most likely to yield reliable judgments.

The Initial Sorting

Most of our teachers prefer to sort out their papers at the start into batches of twenty and then to sort each batch into three piles of approximately five, ten, and five papers on "general impression." They do not expect to hit exactly this proportion of low, middle, and high papers in each batch, but they can come close to it; and by the time they have glanced through sixty papers, they expect to have about fifteen, thirty, and fifteen papers in their three piles—if they have a truly representative cross-section of papers from three grades.

This is the first point at which it is safe to pick out about three papers from the low pile and set them aside tentatively as the very low; then about three papers from the high pile as candidates for an average rating of 5—the very high. Then they leaf through the papers remaining in the three middle piles to see whether they have come reasonably close to placing 12, 30, and 12 papers in these piles. If not, they glance again at the borderline papers in the piles that are too large to see whether some of them may be moved to an adjacent pile that is too small. They may also reconsider the papers that they left protruding from these piles to indicate doubt whether the original placement was correct. If they now decide that some of these are clearly out of line with the other papers in that pile, they move them either up or down and readjust the numbers accordingly.

At the end of this preliminary sorting, there should be pretty close to 3, 12, 30, 12, and 3 papers in the five piles for each set of 60 papers. They can then tackle the rating of these 60 papers with the idea at the back of their minds that sums of ratings for the lowest pile may go from 10 through 14 but should average below 15. Sums for the second pile may go from 15 through 24 but should average about 20. Sums for the middle pile may go from 25 through 34, averaging about 30. For the fourth pile, they may go from 35 through 44 and average about 40. The highest pile should have sums of ratings between 45 and 50 (since 50 is the highest possible sum for one reader). If the sum of ratings for any paper lies beyond the allowable range for the pile in which it was originally placed, one has to reconsider whether it belongs in that pile; and if not, whether some other paper should be substituted for it.

Naturally these limits cannot be observed in any hard-and-fast manner. For example, a paper that clearly deserves the lowest rating in every other respect might conceivably get a rating of 5 on spelling (because there were no spelling errors) and a rating of 5 on handwriting, because it was excellent. The lowest rating it can get on all the other qualities will yield a sum of 8; hence with these two 5's, it will get a total of 18, which puts it beyond the usual limit for the lowest pile. Yet the teacher may decide that it still belongs in the lowest pile because in all the more important aspects of writing competence, it is abysmal.

The Argument over "Halo"

This procedure, which has gradually emerged from three years of practice in the rating of test papers, but is by no means universally accepted, may seem to impose too much "halo effect" on the ratings. That is, it decides on the basis of "general impression" within what range the sum of ratings must lie; therefore it decides at one fell swoop that most of the ratings will lie at one of the five scale positions and allows only a few deviations up or down from this position so that the sum will lie within the expected range. Some teachers argue heatedly that one ought to put down each rating with only the definitions of high, middle, and low points on that quality in mind, and with no preconceived idea of the total merit of the paper. One should arrive at the total merit from the eight separate ratings—not vice versa.

This is certainly a logical and defensible position, and there are only two telling arguments against it: it takes too long, and it is less reliable than proceeding from the whole to the parts. From years of practice in dealing with student papers, teachers have a pretty firm idea that this paper is better than that, and even whether the superiority lies in the larger aspects of writing or in mechanics. But when they get down to deciding whether *this idea* is better than *that idea* for the purposes of these writers, or whether this *organization* is better than that, there are no very firm guidelines and the raters are likely to guess wildly. Besides, all that we are really telling the writer is that his paper is, in general, superior; but it is outstanding in some one quality (for example, the cleverness of its ideas); it is no better than average in usage, and it may be very poor in some one quality such as punctuation or handwriting.

At any rate, that is all that most students learn and remember from these ratings. They get a general idea of where they stand as writers in relation to their competition. Beyond that, they may remember that their best rating was in X and their poorest in Y. It may be just as well that they do not follow the diagnosis any further than that, for the finer points are not likely to be very reliable. These points are better conveyed by the comments written on regularly assigned papers by the teacher or reader, or by comments made in conferences or in class discussions of selected papers. Such comments deal with more particular merits or defects than ratings on the most common characteristics of students' papers, and they can use the full resources of the language.

Hence we regard it as a defensible as well as an efficient and reliable procedure to start rating a paper with the idea in the back of one's mind that the sum of ratings is going to be somewhere near 40, and hence to encircle at once the fourth scale position for all those qualities that led to this general impression. Then one may note that in one quality the paper was better than this; in another it was average; and possibly in another it was poor. That comes pretty close to the way in which people respond to written communications in real life.

After the first sixty papers have been sorted out and then rated in this fashion, the teacher will have his standards for this set of papers on this topic pretty well in mind. The remaining papers may then simply be placed in the piles they most nearly resemble in quality and rated accordingly. One ought to check at the end of every twenty papers, however, to make sure that one is not straying too far from the intended proportions.

The Second Rating

After each teacher has finished this first rating of his set of papers, he returns both the papers and his rating cards to the department head. For the second rating, we have found it expedient at this stage to return the papers to the teacher of origin—but all in one bundle (not separated out by classes), and without the rating cards of the first rater or the name-slips. From the standpoint of research, it would be preferable to have both ratings made by teachers who have not taught these students and will not recognize handwriting, because as soon as one guesses the identity of a writer, one's judgment of his writing is contaminated by one's opinion of his character and conduct and by one's knowledge of his background, circumstances, aspirations, etc. Such considerations must temper our judgment of the writer at some point but should not bias a judgment of his writing.

At the present time, however, most English teachers are already overburdened, and this double grading of unidentified papers strikes them as an extra burden that they simply cannot accept. Besides, what it comes to in the end is that the papers are read *three* times: after they are returned to the teacher of origin, he feels a compulsion to reread them to find out how his students fared and to see whether there are any grades that he wants to protest. When we discovered that the teacher of origin would reread the papers in any case, we decided to make this the second reading but to preserve as many conditions of independent grading as possible by returning all his papers in a random order and by withholding name-slips and first ratings until he had handed in his own ratings. Since he will now have his standards firmly established by his own first reading, and since he knows that his ratings will be compared with those of the other rater, he will not go far astray in rating even those few papers that he is sure he can identify from the handwriting. At any rate, this comes as close to a second independent rating as we have been able to get under normal operating conditions—without the subsidy and incentive of a research project.

Incidentally, no one has yet figured out a quick, efficient way to make sure that each teacher does not receive some of the papers of his own students in the bundle he picks up for the first rating. But when the papers are sorted out after the first rating to be returned to the teacher of origin, a glance at the rating card will reveal which of them he has already rated. These papers must be turned over to some other teacher for the second rating, while he will receive some of theirs. Hence his possible recognition of papers in his second rating will be further complicated by the knowledge that a certain proportion of them will not be those of his own students at all, but rather those that could not be returned to the teacher of origin at this point because he had already rated them.

After all the papers and second rating cards have been returned to the department head, he will have them sorted out again. Then each teacher will finally receive all the papers written by his students together with the name-slips and the two rating cards—his own and that of some other member of the department, identified only by a rater-number chosen for this particular test. The teacher will compare the two ratings of each paper and set aside all pairs of ratings that differ in their sums by more than ten points on the scale we have previously discussed, in which 10 is the lowest possible sum for one rater and 50 the highest.

Protested Ratings

We have selected a discrepancy of ten points in the sum of ratings as the cut-off point because it yields a manageable number of papers for further consideration (in one study it turned out to be only one paper in twelve), and because if the difference is no greater than this, the average of the two ratings will be no more than half a grade-point (on the usual scale of five points) from the opinion of either rater; and this is a variation that both teachers and students will accept as normal and tolerable. But if the discrepancy is greater than this, the average of the two may throw the paper into a grade-bracket that the teacher of origin cannot accept.

He does not automatically protest all such discrepancies but re-reads the papers to which they refer, considering carefully whether they represent normal variations in grading standards that are likely to be offset by a variation in the opposite direction next time, or whether the discrepant rating represents a serious error in judgment. If it is the latter, he returns the paper and the two rating cards to the department head, who has these protested papers read by a small committee of the most experienced and reliable readers in the department. Some member of this committee will give this paper a third rating and then pass it along to another member to see whether he agrees. At the end, this third rating is substituted for whichever of the two previous ratings was more aberrant—and in some cases this may be the teacher's. The committee's rating is then copied in red on the rejected rating card, which is filed under the name of the rater.

The purpose of this dossier is not punitive but corrective. All teachers must expect to have some of their ratings rejected, but if one or two have a large number, a member of the review committee will call on them and explain in a kindly manner why the committee felt obliged to change some of their ratings. He will go over a few papers, explain why certain ratings were judged too low and others too high, listen to their objections, and try to clear up any misunderstanding. He will leave the remaining papers and altered rating cards with them to go over at their leisure, and he will invite them to talk over any changes that they question.

These quiet sessions that no one else need know about are often the first training these teachers have ever received in rating papers by standards prevailing in the department. While one must admit the possibility that the "aberrant" reader may simply be wiser than all the rest, the odds against it are high. To qualify for this sort of private tutoring, a rater must have had some of his ratings protested by most of his colleagues and altered by a committee of the most experienced and trusted readers. Hence it is not a case of one judgment against another; it is one judgment against the consensus of the department.

In practice it is usually found that those who need this coaching are the newer members of the department who have not yet assimilated its standards. Most of them learn quite rapidly, and the department head must go out of his way to congratulate them. But a few never develop a discriminating palate for student writing, and these must ultimately be transferred to other duties—usually to their great relief. In these days of team teaching, teachers are no longer expected to be equally good at everything. It may be their passion for the greatest literature that makes all student writing look alike to them. They may be given additional responsibility for the teaching of literature, the production of plays, programmed instruction, the objective items in English tests, or anything else that does not involve judgment of the whole gamut of student writing.

The Three Converted Scores on Writing

Since the sum of ratings on any one test paper may range from 20 to 100 points and cumulative totals from 80 to 400 points, and since these numbers have different meanings for first, second, and third year students and for different curricula, they must be translated into "converted scores" before they will have meaning for the student, his parents, his faculty adviser, and ultimately college admissions officers.

After each test, a clerk makes a distribution of cumulative ratings to that point for the total population of the grades tested. For example, after the second test, the clerk starts with a list of numbers from 200 down to 40 (the maximum possible range at that point) and puts a tally after each number for each student who has that total. He draws lines across this distribution to mark off the top 5 percent, the high fifth, the middle half, the low fifth, and the bottom 5 percent. With these cutting-points in mind, he marks the first line in the cumulative rating cards of all students:

Standing in total population of grades xyz 1 2 3 4 5

Next, he makes a separate distribution for each track or curriculum within each grade and marks off these five achievement levels as before. Then he can mark the second line in the cumulative rating cards:

Standing in own grade and curriculum 1 2 3 4 5

This is the most appropriate indication of status as a writer and corresponds most closely to a conventional grade on writing. A tenth grade vocational student who gets only a 2 in the first line may get a 5 in the second, indicating that he stands in the top 5 percent of tenth grade vocational students.

At the end of the year, the clerk subtracts each student's cumulative total for the previous year from his cumulative total for the present year and calls the difference his "gain." He makes a separate distribution of these gains for students who started at each of the five achievement levels recorded in line 1. He draws lines across these distributions in the proportions previously specified and marks the third line in the cumulative rating cards:

Growth from last year's cumulative total 1 2 3 4 5
(among students who started at the same level in line 1)

This third line cannot be filled out for first year students unless the school has developed some way of equating totals for the last year in the feeder school with totals for the first year in the present school.

The reason for comparing the gains of only those students who started at or near the same point is that students who start high are more severely handicapped than most school people realize. They tend to think only of "ceiling effect" (relatively little distance left to travel) and ignore the "regression effect" that often makes superior students appear to gain nothing at all.

Regression

In repeated applications of any measure that is not perfectly reliable, those who start high get there partly by ability and partly by luck. The ability will carry over to the next measurement but the luck will not. It may for any one person, but the average of all those who start high will regress toward the mean of the population by a spurious amount that is proportional to the unreliability of the measure. The same will happen to those who start low; hence their gain will look better than it actually is, while that of the high-starters will look worse.

We can show the magnitude of this chance effect by the following oversimplified example. Suppose one student starts with a cumulative total of 100 points (here assumed to be 100 points below the mean),, another with 300 (100 points above). The reliability of these cumulative totals is unlikely to exceed .8; hence we may regard .8 of their initial distance from the mean as "real" and the remaining .2 as the effect of chance. If neither student learns anything or forgets anything about writing, the best estimate of next year's cumulative total will be 120 for the first and 280 for the second, since both will regress .2 of the distance toward the mean. This is due to the automatic operation of the laws of chance and has nothing to do with any actual regression in ability.

Now suppose both students actually improve 20 points in writing ability. This true gain is simply added to what is apparently gained or lost by regression. Hence the first student will have a cumulative total of about 140 points the following year (an apparent gain of 40 points) while the second will have about 300 (right where he started—apparently no gain at all). Yet in reality both students gained exactly the same amount.

This is why—whenever growth-scores are used in evaluating an experiment—we hear so many cries that instruction was apparently pitched at the level of the least able; the superior were not challenged and gained little or nothing. In most cases this is simply the effect of regression. Reputations have been made by taking the lowest 10 percent on any fallible measure (such as an IQ test), using some gimmick, retesting, and publicizing the fact that the average gain was so many IQ points. The gimmick is unnecessary; regression would do it if there was no true gain at all.

It is possible to compensate mathematically for the effect of regression but not by the simple-minded procedure used here to illustrate what happens. The actual formula is quite complicated, and we do not recommend its use because the result often appears to be trickery with numbers. That is, it can happen that the student who gets the prize for the largest gain has the same numerical total this year as last.

A more understandable way to deal with regression is the one we suggested: compare gains of only those students who started at or near the same level (as recorded in line 1 of the cumulative rating cards). Even so, growth scores are tricky and often need to be interpreted by a comment. For all that, the changing position of a student in relation to the total school population as he moves from grade to grade provides a far more solid measure of improvement in writing than anything else that is available to English teachers.

Feasibility and Benefits

It has taken so long to explain the rating procedure in sufficient detail to enable schools to follow it that the reader may now have the impression that, if an English department rates four test papers per year, it will have little time for anything else. One indication to the contrary is that over a hundred English teachers in twelve school districts in the state of New York have just completed a three-year project in which they rated *eight* test papers per year in this fashion—and no one complained. They simply substituted the test paper for a homework assignment once a month and found that it was quicker and easier to rate the test papers (even though they were rated twice) than to grade, correct and annotate the longer homework assignments.

Another way to size up the magnitude of this task is to consider that very few schools will have more than 150 test papers per teacher. After a little practice, most teachers can rate that many papers in five to six hours. The second rating (with standards already established by the first) will take only four to five hours if all are encouraged to work rapidly. With a more normal teaching load, the average expectation is four to five hours for the first rating and three to four hours for the second. This is no more than teachers spend over an ordinary batch of homework papers from all their classes—and there must be no homework papers at the time of these tests or students will rebel. Doing this just four times a year is surely not too much to expect.

Now consider what the teacher gets in return. He is assured of getting scores on both status and growth in writing ability that are far more reliable than most school marks and that represent not merely his own judgment but the consensus of the department. If so, why should he bother to put a grade on the homework papers? It is an axiom of measurement that, once you have a measure that is sufficiently reliable for the purposes for which it will be used, there is no point in piling up additional measures of the same ability. Hence a department might well adopt the policy that homework papers are to receive comments but no grades. At first both the students and their parents are likely to protest, as they protest any change; but after they get used to the new policy, they will like it better.

If the homework papers are not graded, will students write them? Will they put in the time necessary to write them well? Yes, indeed; they respect the teacher; they know that assigned work must be turned in; and when these papers are read and discussed, they want their papers to be well received. If all else fails, they will have to fill out a "Record of Incomplete and Unsatisfactory Work" (discussed in Chapter 6), and if they accumulate very many of these records, they may get into serious trouble. In extreme cases, they may have to write the papers they missed after school and under supervision. But this will enter their record in the proper place (under "Insubordination"); it will not be confused with a measure of their writing ability.

In this era of mounting pressure to get into colleges of high prestige, some students contest almost every grade—from that on a homework assignment to that on the final examination. Some argue, some bluster, some wheedle and some cry. Hence the elimination of grades on homework papers reduces nervous tension, and the ratings on test papers (in which the raters are never identified) obviously cannot be altered by argument, persuasion or pressure. They are already recorded in the departmental office before they are returned to teachers and made known to students, and teachers have no power to alter them. They may commiserate with students and offer to help them to do better next time, but there is nothing they can do about the present rating. Students recognize the difference at once, and if they complain at all, they say, "Look at what *they* did to me!"—never "Look at what *you* did to me!" This practice puts the student and the teacher on the same side of the fence. Both are concerned to make these ratings as high as possible, but it has to be done by merit, not by cajolery.

The Study of Modern Grammar

It is hard to remember at this point that the first "guiding question" in our evaluation of writing was: "What accounts for the large amount of growth in writing ability that is discernible from one grade to the next?" We have now established the fact that such growth occurs and have provided a feasible and reliable measure of its amount for both classes and individuals. Yet what accounts for it? What elements of the English program contribute to it?

Although we have not yet found an answer, we have investigated two possibilities. The first is the study of modern grammar (structural linguistics). Since our school district was among the first to adopt this new approach and has used it long enough to overcome the initial resistance and confusion, it seemed a good place to find out whether this way of thinking about language contributes anything to improvement in writing. To be sure, modern linguists make no claim that any grammatical system—traditional or modern—will improve the written or spoken language of a native speaker. They say that any child with a reasonable amount of curiosity will want to know something about how his language works, just as he wants to know how an automobile works, but it is doubtful that such knowledge will improve either his language or his driving.

The publication of the National Council of Teachers of English, *Research in Written Composition,* concludes a review of studies of the effects of grammar on composition as follows:

> In view of the widespread agreement of research studies based upon many types of students and teachers, the conclusion can be stated in strong and unqualified terms: the teaching of formal grammar has a negligible or, because it usually displaces some instruction and practice in actual composition, even a harmful effect on the improvement of writing.[1]

The only loophole left by this "unqualified" statement is the term *formal grammar.* By the early 'thirties, evidence against its utility had piled so high that most teachers were ready to admit that *formal* grammar had no effect. So what did they do? They changed the name to *functional* grammar and kept on teaching it exactly as before.

Now that a really different grammatical system is in process of development, there is renewed hope that this way of thinking about language will have at least a stimulating effect on composition. One reason is that the new system claims to be teachable and learnable, while the terms and concepts of traditional grammar were so fuzzy and intuitive that one linguist remarked that no one with an IQ lower than 120 could possibly master them.

This seemed to be a point that we could test. The elements of the new system were all covered in grades 7, 8, and 9 and had been taught so long that a reasonable mastery seemed assured. To what extent did students know these elements at the end of grade 9?

As a test, we asked for a complete grammatical analysis of a single sentence: "I have a little shadow that goes in and out with me, and what can be the use of him is more than I can see." There were 26 multiple-choice questions like the following:

> 6. What is *and what can be the use of him?*
>   1—The second independent clause.
>   2—A subordinate clause modifying *shadow.*
>   *3—A subordinate clause, subject of *is.*
>   4—A subordinate clause, object of *see.*
> 12. How many subordinate clauses are there in this sentence?
>   1—One
>   2—Two

[1] Richard Braddock, Richard Lloyd-Jones and Lowell Schoer. *Research in Written Composition.* Champaign, Illinois: National Council of Teachers of English, 1963. p. 37-38.

           *3—Three
           4—Four

18. What is *shadow?*
    1—Subject of the whole sentence.
    *2—Object of *have.*
    3—A linking-verb complement.
    4—Object of the preposition *little.*

24. *Can be* is a different form of the same verb as
    1—*have.*
    2—*goes.*
    *3—*is.*
    4—*can see.*

These grammatical terms and concepts are equally familiar in traditional and modern grammar. This was intentional, since no useful descriptive term of the older grammar had been discarded, but the test was edited carefully for consistency with the modern approach.

After these multiple-choice questions, students were asked to rewrite the sentence in eight different ways, starting with

I had a little shadow	What can be the use
I cannot see the use	Going in and out with me
The children had	More than I can see
Do you have	Go in and out.

Their rewritten sentences were scored as correct if the necessary changes in form, tense, word order and the like were made, without any penalty for other errors. For example, the first sentence would be scored as correct if the four italicized words were written correctly: I had a little shadow . . . that *went* in and out with me, and what *could* be the use of him *was* more than I *could* see.

The results of this test were discouraging. The top 5 percent of the ninth graders had mastered this system completely; they made no more mistakes than a teacher or a superior adult might make. The high fifth had an acceptable command of the system: they got about three-quarters of the questions and the sentences right. The middle half were wrong as often as they were right: they got only half the questions and sentences right. The low fifth had a smattering of grammar: they got a quarter to a third of both questions and sentences right. The bottom 5 percent were completely lost; they were below the chance level, and they fell for the absurd responses such as treating *shadow* as "object of the preposition *little*" in question 18 above. In spite of the emphasis on "pattern practice" in the new grammar, no one in the lowest fourth of the ninth grade was able to rewrite more than one sentence correctly and 13 percent got none right.

That, at any rate, answers one question: the new grammar is not yet teachable or learnable. These were not "culturally deprived" students; on the contrary, they were well above average in socioeconomic status and home background. The teachers were also well above average in intelligence, scholarly preparation, and teaching skill. No school district could be expected to be more wholehearted in its acceptance of the new grammar or more energetic in teaching it. Yet after three years of exposure to this grammatical system and practice in using it, only a fourth of the students were better than half right in their diagnosis of a sentence that is surely not unduly complicated.

Such a finding obviates the need for a controlled experiment on the effects of learning the new grammar on composition. If it is only half learned by the great majority, the effect on writing could hardly be desirable.

The obstinate refusal of most students to learn any system of grammar, traditional or modern, in spite of the inordinate number of class hours devoted to it presents an interesting test of character to English teachers: at what point do we admit failure and give up? It should be clear by now that we are confronted not by inability to learn but by refusal to learn. The whole corpus of basic grammar is neither so extensive nor so difficult as to baffle a student of average intelligence. The relatively few college students who clearly "know their grammar" are usually able to point to a single teacher who taught it to them, usually at some point below grade 10. This may have been their first, second, or third attempt to learn it, but they finally got hold of the system in one particular grade and remember it vividly.

This suggests that the teaching of basic grammar belongs in a single course: a year, a semester, or possibly as little as six weeks. It also suggests that it ought to be elective because only a minority will ever learn it, no matter how it is taught; and if they are not held back by the majority who refuse to learn it because they see no point in it, they ought to master it quickly. The results of our little "shadow" test suggest that not more than a fourth of the students should be expected or encouraged to elect this subject at some point in junior high school, but a solid recommendation must wait upon further study. Incidentally, if students must pass some test of linguistic aptitude in order to be admitted to an elective course in grammar, its privileged status will contribute to its effectiveness.

The rank and file of both parents and teachers will surely oppose any such change since they equate learning grammar with learning to write. Perhaps their resistance may be lessened by representing the elective as a special advanced course in grammar and retaining a smattering of grammatical terms (all that parents remember) in regular courses: independent clause, subordinate clause, phrase; subject, verb, object, complement; nouns, pronouns, verbs, adjectives, adverbs, and "structure words"; singular, plural, possessive; tense, active, passive, connective; "modify" and "agree." Perhaps these 22 terms are too many; certainly they are more than most students can apply unerringly at present; but some such list must be adopted and other terms rigidly excluded.

Meanwhile we may spread the word that many people have learned to write with no knowledge of the grammar of their mother tongue: Shakespeare, for example, and all the great Greek and Latin authors. Grammar was developed only when it became necessary to teach Greek and Latin to foreigners, and for centuries it never occurred to anyone that grammar could be of any use to native speakers. Since our schools have had to teach English as a foreign language to successive waves of immigrants, grammar is still widely regarded as a set of rules to enable a foreigner to get hold of the language quickly and correctly, and for some students this is still needed. The new grammar represents the first serious break with this tradition and we must recognize the consequence: it is now a cultural subject, an intellectual luxury—nice to know for those who are interested but not a necessity for native speakers. Those who still believe that correct usage is impossible to achieve without knowledge of grammatical classifications may be referred to the numerous studies that have found little if any connection between them.

Actually we have no immediate intention of making grammar an elective on the basis of the evidence presented here. We brought up this possibility to illustrate the point that if evaluation is to feed back into the curriculum, we must be prepared to take the bitter with the sweet. We cannot accept only those findings that support the present program and ignore those that reveal persistent failure to learn a body of subject matter that cannot be regarded as necessary for all. We must not act hastily, for there may be something wrong with our present evidence, but if the situation does not improve, there must be a point at which we write *finis* to a program that has failed. Let it be clearly understood that the "program" in question is not the new grammar but any sort of grammar as a requirement for all; and the alternative is not to give it some new name (such as "visceral grammar") and continue teaching it but to turn to something entirely different that gives promise of contributing something to the ability to write.

"Pesky Errors"

Whatever the limitations of the evidence provided by the "shadow" test, it was obvious at this point in our evaluation that all the time spent on grammar could not possibly account for the massive improvement in writing ability that we had found from one grade to the next. Hence we turned to the second most time-consuming element in our writing program:

the corrections and comments written on the compositions usually assigned as homework. Here we had the benefit of the experience of some larger studies that had been in progress for some time: the previously mentioned New York State Composition Project, the NEA-Langmuir Composition Project, and the continuing efforts of several cities to evaluate the effects of employing readers to assist high school English teachers in grading and correcting compositions.

The first efforts to find significant differences between reader-assisted and unassisted groups in growth in writing ability failed because the measure used was not sufficiently reliable to detect the difference that might reasonably be expected. This led to the development of the measure of growth outlined in this chapter. With this improved measure, some significant differences were found, but they were always less than had been anticipated. This led to a study of what the teachers and their readers were doing with the papers, and it turned out that more than 80 percent of what they wrote were corrections of specific errors in usage, wording, and punctuation.

This finding suggested a study of the rate at which such errors were being eliminated. Since it was known that counting errors in student writing is expensive and time-consuming, some easier way of measuring this sort of improvement was sought. John Hodges of the University of Tennessee had provided a list of errors that occurred most frequently in 20,000 college freshman themes. Each of these errors was embodied in a sentence; each sentence was printed in three lines of about equal length (with the whole error in one of the three lines); and students were directed to mark the line that contained an error (or 0 if there was no error). This format approximated the act of proofreading one's own work more closely than most objective tests, since there was no underlining to direct attention to parts of the sentence that might be faulty; there was no indication of the kinds of errors to expect; and students were not asked to label errors— only to detect that something was wrong.

There turned out to be 580 of these sentences, and so the complete inventory was broken up into ten forms of 58 items each. These forms were so piled that the first student in each class received form 1, the next form 2, and so on. Hence it was possible to report only the percentage of errors *missed* (marked incorrectly) by students in successive grades. The following is a typical result for college preparatory students in a large public high school with high academic standards:

Average Percent Wrong

	Grade	9	10	11	12	Gain
Diction (word-choices)		45%	42%	38%	37%	8%
Usage and Punctuation		44%	41%	38%	35%	9%
Spelling (two-choice items)		23%	19%	17%	16%	7%

The spelling items were drawn from Pollock's list of 430 words that were misspelled twenty times or more in 31,375 misspellings found by 600 English teachers in 52 colleges in 27 states (1954). Each word was spelled correctly in one form and given its most popular misspellings in others. Each form had 100 different words spelled correctly or incorrectly, and students were to mark each word *right* or *wrong*. Hence the percentages on spelling are lower because one would get 50% right by chance. But note that the average gain over four years in all three categories was only 8 percent, or 2 percent per year. The dropout rate is more than enough to account for this much gain if the teachers had ignored these errors completely.

Since it may be suspected that these errors were presented in some tricky or obscure context that minimized gains in detecting them, the following items stood exactly at the average in difficulty:

Diction (word-choices)

Steve Ramsey, the swift halfback,
busted through the center of the
line for a gain of fifteen yards.

39%, 45%, 29%, and 37% in successive
grades failed to mark line 2.

Usage and Punctuation

I wanted very much to talk to Jim before he left,
but I could not find him. Finally I saw him
carrying his trunk through a crack in the door.

31%, 32%, 48%, and 29% in successive grades failed
to mark the misplaced modifier in line 3.

Spelling

boundery

21%, 14%, 5%, and 16% in successive
grades marked this spelling "right."

One may quarrel with the first example on the ground that "busted" might be an appropriate form to use on the football field. But this was an English test, and students were directed to look for errors. They had 58 items to consider, and the question of levels of usage might arise at most in two or three. If, in this context and with this mind-set, they failed to notice anything wrong with "busted," their standards of appropriateness in diction leave something to be desired.

It is also straining a point to argue that ability to detect errors in this format is not quite the same thing as ability to avoid them in one's own writing. There is no question that students make such errors in their own writing; the list was drawn from the most common errors that persist through the freshman composition course in college. Hence a goodly number will appear in first drafts, and the student who writes correctly is the one who spots them as he is proofreading and corrects them. He might spot them and still be unable to correct them, but if he does not even notice them when they are displayed nakedly in this format, the argument that he would not commit them on his own seems quite far-fetched.

The results of these inventories call into question the efficacy of all present means of getting rid of these "pesky errors." We pour red ink on them and expect them to wilt—but they don't. Red ink seems to be a terribly inefficient pesticide, and it has the undesirable side-effect of causing large numbers of students to hate and fear writing more than anything else that they are expected to do in school. It is not the errors that wilt but the writers. A heavy dose of red ink wounds a writer's pride so severely that we may have to develop the ability to spot and correct these errors chiefly by editing papers written by someone else.

One device is to duplicate one paper on each assignment with wide spaces between lines and ample margins. Whenever possible, it should come from a class other than the one that will dissect it so that students may say whatever they like about it without fear of hurting the writer's feelings. They study this paper as homework, rate it, and mark it up with corrections and suggestions for improvement as well as appreciative comments on anything that is well done.

In class next day they argue with one another over their ratings, corrections, and comments, and the class accepts some and rejects others. This gets around the difficulty that some students notice only one or two errors in a paper. The class as a whole notices almost as many as the teacher, and like the teacher it notices some that are not really errors at all. But these will be defended by other students, and both sides will appeal to the teacher for a verdict in their favor. If the point is one that they may reasonably be expected to find in a handbook, style book, writer's guide, dictionary of synonyms, or the *Dictionary of Contemporary American Usage,* the teacher may tell the hottest disputants to find a ruling in one of these sources and report back. They soon learn to take pride in being able to back up their opinions by citing one of these sources.

Whenever we mention this practice in other schools, some teachers say, "We have tried it, but we project the paper on a screen with the overhead projector. It doesn't work very well." Of course not. In the first place, the students cannot take the projection home with them to study and mark up before they come to class; hence their comments are off-the-cuff. In the second place, one cannot project the whole paper at once and thus enable the students to discuss the larger elements in writing (such as organization) or even smaller elements in relation to the whole. This is a very poor substitute for reproducing enough typed copies for each student to have one to study in advance, and teachers must not judge the effectiveness of this practice by the results of using the projector.

After students have had some practice editing papers in class, they may pair off and edit one another's papers before submitting them to the teacher. If a student does not agree with a correction or suggestion of his editor, he is not obliged to accept it. They argue over these disputed points and try to find support in the sources already mentioned. Teachers report considerable success with student editing in classes of average or above-average ability but have not yet found a way to make this work well in classes of below-average ability.

Another device that is just beginning to be used is to have students read their papers aloud into a tape recorder, play them back several times, and mark anything in the script that does not "sound right." This practice appears to be even more effective in getting at the larger elements in writing (organization, development, support, proportion, emphasis, adaptation to audience, etc.) than mechanical errors, but the latter may also be spotted as students play back single sentences that do not sound quite right. After correcting these parts, they read and play back the revised version to see whether it sounds better, and if they cannot decide, they often ask some other student to listen to both versions and say which one he prefers. This use of the tape recorder in revising first drafts may be developed much further when English teachers gain access to the language laboratories thus far monopolized by foreign language teachers.

This device also suggests the possibility that some obstinate mechanical errors may have to be "programmed out" through the ear before they will reach the eye or the hand. Unless the errors "sound wrong" to the student, he is unlikely to avoid them or to detect them in first drafts, even though he has been told repeatedly that they are wrong. Such tapes must be prepared by experts, not by students reading their own papers. Students must hear the right thing over and over in different contexts and voices; then the same sorts of contexts again with pauses in which they must say the right thing, followed immediately by the right thing on the tape. This sort of practice has been so effective in foreign language teaching that it offers great promise of similar effectiveness in English.

Whatever means of eradicating "pesky errors" finally prove their worth, it should be clear that we do not yet know what they are likely to be; and the greatest enemies of progress are those who are quite sure that they know the answer already: "Get back to formal grammar, teach it thoroughly, mark all errors, make students correct them, get tough—then we'll be all right." That is what we have now and have had for a hundred years, and we are *not* all right.

Other Possibilities

Neither the teaching of modern grammar nor the application of red ink to "pesky errors" can possibly account for the substantial improvement in writing that we have found from grade to grade. These are the only elements of the writing program that we have investigated thus far, but as time and ingenuity permit we hope to study other elements such as:

Frequency of practice in writing
Types of writing assignments: e.g.,
    Topics based on independent and required reading
    Topics based on personal experience and observation
    Topics based on current happenings in or out of school
    Topics based on historical events
    Topics based on issues, problems, and proposals
    Topics based on imaginary situations
Methods of introducing writing assignments
Writing done in school vs. writing done at home
Consultation during the process of writing
Theme conferences on completed papers
How students get ideas that they want to express
How students develop and support these ideas
How students recognize and discard "deadwood"
Ways of teaching organization
Ways of cultivating awareness of an audience
Ways of securing or simulating an audience response
Ways of motivating revision: e.g.,
    Accepting a revision of an earlier paper in place of a new paper
    Class editing and "buddy" editing
    Publishing revised papers if accepted by student editors
    Shortening papers to fit a given space in a publication
Ways of developing interest in deft wording and phrasing
Ways of expanding the writing vocabulary
Practice in combining sentences without loss of clarity
Practice in manipulating sentences: e.g.,
    To put a given element first or last for emphasis
    To get qualifications out of the way first
    To bury these qualifications in the middle
Effects of independent reading on growth in writing
Effects of imitation of literary models
Effects of associating with more mature students
Effects of disbelieving ideas accepted by associates
Causes and effects of an "intellectual awakening."

Although this list is off-the-cuff and could easily be expanded, it is already too long to cover by the clumsy machinery of controlled experiments. We must invent shortcuts like those already illustrated. Meanwhile, our best guess is that the basic cause of improvement in writing is simply being alive. If it depended on teachers or textbooks, probably no one would learn to write. Still, some of the things that go on or might go on in school may help, and our evaluation program must keep trying to find out what those things are.

The Final Product

Our second "guiding question" about writing was "Why is it still so unsatisfactory in the end?" There is little doubt that it *is* unsatisfactory since there is widespread complaint about it, not only among English teachers but also among teachers in other departments, employers, and the public. But are these complaints justified? Let us examine some representative twelfth grade papers to find out.

Yet where can we find "representative" papers? Not in our own senior high school, since it is well above the national average in socioeconomic indices and test scores that are highly correlated with writing ability. Not even among the "writing samples" secured by the College Board, for this also is a select population. But when Educational Testing Service initiated the movement to employ readers to assist high school English teachers, it prepared some training materials to show the readers what levels of writing to expect in homework assignments and how such papers were corrected and annotated by experienced teachers. It secured these papers in schools that were at the national average and hired a large number of experienced teachers to sort the papers into five piles corresponding to conventional grades of A, B, C, D, and E. Then each teacher picked out the three *lowest* papers in the piles marked A, B, C, and D, and ETS duplicated one paper at each borderline that had been chosen by the largest number of teachers. Although we may quarrel with their choices, these papers probably represent national levels of writing achievement as well as any we are likely to get, since these teachers had no motive for selecting papers that were either better or worse than those likely to be encountered by readers in all parts of the country.

There were 32 sets of such papers for grades 10, 11, and 12, but we shall look at the first assignment for grade 12:

Write a paper on aspects of life in America that you think are good: for example,

Our standard of living
Our economic system
Our system of government
Our scientific progress
Our literature, music, art, or architecture

Our system of education
Equality of rights and opportunities
The natural beauty of the country
The character of our people
Our interest and achievements in sports
Our contributions to mankind.

The following paper was chosen to represent the borderline between A and B:

The Light of Freedom

No one knows where the dream began or in whose mind the spark first flickered. But as strong men built power upon a foundation of slavery and human suffering, men of courage voiced the cry for freedom—"Let my People Go!"

The Pharoh of Egypt, mightiest ruler of the ancient world, commander of one hundred thousand men, let his gaze wander across the white marble throne room and then looked down at the bearded shepard who had made this plea—and Pharoh laughed.

Yet Moses was not to be denied. Israel gained its freedom, and a spark of light appeared in a world of darkness. Again and again, the iron hand of tyranny smothered the spark and crushed its defenders, but you can't kill an idea, or murder a dream. For the men with the dream were everywhere. In Greece, testing a new idea called—democracy! In Rome, braving the wrath of emporers to uphold their belief in man's equality before God. All over Europe, fighting for truth and for the freedom to seek that truth. Socrates, Spartucus, Peter, Paul, Copernicus, Galileo, Luther, Calvin, Wesley, Knox, Voltaire, Rousseau, Montaque, their names illuminate the history of mankind; for each in his own way championed one of the freedoms which was to become an essential part of our modern democracy.

The strong men of Europe began to realize that the establishment of a free and democratic state had become inevitable, only a matter of time.

"Give me liberty or give me death!"—this plea echoed through the Virginia House of Burgesses with the same intensity as that uttered four thousand years before in the throne room of the Pharohs, and like the plea of Moses, Patric Henry's was not to be denied. The American Colonies faced the armed might of the British Empire, but theirs was a weapon more powerful than armies, it was an idea, whose time had come!

As the first ten amendments were ratified, the world saw its dreams of religious, political, and intellectual freedom become realities, protected for all time by the strength and stability of the Constitution of the United States.

The passage of years has brought, not a decline in American liberty, but instead, the growth of new freedoms, social and economic, giving Americans more elbow-room in an ever-changing world.

The spark that was lit when the first man dreamt of equity has never really gone out. It burns in the torch of the Statue of Liberty proclaiming to all men everywhere that here is a land where freedom will never die!

Although there are a number of points in this paper that need correction and probably would be corrected after editing by a "buddy" or by the teacher, it is a creditable performance. It shows good judgment by dealing with a central value in American life; it also shows awareness that freedom was not invented in America by relating it to the plea of Moses, "Let my people go!" It gets from that plea to the Statue of Liberty in just a few bold steps, covering a mighty span of centuries with a catalogue of great names. This is an interesting list in which Calvin, Wesley, and Knox rub elbows with Voltaire, Rousseau, and "Montaque" (Montaigne?) in the ranks of freedom-fighters. Was the student brought up in an uncommonly liberal parsonage? Incomplete sentences are used in this section to good effect.

The last paragraph makes good use of the device of relating the end of a paper to its beginning: the spark kindled long ago now shines in the torch of the Statue of Liberty. The tone of the paper may be a bit more excited than most professors would like, but this youthful enthusiasm is a valuable trait, and here it lifts the paper above the dullness that characterizes much student writing. If more students wrote as well as this, we should have nothing to fear.

But here is the B- paper:

The American Standard of Living

As you probably know we, the citizens of the United States, have the worlds finest standard of living. We possess more money per capita, more luxuries, and more time and labor saving gadgets than any other country in the world. In addition to these tangible assets, Americans also possess the most valuable and the most cherished thing in the world, freedom.

Our standard of living is unprecedented, never before have people enjoyed such freedom or had their lives made more comfortable. Some of the people in Brazil have a very high standard of living, but only a few. The average Brazilian is still without much beyond the bare necessities of life. Only in such places as Rio de Janeiro, Sao Paulo, and Buenos Aires do we find a standard of living on a parallel with our own; however even in these great cities it is enjoyed only by a select few. More than half the world is without adequate lighting and plumbing facilities, and it wasn't more than one generation back that the United States used the kerosene lamp and the outhouse.

Our standard of living is improving every year especially in the field of luxeries. Television and radio are only two of the many sources of entertainment that have been added recently to the American scene. The American housewife does less work than any other housewife in the world. The steam iron was invented to relieve her of the task of sprinkling her family's clothes, before ironing them; the electric mixer enables her to combine foods in a matter of minutes with very little effort; the pressure cooker is available to cut her cooking time down to a few seconds. The man of the family also is aided by many modern conveniences; he goes to work in his own automobile; to help him with his work he may have a typewriter or an adding machine; when he gets home he may heat his house by merely tuning up the thermostat. Many of these luxeries we take for granted. In another part of the world these same luxeries are looked on as modern marvels.

Our standard of living is the best in the world, and the finest the world has ever seen. This has been the accomplishment of American private industry, and our standard of living will improve mainly through their further efforts.

The point of view expressed in this paper is so appalling in its complacent acceptance of gadgets and "luxeries" as tokens of the quality of living in America that one hates to see its relatively high rating. It was probably so rated because its crude points are fairly well developed and supported. While there is one glaring comma-splice, there are fewer gross errors than in the other two papers in this set. The long sentences in the third paragraph show a command of complicated sentence structure.

Apart from these merits, the paper is dull and tasteless. One wonders why Brazil is singled out as the only example of another country that does not enjoy our standard of living; why the writer did not check the location of Buenos Aires; and why the comparison is weakened by the plight of the United States "one generation back." The list of gadgets and "luxeries" in the next paragraph is not impressive and seems to equate the good life with laziness. Steam iron, electric mixer, pressure cooker, automobile, typewriter, adding machine, thermostat—and, oh yes, we have freedom, too. The plug for private industry in the last paragraph at first seems irrelevant, but the writer evidently felt the need for some sort of generalization to serve as a conclusion.

Both of the remaining papers in this set are so poor that there is no strong reason to regard one as better than the other. But by some quirk of the sample, this one turned up at the borderline between C and D:

America's Educational System

The educational problem is one of the most important achievements in the United States today. Education is a necessary step to make the people powerful and literate under provisions of the democratic government. In the following paragraphs, different phases of education will be exemplified.

The first important thing in education is to know just what it means. The definition is "the realization of one's highest self." Education is brought out by vocational interests, government, and to make people understand and live a better life.

Nowadays, it is very hard to get a job with just an elementary education. This paved the way for the necessary building of high schools, not only for better jobs, but preparation for college. There you can take up a profession, such as doctor, lawyer, engineer; or, you might take an advanced course in business. All these advanced schools are to the advantage of the individual person, and should enter them if the opportunity arises.

Since the United States is under a democratic government, it is very important that the population knows how to read and write. Included in the nineteen-fifty census, reports showed that two and one-half per cent of the people could not read or write in any language, thus these people are defined as illiterate. Because the American government and constitution is for the people, by the people, and of the people, it was sought that every person over fourteen years of age be able to read and write. The reason for literate people is that they must be informed about the progress of their government, elect the right people to represent them, and help build a better community in which they live.

Another good purpose of education is the objectives in life to which they stress. The important ones are good health habits, points of life you will need to know after your schooling, how to get along with others, how to become a good citizen, facts about the government under which you live, suggests ideas of what you should do with your leisure time, and try to develop a good character. Boards of Education were established and the individual states took over the control of their school systems. This made them better suited to make rules which should furthur the education in that part of the country.

As you can see, America must have people with a basic education. It could not continue the world supremacy in production, power, and the center of most alliances or conferences concerning other nations. By being a literate population, America has become the leading modern nation of the world.

This belongs in the Department of Utter Confusion; we may also suspect that English was not the native language of some members of this family. Several of the absurd statements could be straightened out with a slightly better command of English vocabulary and idiom. In the first sentence, for example, he writes "educational problem" for "educational system," possibly to avoid repeating "system" from the title. He does not think it will make any difference, but it does. Even when he throws in a hard word like "exemplified" in the third sentence, it backfires on him.

The lofty definition of education in the second paragraph was evidently put in for decoration, since he makes no use of it in what follows. The next sentence announces (in violently non-parallel form) the three phases of education that he intends to discuss—vocational, civic, and cultural—and, oddly enough, he does. Only the last two sentences of the fifth paragraph lie completely outside this framework and should be discarded.

The two hardest things to take in this paper are probably the identification of education with simple literacy and the spectacular violations of parallel structure, especially in the fifth paragraph. It may seem hopeless to teach this student anything about parallel structure, but he might be able to state the rest of his objectives in -*ing* form given this start: "*taking* care of your health, *learning* things you will need to know," now:

(how to get) .... along with others,
(how to become) .... a good citizen,
(facts) .... about the government,

(suggests ideas of what you should do) .... leisure
time,

(and try to develop) .... a good character.
Would he recognize the neatness and clarity of lining them up like
West Point cadets? Or would he be hurt if we did not recognize that he
was striving for variety in sentence structure, as his teacher recommended? If the latter, he needs a good rest before attempting to learn
anything more about the bewildering art of writing.

Finally, here is the D- paper, probably so rated because its boners
are so obvious, even though the writing is a bit smoother:

America's Contributions to Mankind

America has made significant contributions to the welfare of mankind in
government, in science, and in the arts.

America has always been a country that, if it believed in something it would
fight for it. Mabe that's why she is better off now then most other countries.
When America wanted a represenative government she fought for it. And when
she wanted freedom of the press and freedom of speach she revolted against her
leaders and came out on top with what they wanted.

In science America has made many improvements and inventions. Although
the Germans will dispute this statement, the Americans were the first ones to
succeed in getting a plane off the ground any length of time. This happened
when Wilber and Orval Wright took their plane off the ground on that gray and
dismal day back in 1904.

America, also, was the first country to drop the Atomic bomb. That's one
contribution the people on Hiroshima will never forget.

The farmers of the United States have been helped out a great deal by inventions that came from this country. Eli Whitney had one of the bigger inventions of his time when he invented the cotton gin.

After Whitneys invention there were inventions in other fields that were
equally important. The spinning jenny was one of those and it was invented by
a man named James Hargreaves.

As far as contributions in the arts go, I'm afraid I'm not quite up to date.
But there must have been some American who invented something useful in the
field of Architecture.

There is one thing I know about music. The American people started the
form of music known as "Jazz. This music started back in the 1920's when everything was Jazz and drink. This era was known as the "Jazz Age."

There isn't too much to say about painting in the United States but Alex
Brook and Lloyd Wright were both born in the United States.

Although it may be difficult to say in which of these fields America has
made the greatest contributions, most Americans would probably contind that
our system of government has been the keystone of success.

Before we condemn this composition, let us consider what it does
well. It begins with a "program paragraph" announcing the three points

it will cover, and it emphasizes these points by repeating the *in: in* government, *in* science, and *in* the arts. This program is faithfully carried out in this order, and the transitions to science and to the arts are clearly indicated. Nothing extraneous to these three points is included. The conclusion is also well marked and attempts an assessment of our contributions in these three fields. Although the metaphor "keystone of success" is unfortunate, the decision to give first place to our system of government is a sound judgment.

Some teachers commenting on this paper say that they automatically fail any paper with a single-sentence opening paragraph, and they suggest combining it with the second paragraph. This paper illustrates the danger of such fixed rules. In view of the shortness of the other paragraphs, this single-sentence opening is entirely justified; in fact, it is probably the best thing in the paper. It cannot be combined with the second paragraph because it gives the plan of the whole paper, while the second paragraph deals with point 1.

This second paragraph ends so comically that we may overlook its most serious weakness. We note that America is first *it*, then *she*. When this happens, we begin wondering what it will be next: *we, you,* or *they*. In the last sentence of this paragraph it becomes *they* with disastrous effect: we revolt against our leaders and come out on top with what *they* want. This sounds like a communist description of a typical bourgeois revolution but actually is only a matter of a shift in pronouns.

Since our attention is fixed on this technical problem, we may forget to ask, "How did we establish and guarantee freedom of speech and of the press?" By passing the First Amendment to the Constitution. Did this involve any revolt against our leaders? No, they favored it. Did we secure this right by fighting? No, by reasoning with one another and then by voting. Not a drop of blood was shed.

The student knew this well enough since he had just had a good course in American history, but he did not stop to think whether what he was writing was true. The whole paragraph expresses the little-boy attitude that we get what we want by the process of fight-fight-fight. That sounds good to him, and he might object that the inconvenient truth ruins his point. So it does, but in a matter of history, if it isn't true, it isn't a good point. He must go back and try a different angle. The opening sentence of this paragraph now seems a poor way to begin.

The other misstatements might have been avoided by even a superficial check. If nothing else was available, the *American College Dictionary* would give him the spelling of Wilbur and Orville Wright and tell him that James Hargreaves was an Englishman and Frank Lloyd Wright an architect, not a painter. One wonders why he abbreviates the honored names of "Alex" Brook and "Lloyd" Wright. Was his art teacher on such familiar terms with them?

The most disheartening thing about this paper is that a student who had lived seventeen years in the United States and gone through eleven grades of its schools should know so little about its contributions to mankind. We know that this assignment was made at least one week before the paper was due. If the student did not already know what his countrymen had accomplished in at least one field, there was time to find out enough to make a short paper without such ridiculous boners. The underlying attitudes and values, of course, take longer to develop, but what had he been doing all this time? Why does he identify progress in government with fighting, science with a few inventions, and music with jazz?

If this is the outcome of eleven years in our public schools, it makes one wonder whether the country is safe in such hands. So do all the papers, in fact, except the first. In other countries, only this first student would be regarded as a candidate for higher education. We try to include the second and sometimes either the third or the fourth. It is to be hoped that they have sterling qualities that were not brought out by these papers. The third might find a place in one of the smaller teachers colleges, for some of their graduates write not much better than this. The horrifying thought is that some of them try to teach English. Some of these writers may have been their students.

We included this cursory examination of a representative set of twelfth grade papers to show the distance we have yet to travel and the kinds of weaknesses we must overcome before we can be proud of the writing of our students. Notwithstanding the growth we have detected from grade to grade, the final product leaves much to be desired. Although the "pesky errors" are numerous and effective means of eradicating them have yet to be invented, an even greater cause for concern is the appalling immaturity of the thought. We need to give far more attention to this weakness because many teachers do not even recognize it as a problem. Their first defense is that good ideas are the product of God-given intelligence, and if a student is not blessed with it, what can one do? For one thing, one can give far greater prominence to the soundness of the ideas in one's comments on the paper and in class discussions of papers.

We have counted and tabulated dozens of types of comments scrawled on papers, but one that we never find is "Nonsense!" Why not? It is the right word to describe a great deal of what our students write, even when they know better. We cannot believe that teachers are squeamish about hurting the writer's feelings since many of their comments are more devastating than this. Anyway, if the comment goes on to explain what was nonsensical, the student is often flattered to find that his views are taken seriously. He often comes in to show the teacher a revised version that plugs up the hole in his argument, and he wants to know whether it meets the criticism. At any rate, he is far more interested in an attack on his argument than in an attack on his syntax. Yet many teachers have the curious notion that the ideas are none of their business; they can only touch up the expression. Nonsense! The factor analysis reported in this chapter showed that more readers were influenced primarily by the ideas expressed than by any other aspect of skill in writing. How can students at any intelligence level be stimulated to sharpen their ideas or find better ideas unless they are continually challenged?

A second defense is that almost any topic of general concern (like the one we have been examining) is a "social science topic" and therefore inappropriate for an English class. It is odd that a student cannot be asked to discuss something he likes about living in America without being accused of invading the social sciences. Remember that the first got most of his material from Moses, a list of religious reformers, and a work of art—the Statue of Liberty. The second took up gadgets and "luxeries"; the third, education; and only the fourth tried a bit of garbled history and then went on to inventions and the arts. Yet this is the sort of topic that is often condemned as "social science"—as though English students should not be expected to know anything about the land of their birth. What such teachers prefer is a "literary" topic: a discussion of some point in a chapter or poem that has just been studied. A few such papers are indispensable in the study of literature, but a whole program devoted to writing about books is deadly. Writing about writing is probably the worst writing that most students ever do.

A third defense is to turn back to the types of writing that students have already developed to a point of diminishing returns by the end of junior high school: relating an incident, inventing a story, or telling about a person. These make excellent practice in writing for the younger students, but most of them have gone as far as they are likely to go in these directions by age 13 or 14. To go on to more mature types of writing, they must learn to support a position on some issue, to analyze a problem and propose a solution, to explain why something happened, to attack an argument or practice that they regard as indefensible, to compare various alternatives, and the like. In other words, they must learn to handle ideas.

Why should they? After leaving school, most students will write very little except personal letters, and these will get by on family anecdotes that are written well enough for this purpose by thirteen-year-olds and by people who never read a book. The ability to express a defensible thought in writing is not, strictly speaking, a necessity for all, but a civilized human being should be ashamed if he is unable to do it. Students of this age are concerned about their appearance. Even if the effect they try to achieve is "a sweet disorder in the dress," the disorder is prescribed by teenage mores and they conform meticulously. What about the appearance of their minds? Many seem unaware that the contents of their minds are exposed to the gaze of their fellow students whenever they put pen to paper. If someone whispers, "Pardon, your slip is showing," they are embarrassed. But that is a minor contretemps, for the slip is not part of the self, nor are the other "slips" that we have been calling "pesky errors." It should be much more embarrassing for someone to whisper, "Pardon, your mind is showing."

In the next phase of our writing program, we hope to give first place to the discussion and criticism of ideas. When these are as sound, challenging and forthright as the writer and the class can make them, we shall be in a better position to consider how they can be presented most effectively.

Part Four

A Look Ahead

THOSE "Sunday farmers" we talked about earlier in this book did not stop their "work" just because it was autumn and the crops were almost in. As a matter of fact they were at their best then. They loved to saunter around the ripening fields, and if the harvest was a good one they just plain enjoyed the feel of it. But, as they thought back over the year, they also thought ahead to what they could do next, because they had this crop.

We are in a rather similar humor right now. We cannot pretend that the harvest is all in or the problems all behind us. Still, we feel that we have broken some new ground, and we should like to take a few pages to consider the gains that are going to be possible if that ground is cultivated.

It will not be easy. The cramping, distorting system of marking and grading and crediting from which we are seeking to break free has imprisoned men's minds for a long time. Now we believe we have shown that it is feasible to build a road to freedom. If schools have the vision and the courage to open that way, much that has been yearned for as "ideal but impracticable" will suddenly become easy and natural. Even though we cannot yet see all the way ahead, let us take the most thoughtful look we can.

8

The Fruits of Freedom

Fred T. Wilhelms and Paul B. Diederich

ALMOST from its first meeting, this Yearbook Committee has been dominated by one fundamental perception: The traditional system of marking and grading and credit-granting is so inadequate and distorting, such a nuisance to good teaching and learning, that we simply have to throw it out and get ourselves something better.

To get at that "something better" we first analyzed what evaluation is for. We concluded that its fundamental purpose is simply to provide feedback and guidance whenever and wherever feedback and guidance are needed. But we soon recognized that feedback and guidance are needed by a variety of persons—the learner himself, his parents, and his teachers—as well as for a variety of institutional purposes, and that they must take a variety of forms.

In fact, to do its fundamental task, evaluation must perform five tasks. It must:

> Facilitate self-evaluation
> Encompass all the objectives
> Facilitate teaching and learning
> Generate records appropriate to various uses
> Facilitate decision-making on curriculum and educational policy.

These five tasks demand very different types of information and organization. It is almost not too much to say that the products of evaluation must emerge to function in three different "worlds."

In the Private World of the Learner

Of all the forces operating in a school the energy of the learner is the greatest. If it is "turned on" at full voltage—and directed straight into the task at hand—it is almost irresistible. Even if teaching is mediocre and material resources are meager, the youngster will somehow move ahead. But if it is "turned off"—or diverted from the task or opposed to it—nothing else matters very much.

That flow of energy is controlled by the learner's perceptions. It is not very much at the disposal of the school or the teacher, to be ordered about from this to that. It is not always even at the disposal of the child's own conscious will; the intuitive impulses which govern it sometimes lie deeper inside. If a full charge of energy is to be delivered to any learning task, two conditions must prevail: The learner must see the task with clear eyes and sense that it is relevant to his private goals; and he must have faith that he is worthy to tackle it, that he is the kind of person who ought to do this sort of thing and who can do it if he stretches.

Above all else it is the function of evaluation to bring these two conditions into existence and to release the full flow of the learner's energy. No matter how much of a superstructure may be built above it, nothing else is so basic a criterion of evaluation as what happens within the learner himself. Yet it is precisely at this point that the traditional system of evaluation is weakest. Eternally preoccupied with the grading and marking and rating of pupil products, it largely blocks out—when it does not also distort—that quiet, intimate communication that has to do with the individual person. We have all grown so accustomed to this that it is hard to see that it can be otherwise.

We believe we have shown that once the burden of grade/record production is lifted there is freedom for something very different. The teacher's key question can shift from what a pupil's grade should be to what it is that the student needs to know about his work and about himself. "Diagnostic teaching" is a good shorthand term for the result. It means that the newly freed teacher can communicate openly with individuals, small groups, or the class as a whole about what has been accomplished, what remains to be accomplished, and what the next steps may be. The learner can be brought actively into the process, learning to see his present status and to size up what he needs to do. The emphasis moves away from endlessly measuring him to genuinely conferring with him in a helping, guiding relationship. Subject matter can constantly be adjusted to his needs and abilities.

Even so, it would be a bad mistake to interpret diagnostic teaching simply as the nicer adjustment of a body of subject matter to each learner's situation—important as that is. The fundamental thing lies deeper. There are many sets of subject matter which can be used to achieve a given goal. Seldom is any particular bit of content so important in itself that all learners must have it. Perhaps not even all goals are universally relevant to every child. Diagnostic teaching takes the learner-as-a-person into account quite as much as the technicalities of content. It gives him rich opportunities to learn about himself and to feel his way toward what he needs to learn. It helps him to grow in self-acceptance and respect for his own intuitions.

All of this has been said better and more fully in earlier chapters. But it is important to remind ourselves—having just read the complex chapters on evaluation-for-the-record—that the most fundamental gains in the reform we propose go back deep into the private world of the learner. He is the one, above all others, who needs constant feedback to know himself better and to see the job ahead of him more clearly—and help define that job. He is the one who has been cramped and confined by the existing system, all too often cut off from chances to understand himself and bring his own motivations to bear on learning. If we succeed in freeing him, all the rest is only so much bonus—important in its own right, but not so fundamental.

In the World of the Teacher

Freedom to teach is the second great gain our proposed system offers; freedom to put oneself genuinely in a helping relationship to the learner, to figure out as precisely as possible *with the learner's help* what it is that will be best for him and then help him to achieve it. This is what every good teacher wants.

There are many obstacles in the way of this ideal—the size of the group, the exigencies of schedules, etc. Our thesis has been that one primary obstacle has been the pressure upon the teacher to be forever measuring and judging when he should be simply helping. We have sought to take that load off his shoulders by providing plenty of significant measurement-for-the-record through other means.

This has not implied any lessening of the teacher's use of evaluative devices; rather the opposite. But we believe we have achieved a system in which the teacher is free to use every form of evaluation as a means to helping the learner. He will probably wish to use every kind of testing device his ingenuity can conceive, as well as the data supplied by standardized tests. We hope he will swing to an unprecedented use of private and small-group conferences. The distinctive thing will be his purpose. He will have comparatively little need for judgmentalness; he will have enormous freedom for helpfulness.

Once more, it may be well to point out that one important purpose of the elaborate structure of evaluation-for-the-record built up in the later chapters of this book is simply to get the record-producing function "off the teacher's back." We believe that the instant that is achieved a teacher's energies can go directly to his true functions.

The world of the teacher and the world of the learner are intimately intermingled. In our proposal we are struggling to help that joint world take on a new character. Breaking the old shackles of test-measure-and-judge, we hope to open up genuine communication. We want to see teacher and learner planning together, testing together, deciding on next needs together. We want them able to talk about themselves as persons, with all their hopes and doubts and frustrations and aspirations. We want them able to explore possibilities, relish successes, evaluate failures together, and decide how to move on.

All this may sound almost sentimentally soft. It is not so. The key to hard, constructive work, to throwing oneself boldly at the barely possible, lies in mutual understanding and acceptance of needs and purposes. It is *not* mere nice-Nellyism to estimate that a classroom, freed of the old loading of judgment-making, can become the kind of place where learners can mobilize their energies because they believe in their purposes.

In the Larger World of the Institution

Even though the most fundamentally important uses of evaluation lie in the world of the learner and of the teacher, there are also absolutely essential services it must perform in the larger complexes of the schools and society.

The most *visible* of these needs has to do with college entrance. To put it bluntly, any system of evaluation and record-keeping which failed to facilitate the entrance of a school's graduates into appropriate colleges would not have a ghost of a chance of surviving, no matter how ideal it might be in other respects. To state the matter in this way is to reduce things to their lowest common denominator. But responsible realism has compelled the committee to crack this problem, for it is the rock on which any discussion of evaluation reform is likely to break up.

Nevertheless, this seemingly negativistic approach should not obscure a set of real and important educational needs. It *is* essential for a school to have data on each student so organized that it can report intelligently not only to the colleges but also to any other institution to which a student may transfer at any point, as well as to parents and prospective employers. There is no question but that such data and such reporting are essential; the question is, rather, how the most significant data for any purpose can be identified, how the reporting can be made most meaningful, and how the whole process can be carried out in consonance with good learning and teaching.

Furthermore, within the school itself, there is tremendous need for feedback so organized that it can provide guidance for curriculum improvement and every sort of educational policy making. Therefore, the committee, having searched long and hard for evaluation most relevant to the learner and his teacher, had to search equally long and hard for evaluation relevant to the needs of the educational system.

As the reader already knows, this phase of the inquiry was largely cast in the form of an experimental development in a cluster of junior high schools. That development is still by no means complete. But it has proceeded far enough to get a sense of direction. Perhaps the best way to test it now is to ask ourselves, "When we have this new system going, what sorts of things will it enable us to report about each student when he transfers from one school level to the next?" The reader is asked to understand that the selection of this question does not mean that such reporting—say, from high school to college—is the *only*, or even the *most important* reason for the data-collecting system. The question merely provides a handy way of looking at the assemblage of data which becomes possible as we swing from the old system to the new.

What Can We Say to the Next Higher Level?

The two preceding chapters should have demonstrated that a cooperative evaluation program of the sort therein described will make available a large body of information about students within any stage or level of education. The actual study was done at the junior high school level, but it could have been done just as well in the senior high school or elementary school.

Everyone who has a right to this information—the student himself, his parents, his teachers, the guidance counselor, the curriculum director—will know where to get it. It will all be sent to the adviser of the student concerned: a teacher, coach, or librarian who has regular contact with that student and who is responsible for keeping track of all approved information as to his progress and difficulties. This will be possible because no adviser will have an advisory group of more than thirty-five students and most will have between twenty and thirty. It will also be possible because the information that reaches advisers is carefully screened. It must be approved by the head of the department that secures the information and ultimately by the Evaluation Committee of the school or district; it must represent the independent judgment of more than a single individual; and it must be related to some major goal of instruction that is officially recognized by the department and by the school.

The adviser will not only receive and scan this evidence but will also file it in an appropriate slot of the record folder of the student concerned after sending one copy to his parents—with interpretive comments whenever they are needed. This bit of machinery insures that all significant information about a student will pass not only through the hands of a single person who knows the student but also through his mind. If any adviser is asked how one of his advisees is getting along in any of his courses or activities, he will usually be able to answer in general terms without consulting his records. If more detail is needed he will know precisely where to locate the information in his file of record folders. That is why each department sends reports on all measures "for the record" to the advisers of the students concerned rather than directly to parents. If the departments bypassed the advisers, then no one person in school would have in his head and in his files a comprehensive picture of how each student was getting along.

One payoff of this channeling of information is that if any teacher is puzzled by the behavior or the difficulties of any student in his classes, the quickest and easiest way to find out about him is simply to ask the student's adviser. The adviser can usually supply the missing parts of the puzzle offhand, or he can reach for the record folder and read off the relevant scores and other indices. If the teacher wishes to study the case in greater depth, he can borrow the record folder and make notes of all pertinent information sent in by former teachers in his own field and current teachers in other fields. Similarly, if a parent wants further information about any problem that his child has encountered in school, he knows precisely where to go. The adviser has more information about his child from more independent sources than any other person in school, and after telling the parent what he knows and discussing the hypotheses he has formed, he can send the parent along to the teachers who know the problem at firsthand.

So far so good. But how much of this information can we or should we send along to the next higher level of education? If we tried to send all of it in the person of the ninth grade adviser with a suitcase full of record folders, it would take hours of conferences for him to tell all he knew to the teachers who might be concerned. There would be no way for them to tell in advance which information would prove to be pertinent, and they would be overwhelmed by the sheer mass of it. Even if we sent along the record folders with the original reports on all measures "for the record," they would be so bulky with the accumulation of three years and so detailed that no one would be likely to read them with enough care to reach defensible conclusions. A teacher at the next higher level would be more likely to reach for isolated bits of information, and these can be misleading without the larger context that the adviser of the previous year has had time to build up. Hence the school has an obligation to develop some kind of record form in which the salient features of the information thus far gathered about a student can be displayed in a way that the mind can grasp in a reasonable length of time. Then the adviser of the last year must fill out this record from the more copious information in the record folder, since only the adviser knows enough about the student to select the pertinent data and to supply interpretive comments as needed.

We have indicated earlier that the actual development of a record form in the school district that tried out this program would only begin six months after the writing of this report. Hence we have no actual knowledge of how it will be done, and our summaries of actual data are likely to differ in important ways from our projected summaries of imaginary data. For one thing, they are likely to be simpler, since the data that even the most energetic school district can collect usually fall short of what it regards as possible and desirable. Still, we owe it to the readers of this volume to attempt some extrapolation of what the junior high school record of a student may look like by 1970. Hence we shall present the proposed record in the following pages as a reasonable image of the future, based on data already collected and on data that we hope to collect within the next two years. Not all blanks would be filled for any given student, but no section of this record would be completely blank. The form itself is of no particular consequence here. It will undoubtedly be modified in many ways. What we are attempting to portray are the *sorts of information* we shall be able to report in an organized, intelligible way.

A PROJECTED JUNIOR HIGH SCHOOL RECORD

1. BIOGRAPHICAL INFORMATION

2. ACADEMIC RECORD
   Previous schools attended
   Courses taken each year in this school
     Course grades (while these are still given)
   Extracurricular activities
   Honors, awards, offices
   Noteworthy experiences, achievements, or difficulties

   Explanation of the Scaled Scores Used in the Remainder of This Record:

   The scaled scores used in this record are based on the total district population in the grade tested with separate norms for boys and for girls where indicated. The mean is 3, the standard deviation 1; second digits (when used) refer to tenths of the standard deviation. Scores of selected groups are equated to the district population by relevant aptitude scores. The district population is half a standard deviation above the national in aptitudes and basic skills. The following table may assist interpretation:

	Rare	Low	Middle	High	Rare
Scaled scores on district norms:	00 05	10 15 20	25 30 35	40 45 50	55 60
Standard deviation equivalents:	-3	-2 -1	Mean	+1 +2	+3
District percentile equivalents:	0.1 1	2 7 16	31 50 69	84 93 98	99 99+
National percentile equivalents:	1 2	7 16 31	50 69 84	93 98 99	99 99+

For less precise measures: L = low quarter, M = middle half, H = high quarter.
When quartiles are unknown, L = deficient, M = acceptable, H = outstanding.
In ratings 1=lowest 5%, 2=low fifth, 3=middle half, 4=high fifth, 5=top 5%.

3. GUIDANCE

Aptitudes: (weighted average of best predictors, district norms by sex)
Verbal............, Math............, Languages............, Clerical............, Mechanical............, Spatial............
Academic interests: (Interest Index standings, grade 8 norms by sex)
English............, Social Studies............, Biology............, Secretarial............, Home............, Art............,
Languages............, Math............, Physical Sciences............, Business............, Shop............, Music............
Sociometric ratings: (grade 9 within-school norms by sex)
    Acceptance by classmates: L M H; of classmates: L M H
Record of behavior problems: (verbal summary)
Record of incomplete and unsatisfactory work: (verbal summary)
Record of guidance conferences: (verbal summary)

4. MATHEMATICS

Departmental exams. cumulative totals in each grade, district norms by sex:

	7	8	9		7	8	9
Computation	....	....	....	Concepts and processes	....	....	....
Problem solving	....	....	....	Mathematical reasoning	....	....	....

5. SCIENCE

Knowledge and understanding: (departmental exams, district norms for grade)
    General Science............, Biology............, Elective (   )............
    (Physics and Chemistry not offered in junior high school)
Critical thinking: (standardized and local tests, essays, records)
    Inductive processes............, deductive processes............, seeing relationships............,
    Awareness of assumptions............, of definitions............, of axioms............,
    Formulating hypotheses............, verifying hypotheses............, concept of proof............,
    Analysis, interpretation, and criticism of data and arguments............,
    Detection and refutation of logical fallacies............, of statistical fallacies............
Scientific attitudes: (reasons given in tests, essays, reports, discussion)
    Questioning............, faith in the possibility of solving problems............,
    desire for empirical verification............, desire for precision............,
    acceptance of new ideas............, willingness to change opinions............,
    objectivity............, suspended judgment............, avoidance of dogmatism............,
    aversion to superstition............, awareness of limitations of knowledge............,
    judgment of what is of fundamental and general significance............,
    respect for theoretical structures............, respect for quantification............,
    acceptance of probabilities............, of warranted generalizations............
Independent research: experiments, construction of models, exhibits, etc.
    (verbal summary, laboratory skills noted)

6. SOCIAL STUDIES

Knowledge and understanding: (departmental exams, district norms for grade)
History..........., Geography..........., Government..........., Current events...........,
Sociology..........., Anthropology..........., Psychology..........., Economics............
Social attitudes: (statements of opinions and reasons, grade 9 district norms)
Consistency..........., quality and relevance of reasons...........; tendency toward
(check): authoritarian........... conservative........... middle........... liberal........... radical............
Democratic behavior: (tests, essays, questionnaires, records, observations)
School voting record: extent..........., quality of reasons...........
Knows about, reacts to, and discusses important issues and events...........
Awareness of and concern for social problems..........., avoids glib solutions...........
Relates present issues to their historic background...........
Can discover, evaluate, and present facts relevant to social issues...........
Is willing to devote time and effort to school and community affairs...........
Accepts majority decisions..........., respects law and its agencies...........
Values, respects, and defends basic human rights...........
Knows in general how economic systems operate...........
Respects property rights, contracts, and regulations...........
Understands cultures and ways of life other than his own...........
Expresses commitment to democratic principles in words and action...........
Knows about, critically evaluates, and supports efforts to prevent war...........
Shows interest in the development of backward nations...........
Sees real dangers in world situation..........., rejects imaginary dangers...........
Is willing to defend country against aggression and tyranny...........

7. ENGLISH

Reading skill: (standardized and local tests, district norms for grade tested)
Comprehension..........., speed..........., adaptation of speed to material and purpose...........
Record of independent reading: (district norms for 3-year cumulative total)
Quantity..........., maturity..........., variety..........., special interests (line below):

....

Literary competence: (Standardized and local tests, district norms for grade)
  Tests on major literary works: (listed below; total and part scores)

  Literary aquaintance: (grade 9 district norms, total and part scores)
  Tests and records of ability to cope with difficulties in adult reading:
  Vocabulary..........., longer and more complex sentences...........,
  longer and more complicated story line..........., more complex characters...........,
  literary forms and devices..........., relation of parts to whole...........,
  interrupted time sequences..........., disagreeable incidents and characters...........,
  nonliteral meanings..........., irony and satire..........., imagery and symbolism...........,
  views contrary to one's own..........., unfamiliar periods and settings...........,
  author's purpose..........., depth of experience, insight, and emotion...........
Writing: (four test essays per year rated anonymously twice; grades 7-8-9 mixed
  together without identification; scores show standings in grades 7-8-9 combined)

MERIT	7	8	9	MECHANICS	7	8	9
Ideas	....	....	....	Usage	....	....	....
Organization	....	....	....	Punctuation	....	....	....
Wording	....	....	....	Spelling	....	....	....
Flavor	....	....	....	Handwriting	....	....	....

Total ratings in grade 9: standing in district............, in own group............
Growth in totals from 7 to 9 among those who started at same point............
Test of ability to detect common errors, grade 9 district norms............
Test of grammatical knowledge and skill, grade 9 district norms............
Speech: (within-school norms for grade 9)
 Ability to speak before an audience............
 Ability to participate effectively in small-group discussions............
 Ability to entertain others in conversation............
 Quality of voice............, standard pronunciation............, standard usage............
Listening: (test of listening comprehension, grade 9 district norms)............

8. FOREIGN LANGUAGE: .... (Cooperative MLA Tests, grade 9 norms)

 Speaking............, listening............, reading............, writing............
 vocabulary............, grammar............, cultural acquaintance............

9. FINE AND PRACTICAL ARTS

 Departmental tests, ratings, etc.; district norms for grade and sex:

	Theater	Dance	Music	Visual Arts	Shop	Home Arts
Performance	....	....	....	....	....	....
Appreciation	....	....	....	....	....	....
Knowledge	....	....	....	....	....	....
Interests	....	....	....	....	....	....
Attitudes	....	....	....	....	....	....
Preferences	....	....	....	....	....	....
Totals	....	....	....	....	....	....

 Practical competence: (performance tasks, records, observations)
 Making things............, making repairs............, cleaning, keeping things in order............,
 grooming............, care of house, grounds, etc............, care of children............
 care of pets............, care of tools............, of materials............, of money............,
 shopping............, cooking............, serving............, dining out............, traveling............

10. VOCATIONAL EDUCATION

 Vocational interests: 1.. 2..
 Local test of acquaintance with work of community and region............
 Vocational knowledge............, skill............ in............
 Work habits: (records, ratings, observations)
 Self-direction, initiative............, industry, perseverance, thoroughness............
 honesty, responsibility............, orderliness, system, neatness............,
 good judgment, decisiveness............, can lead............, can follow............,
 can work and play with others without quarreling............,
 completes assignments satisfactorily and on time............

11. PHYSICAL EDUCATION AND SPORTS

 Record of physical development and health; absences due to illness
 Participation in sports and outdoor activity: extent, variety, skill
 Health knowledge: physiology, psychology, hygiene, etc.
 Health habits: diet, play, rest, cleanliness, medical care, etc.
 Healthful attitudes:
  Security: self-confidence, poise, independence, flexibility, cheerfulness
  Affection: gives and receives affection freely, shows good will to others
 Safety: obeys safety regulations, takes reasonable precautions, etc.

12. PREDICTIONS (Consider also the aptitudes reported in Section 3.)

Weighted average of best predictive measures of achievement in:

Mathematics............   English...........   Fine arts..........
Science............   Languages..........   Practical arts..........
Social studies..........   Music..........   Business education..........

Academic Promise: rank in class of.......... students:..........

(based on weighted total of the foregoing averages).

Comments on the Projected Record

The first reaction of any practical schoolman to this projected record must be that it would be impossible to collect such voluminous and detailed information about any student in the three years of junior high school without spending more than half the time in testing, rating, and record-keeping. The reaction of members of the Evaluation Committee that directed the tryout of our Cooperative Evaluation Program during the past two years, however, is that it is amazing how many of these blanks we can already fill and how many more we already know how to fill on the basis of a perfectly feasible extension of our present procedures. When we started out, we thought it might take at least a generation to replace subjective course grades with actual measures of growth toward the major objectives of each field. After starting from scratch and accumulating data on these objectives for just two years, we now think we shall have something substantial to report in every section of this record by the end of the fifth year—three years from now. We are also confident that no teacher and no adviser will be overwhelmed by the job of securing all this evidence, assembling it in the record folders, and analyzing it for feedback into the curriculum.

We intend to hold to our present standard of having each department or team do something quite definite about measurement for the record on an average of not more than six scheduled occasions each year. Some departments with complex measurement problems (like English) may require as many as eight while others (like mathematics) may require no more than four. Even in English the load on any one teacher will not be excessive because some will have primary responsibility for reading and literature, others for writing and grammar, and others for speech and listening. All may lend a hand in scoring or grading these measures, but the harder job of preparing, revising, and analyzing the results of the measures may gradually be assumed by small committees. After we have prepared several forms of the more important objective tests and can use them repeatedly in successive classes, the burden of evaluation will be further reduced.

After reading the two preceding chapters, one can see how the main blocks of this evidence can be secured and recorded in little time with little effort. For example, the twelve scores on Academic Interests in Section 3 are secured, recorded, and interpreted by the students themselves in little more than one class period. Then the answer sheets will be forwarded to advisers with the interest scores in each field already labeled H, M, or L (high, middle, or low) by reference to the norms for boys and for girls that are printed right on these answer sheets. The sociometric ratings can be secured in fifteen or twenty minutes, but it will take a few hours of clerical work to count the number of checks given or received by each student—until we can get such ratings on IBM mark-sensing cards and secure the totals by machine. Rating test essays on eight aspects of writing competence has already been explained in great detail. Some of the measures now being prepared for use in music and art to get at some of the hard-to-measure objectives of these fields have also been explained and illustrated, so it should not be hard to imagine how the blanks for these fields in the record will be filled.

What may still boggle the imagination, however, is how the clusters of very specific behaviors under critical thinking, scientific attitudes, democratic behavior, ability to cope with difficulties in adult reading, practical competence, and work habits will be measured. In general, these are checklists that we use in devising tests, analyzing written statements, and preparing records of performance tasks, independent study, creative products, and the like. Hence these specifics are more likely to be tested at the item level than at the level of whole tests. For example, in every test on a suitable literary work or selection, we try to include a few items on the author's purpose. At this stage this is seldom the author's purpose in the work as a whole but his reason for doing this or that. Why did he start with a fable? Why does he use New York as his first example? Why does he capitalize *Modern* in this sentence but not in that? In a whole series of these tests there may be a total of twenty or thirty items of this sort. Only after the series is complete will the subscores on these specifics be tallied for each student by part-time paraprofessionals—college-educated housewives, teaching interns, or clerks. These paraprofessionals will also use these checklists in tabulating specific kinds of statements or reasons that appear in student essays: for example, in commenting on passages in books, how often does he consider the author's purpose? Of these inferences, how many are reasonable and how many are unreasonable? The totals thus accumulated may not be sufficiently reliable to apply the scaled scores that are explained in the record, and the degree of proficiency may be indicated as H, M, or L—high, middle, or low.

Even so, we may not be able to accumulate sufficient data to record anything at all on some of the specifics in the clusters previously listed. That is all right; we included all the specifics that we thought might eventually yield pay dirt. If some do not, they will be left blank until the record is revised; then they may be deleted. They will not be deleted, however, if we get sufficient evidence to record for some students but not for all. It is expected that some students will exhibit the category of behavior in question by some of these specifics and other students by others.

The ingenuity thus far shown in devising various measures of objectives that are hard to measure should clear us of suspicion that we intend to put down subjective global ratings of these characteristics based on hazy recollections of what the student has done over a period of several weeks. For example, the heading *Democratic behavior* is reminiscent of the old ratings on *citizenship* in which a student was often marked low if he talked in class or left paper on the floor. Such ratings would never be approved by our Evaluation Committee. Instead, one possibility is to look at the voting record of each student. In our small-group meetings a large number of social issues, both present and past, are discussed and debated in the course of each year: for example, should Julius Caesar cross the Rubicon or not? Why? At the close of as many of these discussions as possible, we hope to have each participant indicate the alternative he favors and add a short statement of his reasons. After the social studies teachers examine a sample of these responses, they may be able to categorize the decisions favored (cautious, moderate, extreme, etc.) and the reasons (relevant, informed, shrewd, etc. and their opposites), and paraprofessionals may classify the responses of each student in these categories.

After a long series of these votes we may find it possible to draw some conclusions as to the ability of each student to reason well and make wise decisions on social issues. This again is something we have not yet tried and there is no guarantee that it will work; but at least it indicates that we are not thinking in terms of vague global ratings but in terms of specific decisions supported by reasons, recorded by the students themselves. This comes closer to genuine democratic behavior than never leaving paper on the floor, and it is also entirely feasible without an undue expenditure of time.

We intend to go as far as we can in the direction of securing evidence like this on the clusters of behavior that appear in the record, and we shall not worry if we do not succeed in covering all of them. In fact, we have put down more specific behaviors than we can reasonably hope to cover, expecting that the evidence actually secured will include some surprises: good evidence on some behavior that looked hard to measure, little or none on some other behavior that looked easy. We must confess that the evidence to be secured in the last three fields is extremely sketchy because these fields have not yet become involved in the tryout of our Cooperative Evaluation Program. At the end of the coming year, the evidence actually secured may look quite different.

The only other heading that requires an explanation is the last section on *predictions,* which looks suspiciously like overall grades, culminating in a figure on rank in class. It is possible for us to be more hardheaded than this chiefly because we have good statistical support provided by our outside consultant on measurement. He can have all the achievement data for each student punched on IBM cards, followed at a later date by similar achievement data secured in grades 10-11-12. Then a computer will correlate everything with everything else, which will enable him to set up regression equations that will indicate which of these measures in combination best predict future achievement in the same field, and the relative weight to be given to each measure. Once this is done by refined statistical procedures in this one school district, far simpler procedures can be recommended to other school districts that have comparable student populations. In this way we can regain the old-fashioned simplicity of single course grades (for purposes and situations in which such simplicity is essential) but on a level that is infinitely more sophisticated.

Q. E. D.

And so we come to the end of our venture. To be sure, we have only scratched the surface, and most of the hard developmental work remains to be done. But if our sense of direction is valid, that work can be done; for the schools have constantly increasing resources of sophisticated personnel and tools such as computers, and complexities which only a few years ago looked utterly unmanageable will soon be easy to handle.

What we believe we have demonstrated is that schools do not now need to settle for educationally inadequate and damaging systems of evaluation because of the inevitable question, "What are you going to do about college entrance requirements?" Any sensible reading of the categories of data which the experimental junior high schools feel they will have ready in a few years must show that the senior high schools, in their turn, can provide colleges far more significant data than they have ever provided—and do it without jeopardizing their own educational programs. Of course, it will take time for schools and colleges to negotiate and organize new ways of communicating. But there need be no doubt that college admissions officers will value the kinds of data that can be supplied them in the proposed system more highly than they do the information they now receive. Schools will not need to carry on with their endless preoccupation with marking and grading and the granting of credits just because some college someday will wish to see the result.

And, with that burden off our backs, what can we not do! In the quiet world of the learner and the teacher we can build an open communication based on clear and thoughtful perceptions unpressured by external considerations. We can release the pupil's energy into purposeful learning and the teacher's energy into helping. In the larger world of the school system we can set streams of meaningful data flowing freely to all who need them so that every decision can be based upon significant evidence. The ultimate purpose of the whole process of evaluation is to provide feedback to guide every person who needs to learn and every person who needs to assist learning.

Appendix A:

National Assessment

*Jack R. Frymier**

T HE 1960s will probably be remembered as turbulent times in American education. All over the country school people have worked in an unprecedented manner to master the intricacies of modern curricula, school desegregation, and federal involvement in education. National assessment of education has recently become another area of genuine concern.

What is national assessment? Who is advocating the idea? What has happened to date? What are the implications of such an effort for children? For parents? For school boards? For the public at large? The purpose of this paper is to explore some of these questions in overview form.

The Basic Idea

Assessing the operation has for years been a part of educational practice. In a sense, assessment might be likened to navigation: it enables those concerned to find out where they are and how far and in what direction they need to go. As an aspect of the educational effort, it presumes that the goal desired is clear and the means for attaining that goal available.

The notion of "national assessment" is a natural and logical extension by Ralph Tyler of his own basic ideas about evaluation and the instructional program in a school to assessment and education in America. As Chairman of the Exploratory Committee on Assessing the Progress of Education, Tyler has evidenced a singleness of purpose in this Carnegie Foundation-sponsored project. Those familiar with Tyler's

*The author is indebted to Horace C. Hawn for his assistance on this project.

earlier writings on curriculum [1] and instruction [2] recognize this development as a geographical rather than conceptual expansion; a change in form rather than substance. Tyler says it this way:

The most frequent use of evaluation is to appraise the achievement of individual students. . . . A second use of evaluation is to diagnose the learning difficulties of an individual student or an entire class to provide information helpful in planning subsequent teaching. A third use of evaluation is to appraise the educational effectiveness of a curriculum or part of a curriculum, of instructional materials and procedures, and of administrative and organizational arrangements. . . . There is a fourth use which is to assess the educational progress of large populations in order to provide the public with dependable information to help in the understanding of educational problems and needs and to guide in efforts to develop sound policy regarding education.[3]

At another point he states:

Because education has become the servant of all our purposes, its effectiveness is of general public concern. The educational tasks now faced require many more resources than have thus far been available, and they must be wisely used to produce maximum results. To make these decisions, dependable information about the progress of education is essential, otherwise we scatter our efforts too widely and fail to achieve our goals. Yet we do not now have the necessary comprehensive and dependable data. We have reports on numbers of schools, buildings, teachers, and pupils, and about the moneys expended, but we do not have sound and adequate information on educational results. Because dependable data are not available, personal views, distorted reports, and journalistic impressions are the sources of public opinion and the schools are frequently attacked and frequently defended without having necessary evidence to support either claim. This situation will be corrected only by a careful, consistent effort to obtain valid data to provide sound evidence about the progress of American education.[4]

Throughout these and other papers [5, 6, 7] Tyler makes three central

[1] Ralph W. Tyler. *Basic Principles of Curriculum and Instruction.* Chicago: The University of Chicago Press, 1950.

[2] Ralph W. Tyler. "The Functions of Measurement in Improving Instruction." In: *Educational Measurement.* E. F. Lindquist, editor. Washington, D.C.: American Council on Education, 1951. p. 47-67.

[3] Ralph W. Tyler. "The Objectives and Plans for a National Assessment of Educational Progress." *Journal of Educational Measurement* 3: 1; Spring 1966.

[4] *Ibid.,* p. 2.

[5] Ralph W. Tyler. "A Program of National Assessment." In: *National Educational Assessment: Pro and Con.* Washington, D.C.: National Education Association and American Association of School Administrators, 1966.

[6] Ralph W. Tyler. "Assessing Educational Progress." *School Boards,* December 1965.

[7] Ralph W. Tyler. "Let's Clear the Air on Assessing Education." *Nation's Schools* 77 (2): 68-70. Reprinted, with permission, from *Nation's Schools,* February, 1966. Copyright 1966, McGraw-Hill Book Company, Inc., Chicago. All rights reserved.

points: education is a *national* rather than a state or local problem; there must be *"good data"* available; and these data are primarily for *public* rather than professional use.

These same points were emphasized by the Carnegie Corporation, sponsor of the national assessment program, in its own publication.

There was general agreement [within the group discussing the question] that a national assessment would be valuable. For one thing, it is presumably better to know more rather than less about anything, particularly the way we are educating our children. Knowing more would put us in a much better position to make intelligent decisions about the allocation of resources and efforts. From a practical point of view, it is not realistic to expect the national and state legislatures to appropriate increasing amounts of money for a variety of educational programs if they can never find out what the pay-off is.[8]

Operationally, national assessment would reflect three concepts which differ from conventional evaluative efforts: test "items" would not be predicated upon a differentiating base; sampling procedures would be employed; and data would be reported in non-technical form. Ebel[9] raised very pointed questions about these concepts, but the basic approach apparently remains as follows:

In assessing the progress of education, no individual pupil, classroom, or school shows up at all. Instead, a report would indicate that 90 per cent (nearly all) thirteen-year-old children can comprehend reading paragraphs like these, can solve arithmetic problems like these, can sing songs like these, have citizenship habits like these, and so on. Examples are given of the achievements rather than relative scores. Similarly, the achievements characteristic of 50 per cent of the thirteen-year-old children would be explained and those characteristic of only about 10 per cent of the age group. Reports of this sort are planned for four age groups—nine, thirteen, seventeen, and adult. Samples of children, youth, and adults carefully chosen to represent geographic areas; socioeconomic levels; and rural, urban, central city, and suburban populations would provide data without anyone or any classroom taking full assessment battery or getting a score or report from it.[10]

The Steps Toward Assessment

Innovation in education presumes change over time. National assessment represents a major kind of educational innovation. As such, the evolution from idea to reality can be traced along a time line, if enough facts are known. From the data presently available, five steps toward

[8] Carnegie Corporation of New York. "The Gross Educational Product: How Much Are Students Learning?" *Carnegie Quarterly* 14: 2; Spring 1966.

[9] Robert L. Ebel. "Some Measurement Problems in a National Assessment of Educational Progress." *Journal of Educational Measurement* 3: 11-17; Spring 1966.

[10] Ralph W. Tyler. "Assessing the Progress of Education." *Phi Delta Kappan* 47 (1): 14; September 1965.

national assessment have apparently occurred: a committee was formed, several conferences were held, contracts for instruments were let, efforts to calm fears were undertaken, and plans for tryouts were made. Without doubt other steps have been taken in very recent months to extend the notion toward implementation in American education. In the section which follows, a brief elaboration of these various efforts is described.

Forming a Committee: Tyler reports [11] that in the summer of 1963 several educational leaders asked him to prepare a memorandum on the possibility of assessing the progress of education. "This memorandum was the subject of discussion in December, 1963, by a conference of educational measurement people [and] . . . In January, 1964, a conference of national educational leaders reviewed the memorandum." [12]

Following this, Carnegie Corporation appointed an Exploratory Committee on Assessing the Progress of Education, and Tyler was asked to serve as chairman.[13] This committee met first during August 1964, and planned a series of conferences to be held with school administrators and persons directly concerned with school problems.

Conferences Held: Between September 12, 1964 and October 28, 1964, five conferences were held with superintendents and administrators in Dallas and New York [14]; and on January 5, 1965, a conference was held in Chicago with school board personnel.[15] Participants received a memorandum [16] and correspondence outlining the nature of the meetings and the proposed national assessment plans before the sessions. Throughout all of these communications an unusual blend of private foundation participation and federal government concern was evident. For instance, in a mimeographed letter to conference participants dated October 1964, Stephen Withey, Staff Director for the Exploratory Committee on Assessing the Progress of Education wrote:

> One of the statutes setting up the United States Office of Education states that the office be informed and report on the state of education in the nation. The Office of the Commissioner of Education is interested in filling this requirement far more fully than has been true in the past. As a preliminary step, the Carnegie Foundation has organized and financed an exploratory committee to consider the values and disadvantages in assessing the progress of education in the various contexts and settings found across the nation.[17]

[11] *Ibid.,* p. 15.

[12] *Ibid.*

[13] *Ibid.*

[14] Ralph W. Tyler. "Summary of Conferences with Superintendents and Administrators." Mimeographed. 67 p.

[15] Ralph W. Tyler. "Summary of Conferences with School Board Personnel." Mimeographed. 10 p.

[16] "Summary Memorandum." Mimeographed. 13 p.

[17] Correspondence to members of the conference.

The memorandum itself included these points:

The administration and analysis of the assessment and the reporting of results to be put into the hands of the Office of Education through preliminary developmental administration would be under contracted research auspices. . . . *Initial* reporting would not be by political units smaller than the state.[18]

Contracting for Tests: In February 1965, a seminar involving the major test constructing agencies was held.[19] In April 1965, these agencies submitted proposals to the Exploratory Committee,[20] and by April 20, 1965, contracts were awarded.[21] The Committee

. . . contracted for initial instrument development work in the areas of reading and writing, mathematics, science, social studies, citizenship, vocational education, and literature and the fine arts. These contracts were made with the American Institutes for Research, Educational Testing Service, The Psychological Corporation, and Science Research Associates. In five of the areas, contracts were made with two agencies to get two different approaches. These initial contracts called for the agencies to work with scholars and teachers to identify objectives considered authentic to the discipline by the scholars in that area and objectives that the schools are actually seeking to obtain as of 1965. . . . The sets of objectives developed were reported to the Committee the first part of November.[22]

Following this, various individuals and associations interested in education were contacted, and beginning November 28, 1965, a series of four regional conferences was held throughout the country. "Each group reviewed all fifteen sets of objectives under the chairmanship of one of its members." [23]

Panels were asked to judge each objective in terms of the questions: "Is this something important for people to learn today? Is it something I would like to have my children learn?" . . . Following the fourth regional conference, the chairmen from the eleven panels were brought to New York to pool and discuss the reactions and suggestions of their individual panels. . . . most of the objectives developed by the agencies in their work with scholars and teachers were accepted as desirable for American youth by these laymen.[24] There were recommendations for reworking and rewording some of the objectives and these were taken back to the contractors for reconsideration by their scholar-teacher consulting groups.

[18] "Summary Memorandum." p. 5.

[19] Tyler, "Assessing the Progress of Education," p. 15.

[20] "A National Assessment of Educational Progress." Mimeographed. April 23, 1965. 4 p.

[21] *Ibid.*

[22] Jack C. Merwin. "The Progress of Exploration Toward a National Assessment of Educational Progress." *Journal of Educational Measurement* 3: 7; Spring 1966.

[23] *Ibid.*

[24] *Ibid.,* p. 8.

Calming the Fears: From the outset, the Exploratory Committee seems to have encountered mixed reactions from persons confronted with both the possibility and the probability of a national assessment effort. The proposition was interesting, even fascinating, but to many it "sounded" like a national testing program leading to a national curriculum. The Exploratory Committee, and particularly Tyler, began to communicate extensively with various groups and through different publications to allay the fears.[25] For example, these statements appeared:

There is some misunderstanding. . . . Several common fears are expressed by those who think of the assessment project as a National Testing Program. . . . A second fear is that such an assessment enables the Federal Government to control the curriculum. This is also a misunderstanding.[26]

It has encountered some difficulties in getting understanding.[27]

The two questions that Superintendent Minear has raised are both questions that are highly hypothetical; namely, the possible connection later that the federal government might have with this. Actually, I don't see any necessary connection. Our work has been entirely in the private sector.[28]

A good deal of public confusion has been encountered. The project is being confused with a nation-wide individual testing program. . . . A second fear is that such an assessment enables the Federal Government to control the curriculum. This is also a misunderstanding.[29]

Plans for Tryouts: Although the questions have been continuous, plans to implement a national assessment program have moved steadily forward. Instrument tryouts were set for fall, 1966, and Tyler stated that the Exploratory Committee "would hope to have the material ready for the first national assessment in the fall of 1967." [30]

Assessing the Assessment Effort

Any look at a proposal with consequences as far-reaching as "national assessment" generates questions regarding both the concept and its implications. Some which deserve consideration are described below.

[25] Tyler, "Assessing the Progress of Education." p. 14.

[26] Tyler, "Assessing Educational Progress."

[27] Tyler, "Let's Clear the Air on Assessing Education." p. 70.

[28] National Education Association and American Association of School Administrators. "Panel Discussion on a Program of National Assessment." In: *National Educational Assessment: Pro and Con.* Washington, D.C.: the Associations, 1966. p. 25.

[29] Tyler, "The Objectives and Plans for a National Assessment of Educational Progress." p. 2-3.

[30] Ralph W. Tyler. "Answers to Inquiries." In: *National Educational Assessment: Pro and Con.* Washington, D.C.: National Education Association and American Association of School Administrators. 1966. p. 33.

What Is the Rationale Underlying the Adoption Process? The process by which "national assessment" has come into being seems unconventional if not unorthodox. Why have so few persons participated in either the development or the implementation of the idea? It would appear that not more than a hundred or so persons, at most, have had any real opportunity to do more than simply *react* to the basic concept, which appears to have undergone little change from its initial form. Many persons have *reacted,* to be sure, and others have been *contracted* with to accomplish a particular chore, but there seem to have been only limited opportunities for concerned persons to affect the conceptualizations which are involved.

These limitations seem to have arisen in part because the pace of those who spearheaded the movement was exceptionally fast. For example, a review of the chronology of "national assessment" events indicates that from the time Tyler was first approached (Summer 1963) until the scheduled date for operationalizing the concept (Fall 1967) will require about four years. And if the notion emerges on the educational scene in September 1967, it will not appear in trial form but actually full-blown. Depending upon one's own personal sense of values and urgency, four years may seem "about right," "too fast," or "too slow," but in comparison with other educational innovations, this will be one of the most rapid changes which ever occurred in American education.

The adoption of language laboratories or the PSSC (Physical Science Study Committee) physics program has moved to the point that approximately 50 percent of the American high schools have incorporated these changes into their program over an eight- or ten-year period of time. Acceptance of the provisions of the National Defense Education Act of 1958 and the Elementary and Secondary Education Act of 1965 proceeded much more rapidly than that, of course, but the educational community has generally been reluctant to move too far too fast. The point is, considering the magnitude of the proposition and the potential consequences which might ensue, moving from the formation of an Exploratory Committee to five small group meetings to conferences with test developers to contracts with those same companies in less than eight months seems unnecessarily fast.

If the idea is so important and if it is appropriate and sound, certainly a more extensive involvement and somewhat slower pace would assure a more adequate understanding and more complete acceptance of the proposition as a necessary and desirable kind of educational change.

In analyzing the content of Tyler's and other Exploratory Committee members' responses to questions, furthermore, one gets a real feeling of "sameness" and "inflexibility" throughout. There appears to be a continuous effort to convince the unknowing. Almost never does the critic appear to have been *heard*. It is as if the questions which have been raised were listened to and answered, but not really comprehended or seriously considered at all.

Furthermore, even though the proponents of national assessment made little effort to solicit the thinking of interested persons or to communicate with the profession at large in any meaningful way until the idea had crystallized out in final form, even when they did begin to share their thinking it generally appeared in one basic form. Most of the published statements contain either identical or very similar phraseology and illustrations. It is as if there is only *one* idea and that professional dialogue has not pressed the advocates to use new illustrations or to examine the basic assumptions upon which it is based. All things considered, the involvement and pacing and persistence which have been apparent force one to raise questions regarding the basic rationale underlying the entire adoption process.

What Are the Central Purposes of National Assessment? No aspect of the "national assessment" notion has produced as much furore as that which relates to questions about control. Two basic factors make these questions especially crucial. One concerns the conflicting evidence about control, and the other involves the fact that assessment results will be beamed at lay policy makers rather than professional educators. The heart of the concern, of course, involves the question of possible increases in federal control. For example, Keppel said:

> Because I believe that the theory and technology of statistical sampling have developed to a point where they can facilitate educational assessment, as U.S. Commissioner of Education I encouraged the Carnegie Foundation of New York, with private funds, to explore the matter.[31]

In the "Summary Memorandum" distributed to conference participants during the early stages of the Exploratory Committee's work, these statements appear:

> A Presidential Commission of 19-25 members be appointed to oversee the assessment program, although it might start under private auspices.

> The administration and analysis of the assessment and the reporting of results to be put in the hands of the Office of Education. . . .[32]

Yet Tyler himself maintains:

> The two questions . . . raised are both questions that are highly hypotheti-

---

[31] Francis Keppel. "National Educational Assessment: We Badly Need It." In: *National Educational Assessment: Pro and Con.* Washington, D.C.: National Education Association and American Association of School Administrators, 1966. p. 6.

[32] "Summary Memorandum," p. 5.

cal; namely the possible connection later that the federal government might have with this. Actually I don't see any necessary connection.[33]

The Carnegie newsletter stated

As for federal control, while it does not exist, no sensible person would hold that there is not considerable national and state *influence* over education.[34]

One cannot help but wonder if the problem is more fundamental than semantics.

Suppose, however, that the federal government never exerted any measure of control, but that assessment was completely under the influence and direction of a private corporation such as the Carnegie Foundation. Is it reasonable to presume that such a group, which has *no* direct responsibility to the general public, should be entrusted with such an undertaking? Hand outlines the problem this way:

I wish I had the space to justify the assertion that of two kinds of centralized control over public schools, one (centralized control by a private body or bodies in no way legally responsible to the public) is vastly more undesirable than the other (federal control by legally responsible bodies).[35]

Considering these points, and the fact that the "Educational Compact" idea (a confederation of various states and their governors into a working unit dealing with educational problems) has also been supported by the Carnegie Foundation, the interrelationships of private and public sectors blur. When one adds the fact that the president of the Carnegie Foundation is currently serving as Secretary of Health, Education, and Welfare to the idea that assessment data collected by this private foundation will be made available primarily to policy making lay bodies, the result is naturally disturbing to professional educators who spend their lives in schools working to help children learn.

Educators are not about to forget the fact that policy making in education is rightfully a non-professional role, but neither will they ignore the responsibility inherent in the fact that they are the only group which regularly works at the business of maximizing young people's opportunities to learn in school. School boards, state legislatures, and the Congress have been notoriously negligent in their responsibilities in previous years. One might argue that having meaningful assessment data will enable them to make more intelligent decisions about educational policy than before. That may very well be true. The questions regarding purposes of "national assessment," however, still remain. American

[33] *National Educational Assessment: Pro and Con, op. cit.*, p. 25.

[34] *Carnegie Quarterly, op. cit.*, p. 4.

[35] Harold C. Hand. "National Assessment Viewed as the Camel's Nose." *Phi Delta Kappan* 47 (1): 13; September 1965.

education has been saddled with the "Carnegie unit" for more decades than one likes to name. The reservations regarding *stated* purposes and the concerns about *actual* purposes are both legitimate and real.

Must Content Be the Focus of Assessment? Tyler's own theory of curriculum development presumes that educational purposes should be derived from a study of the learners, from a study of contemporary life outside the school, from subject specialists, from philosophy, and from psychology.[36] In the "national assessment" effort, however, the subject area is the only focal point of concern. Contracts for identifying objectives and devising procedures for assessing objectives were granted by subject matter areas.

A look at any of the many statements of educational purposes in America in the last half century (e.g., *The Cardinal Principles of Secondary Education, The Purposes of Education in American Democracy, Education for All American Youth, The Central Purpose of American Education*) points up the fact that these are always *general* objectives which are actually content-free. In theoretical terms, subject matter content is typically considered a means to an end rather than an end in its own right, and educational objectives should proceed from general to specific in such a way that this means-end relationship can be maintained. To *start with* subject matter areas in terms of instrument development, therefore, raises questions about the legitimacy and appropriateness of objectives which will be identified.

But the distinction is actually more subtle than has been implied. One can begin with content and devise testing instruments which assess critical thinking or creativity or motivation. The question is: will this occur? Critical thinking and creativity and motivation are generally considered worthwhile educational goals, yet most persons would agree that today our schools are less effective in attaining these objectives than they are in imparting information and developing subject matter competence. The central question here is: Will this kind of "national assessment," which is being built upon a subject matter base, increase or decrease the possibility of attaining a variety of important educational goals? Will "national assessment" further the notion of pluralism and diversity among our people, long held to be a noble and legitimate social end, or will it compound the concern of all for purely subject matter ends?

In summary, the idea of "national assessment" is not quite four years old. It is predicated upon the possibility of testing a few scattered persons around the country with newly developed instruments to produce new kinds of data about the educational attainments which policy

---

[36] Tyler. *Basic Principles of Curriculum and Instruction, loc. cit.*, Chapter II

making groups might use. The idea is exciting in that it outlines a whole new kind of educational feedback. It is frightening in that it is fraught with very real possibilities for undesirable purposes and influence and control.

The questions which arise are tough but real. Should assessment be primarily a national or state or local concern? Can we contrive ways of using assessment data creatively and effectively to assure increasing opportunities for young people to learn? Can we examine the basic assumptions upon which both "national assessment" and "education" rest, then use all of the talents of all of the people to preserve the best of the old while incorporating the best of the new for ever better schools?

Appendix B:

Pinhead Statistics

Paul B. Diederich

THIS appendix has been described as "the amount of statistics that can be inscribed on the head of a pin and understood by a head of the same dimensions." It explains just four statistical concepts and procedures: correlation, reliability, the significance of differences, and scaled scores. All of these can be computed in three to five minutes by short-cut procedures that would not puzzle an eighth grader. They are not as precise as the methods used by professional testmakers but precise enough for the purposes indicated in the last three chapters and as precise as the data from classroom tests, ratings, and the like will ordinarily warrant.

Correlation

Let us start with *correlation* because it is not only useful in its own right but is also the most generally acceptable way of computing the *reliability* of measures—especially those that are not objective test scores—and of understanding what reliability means.

A correlation is a decimal representing the amount of agreement between two measures of the same students. The last phrase is very important because the most common error teachers make in regard to correlation is to speak of correlating the boys with the girls or the first period class with the second period class. It simply cannot be done. Whenever you apply the same measure to two different groups of students, the term you want is *comparison*. You can compare the boys with the girls or the first period class with the second period class, and you ordinarily do so by comparing their averages. There is no possible way to correlate them.

To be sure that you are on the right track, always start with a single list of students' names, each of which has two measures after it that you propose to correlate. These measures need not be of the same thing or on anything like the same scale. You can correlate height (in inches) with weight (in pounds), and it may set a standard of comparison to remember that the usual correlation between height and weight—among adults of the same sex—is about .5. That is, tall people tend to weigh more than short people, but the correlation is far from perfect because some are tall and thin while others are short and fat. People who attack tests sneer at a correlation this low, but remember that it is good enough for you to get worried if you are really far from the average weight for your height.

It may also help you to remember that the correlation between the grades given to the same set of essays by two different readers who have had some practice in grading by common standards is often about .5. This amount of agreement on anything as complex as writing ability is creditable. If the readers have had no previous experience with this double grading of unidentified papers, and if they write nothing on any paper that is likely to influence the judgment of the second reader, the correlation between their grades is likely to be between .3 and .4 —which is just a little better than chance.

Most correlations that you see in print are computed by the "product-moment" method, which is too complicated for our purposes. It would take you at least three hours to learn how to compute it, and after you knew how, it would take about half an hour to compute one such correlation for a class of average size—unless you had a desk calculator and considerable skill in using it. Fortunately there is another method called "tetrachoric correlation" that yields a fair approximation of the result that you would get by the more laborious method. A tetrachoric correlation between two measures means approximately the same thing as a product-moment correlation and usually rounds to the same number if the computation is carried only to the nearest tenth. The tetrachoric is simply less precise, and for that reason we prefer to state it only to the nearest tenth whenever that is feasible.

How do you compute it? First, you find the middle score on each measure. This is done by tallying the scores in a list of all possible scores and counting down to the middle tally, or by arranging the papers in the order of their scores and counting down to the middle paper.

Second, you put a check after each score on the first measure that stands above its middle score; that is, you check all scores that stand in the top half of the class on this measure. When you count these checks, you may find that you need two more students who stand at the middle score to take in exactly half the class. It is not fair to pick students who will do your correlation the most good—i.e., those who also stand in the top half on the other measure. You must pick them at random. Since their names are usually arranged in alphabetical order, check the first two students with middle scores that you come to in this order.

Third, repeat this process with the second measure: put a check after all scores that stand above its middle score. This time you may find that you need one more student with a middle score to take in exactly half of the class. Check the first one that you come to in alphabetical order.

Suppose the class has an odd number of students like 33: how do you take in exactly half this number? There are more exact ways of handling this problem, but all we are going to get is an approximation; hence the simplest thing to do is to get rid of that extra student before you start checking. It will not make much difference in the correlation if you cross out the first student with a middle score on the first measure. Then you need check just 16 scores on the first measure that stand above or at its middle score; also 16 scores on the second measure that stand above or at its middle score.

Fourth, count the number of students who have two checks after their names—those who stand in the top half of the class on both measures that you are correlating. Let us suppose that there were 13 such students.

Fifth, reduce this number to a percent of the class by dividing by the total number of students for whom you have both scores—minus the one you left out to make even halves. In this case, divide 13 by 32. It is easy to go wrong at this point by dividing by 16 because thus far you have been concentrating on half the class. But here we do not want the percent of the half-class; we want the percent of the whole class who stood in the top half on both measures. Hence you divide 13 by 32, and it comes out to about 40 percent. Actually it rounds to 41 percent, but 40 percent is the nearest number in the table below. You look for this percent (or the one nearest it) in the table below and read off the corresponding tetrachoric correlation:

Percent in top half on both:	25	27	29	31	33	35	37	40	43
Tetrachoric correlation:	.00	.13	.25	.37	.5	.6	.7	.8	.9

Thus we find that the correlation between these two measures is approximately .8. If you computed it by the product-moment method, it would probably come out between .75 and .84 and hence would round to .8 as the nearest tenth—unless it was close to a borderline to begin with. Then the more exact figure might round to either .7 or .9—but so what? With just 33 cases either figure has a big wobble in it, and all you need to know is that this correlation is high. For ordinary classroom purposes the tetrachoric will come close enough to the exact figure to serve. Of course, if you are doing a controlled experiment, you will need greater precision than this, but then you are likely to have someone handy who knows how to compute product-moment correlations and who will run them off for you on his desk calculator.

Elementary courses in measurement stress the point that correlation never proves causation. It means only that a high amount of one thing is usually associated with a high amount of another; it does not say that the first caused the second or vice versa. Very often the two things are associated by way of some third variable. For example, suppose you had some very good measures of writing ability—a lot of essays rated by a lot of good judges—and you looked through these students' scores on other tests to find which had the highest correlations with the scores on writing. You might find that the highest correlation was with a simple test of vocabulary, and you might conclude that if you could double each student's active vocabulary, you could bring about a vast improvement in his writing. While stranger things than this have happened, you should be aware of the fact that a simple test of vocabulary is one of the best indicators of verbal aptitude or "general brightness." The brighter students just naturally pick up more words —as they pick up more of almost everything else. They also tend to write better than the less bright, since it takes a high order of intelligence to write well. Hence if you take a dull child and merely double the number of words that he knows how to use, you may not improve his writing at all. He may just acquire the habit of using a long word when a shorter word would serve his purpose better, and he would be marked down for it by a discerning reader. Hence you must be wary of believing that a high correlation between any two things in education proves that one causes the other. They may both be effects of the same cause, which is out of sight.

On the other hand, low correlations between reliable measures of different traits or abilities can practically *disprove* causation—especially if such findings have been found repeatedly by different investigators in different circumstances. For example, all sorts of people have been trying for at least fifty years to prove that knowledge of and ability to apply this or that brand of grammar will improve writing. They teach this brand of grammar for a year or more and get a reliable measure of how much of it each student has learned and is able to apply. At the end of this time they also collect several samples of each student's writing and have these rated by good judges who know nothing about the results of the grammar test. In the more sophisticated experiments they have papers on the same topics written at the beginning and end of the experiment and have them rated by judges who do not know which papers are initial and which are final. In the first case they have data on status as a writer at the end of the experiment; in the second they have data on growth during the experiment; but in both cases the correlation of writing ability with mastery of any brand of grammar is usually of the order of .3. This result has turned up so many times in this country and in Great Britain and Canada that the conclusion is inescapable that grammar simply does not improve writing. If it did, those who know more of it would write better than those who know less, but no consistent tendency in that direction has been found by competent investigators.

Correlations have many other uses that ingenious teachers will discover for themselves. For example, when one has a teaching problem, correlations provide one way of finding out what other skills, characteristics, and background items are related to the problem; also the degree of their relatedness. They can also show which measures are so closely related to one another that one is practically wasted and should yield its place to some other measure.

One situation in which tetrachoric correlations are almost meaningless is that in which one measure is a grade on the usual A-B-C-D-F scale without plus or minus signs. Then almost half the students will get the middle grade of C, and checking C's at random until one takes in half the number of students introduces too large an element of chance into this procedure. It is all right to use ratings, but try to get these spread out over a much wider range of numerical scores. For example, Chapter 7 on "Cooperative Evaluation in English" presents a rating scheme for test papers designed to reveal writing ability. It calls for ratings on a five-point scale on eight components of writing ability, and two of these get double weight. Hence the lowest possible total from one rater is 10; the highest possible is 50; and a student who is average in everything gets a total of 30. There are never enough scores of 30 to create any difficulty with this method of computing correlations between the ratings of different readers.

Reliability

Reliability is basically a special case of correlation. We have seen that a correlation need not involve measures of the same thing: height may be correlated with weight. But when two measures try to get at the same ability (for example, two independent ratings of the same set of essays), the correlation between them is the reliability of one measure—in this case, one rating. If you are going to use the sum or average of the two as the measure of record, the reliability is twice the correlation divided by one plus the correlation. For example, if the correlation between the two sets of ratings is .5, the reliability of the sum or average of the two is:

$$\frac{\text{Twice the correlation}}{\text{One plus the correlation}} = \frac{2 \times .5}{1 + .5} = \frac{1.0}{1.5} = \frac{10}{15} = \frac{2}{3} = .66$$

This is called the Spearman-Brown Prophecy Formula. It can also prophesy the reliability of any number of ratings of the same sort. For example, we have recommended four test essays per year each rated twice: in other words, eight ratings on writing ability per year. If the correlation between each pair of ratings continues at the initial level of .5, the reliability of the sum or average of the eight ratings will be:

$$\frac{8 \times \text{correlation}}{1 + (7 \times \text{correlation})} = \frac{8 \times .5}{1 + (7 \times .5)} = \frac{4.0}{1 + 3.5} = \frac{4.0}{4.5} = .89$$

Stated more generally, the reliability of the sum or average of X measures of the same sort is X times the reliability of one measure divided by one plus (X—1) times the reliability of that measure.

Reliability is usually thought of as the correlation between two measures of the same sort, taken at about the same time, that try to measure the same ability or characteristic. Obviously you will have more confidence in your measure if you measure the same thing twice and get about the same result both times. Reliability thus refers to the consistency or stability of measures and should not be thought of as the trustworthiness or general goodness of the measures. For example, some English teachers who are distressed by the unreliability of essay grades on writing ability resort to counting the number of errors per 100 words in usage, punctuation, and spelling. This yields a much more stable or reliable measure than ratings on general merit, but it does not follow that it is a better measure of writing ability than such ratings. On the contrary, it restricts the attention of both the teacher and the student to mechanics and leaves out far more important elements of good writing such as ideas, organization, wording, and flavor.

If the students know that they will be measured in this fashion, they will lose interest in practicing writing and bone up on workbook exercises in mechanics. Ten hours spent in this fashion will produce greater improvement in the scores awarded by that teacher than one hundred hours spent in writing essays. But in the end they are unlikely to write anything worth reading because their attention will be concentrated exclusively on the avoidance of mechanical errors. They will also be disinclined to take chances. If they are not sure that they know how to use a semicolon, for example, they will avoid it and substitute the familiar comma with *and*. Hence a narrow concentration on the reliability of measures without sufficient regard to what they measure may sometimes be a deterrent to learning what is most worth learning. But if we give priority to the measurement of important things, we must still do our best to measure them reliably. If the measures wobble all over the place, we cannot be sure that students are actually improving, and we shall not be able to find out that some ways of helping them work better than other ways.

The reliability of objective tests in which all items have equal weight can be estimated from the "internal consistency" of any one test. You can see why if you take the earliest form of such estimates: correlating scores on odd-numbered items with scores on even-numbered items. The correlation is the reliability of half the test, and it can be stepped up to the reliability of the whole test by the Spearman-Brown Formula given above. This is called the "split-half" method of estimating reliability, and occasionally it is still used. A much easier and quicker method is known as K-R 21, meaning "Kuder-Richardson Formula 21." The reliability by this formula depends on just three quantities: the mean (average score on the test), the number of items, and the standard deviation (a measure of how far the scores spread out). You already have the first two. The third can be a bit tricky to compute, but here is a shortcut suggested by W. L. Jenkins of Lehigh University:

$$\text{Standard deviation (s)} \; = \; \frac{\text{Top sixth—bottom sixth (of scores)}}{\text{Half the number of students}}$$

This is easy to compute because one does not even have to add all the scores; only the top sixth and the bottom sixth, which is usually quite a small number. So small, in fact, that one has to take the formula quite literally. Suppose there are just 28 students. A sixth of 28 is 4⅔. Hence you must add together the first four scores and two-thirds of the fifth. Suppose the top five scores are 98, 92, 87, 85, and 82. Two-thirds of 82 is 54⅔ or (rounding to the nearest whole number) 55. The sum of these five scores is 417. Then suppose the bottom five scores are 21, 26, 30, 35, and 37. Two-thirds of 37 is 24⅔ or, rounding again, 25. The sum of these five scores is 137. The standard deviation is 417—137, which equals 280, divided by half the number of students, which is 14. The quotient is 20—exactly what you get by computing the standard deviation in orthodox fashion.

Now let us return to K-R 21 with confidence that you can get the standard deviation in about two minutes and you already know the other two quantities, the mean and the number of items, that you need.

$$\text{K-R 21} \; = \; 1 \; - \; \frac{M(n-M)}{ns^2} \qquad \text{in which M = mean; n = number of items;} \; s^2 = \text{square of the standard deviation.}$$

Suppose there are 100 items; the mean (average score) is 60; the standard deviation (as computed above) is 20, and the square of 20 is 400. Then,

$$\text{K-R 21} = 1 - \frac{60 \times 40}{100 \times 400} = 1 - \frac{2,400}{40,000} = 1 - \frac{6}{100} = .94$$

The tricky thing to remember is to subtract from one in the end, because your attention will be concentrated on manipulating the large numbers in the fraction. When you find that it reduces to .06, your first tendency is to regard this as the reliability of the test—which would be terrible. It is not; this is just a conservative estimate of the "sampling error." The reliability is one minus this quantity, .94, which is very high indeed. Few standardized tests could approach this reliability in a group as small as 28 students. About the only test that could do it would be a vocabulary test peaked at exactly the right level of difficulty, which is what we have assumed here. Most of the good, usable tests and other instruments worked out by the writer's students have reliabilities between .6 and .8 in the relatively small groups in which they are tried out. With an unconventional instrument or procedure it is unusual to get even as high as .6. Then the thing to do is to secure additional measures of the same sort until the cumulative total for the year hits a reliability of .8 or better. A formula for estimating the number of additional measures required was given in Chapter 6.

The only cases known to the writer in which the shortcut Jenkins. formula for the standard deviation goes haywire are (a) when most of the measures are near a perfect score (as in a mastery test); (b) when the number of scores is very small; and (c) when the scores are letter grades and there is no way to tell how many stand in the top or bottom sixth. In such cases one has to learn the orthodox method of computing the standard deviation. This is not very difficult, but it does take a bit of time.

The K-R 21 formula shows what quantities it is most important to maximize in an objective test in order to attain high reliability. The most important by far is the standard deviation (how far the scores spread out) because this is the only quantity that gets squared, resulting in a very large number. It is also in the denominator of the error term so that, the larger this number is, the smaller is the fraction that one has to subtract from one. One consequence is that the reliability of an objective test is not a fixed quantity that will remain the same no matter what group it is applied to. It depends most of all on the spread of ability in the group tested. Formerly test publishers reported the reliability for the total group on which norms were secured—a very large number ranging from geniuses to morons —and this gave teachers an exaggerated impression of the reliability of the test when administered to single classes within a school. It was E. F. Lindquist of Iowa State University who first set the pattern of reporting a range of reliabilities for groups of class size.

How does one get a large standard deviation in such groups? The first answer goes contrary to the practice of most teachers. They start with very easy items that almost everyone gets right and work up to very hard items that most students get wrong or omit. Hence the first quarter of the test is nearly wasted because too many students get these items right, and so is the last quarter that too many get wrong or omit. It is only the middle half that really spreads the students out, and that determines the standard deviation. A better policy is to include as many items as possible that about 60 percent of the students get right. In practice it is impossible to attain uniform item-difficulty, but if one tries out a large number of items over the years, one can discard those that more than 30 percent get wrong or more than 90 percent get right. The remainder will average out to about 60 percent correct, which is the optimum number. In a publication like this one cannot cite the large number of studies that support this conclusion, but the evidence is substantial.

A second answer is to perform an item-analysis on important tests and discard items that do not discriminate very well between high-scoring and low-scoring students. The usual way of doing this is laborious, but the writer has found it easy—after the papers are scored—to pass out the top half of the papers to his right and the bottom half to his left. Then he calls out "Item 1," and all students holding a paper that got that item right raise their hands. A counter for the high group reports the number of hands in his section—"Fourteen"—and then the counter for the low group—"Eight." The teacher writes these numbers below that item in his copy of the test, and so do the students on the paper that they are holding. Then they add these two numbers together as an index of success on that item (22 out of 40 got it right). Next they subtract the lows from the highs as the index of discrimination: eight more highs than lows got it right. In a class of forty students, the minimum difference between highs and lows that is acceptable by the standards of testmakers is four students—ten percent of the class. This is approximately equal to a "biserial correlation with total test" of .30. This shows the extent to which those who did better on the test as a whole also did better on this particular item. The higher this index of discrimination is on all items in the test, the larger the standard deviation and hence the reliability.

The second most important quantity to maximize in order to achieve high reliability is the number of items in the test—since the square of the standard deviation gets multiplied by that number and hence further reduces the fraction that one has to subtract from one. This is a point on which the demands of teachers are contradictory. They want high reliability but also tests that they can administer within 40-minute periods. The only way to meet both demands is to resort to factual or skill items in some form that goes very fast so that it is possible to get in about 100 items in 35 minutes of working time. Items calling for deep thought cannot be taken at so fast a clip. Such tests should either be divided into two forms that can be taken on successive days or else—as this yearbook has suggested—cumulative totals on each objective should be carried forward from one test to the next until reliability reaches a satisfactory level—here set at .8.

Why do we want high reliability? Because we shall never find out that one thing works better than another if the measures wobble all over the place. Suppose you were trying out various reducing diets and your bathroom scale told you one morning that you weighed 120 pounds, next that you weighed 180 pounds, next 94 pounds, and so on. You would never find out which reducing diet was best for you. Moreover, if 100 men and 100 women selected at random weighed themselves on this unreliable scale, you might conclude that there was no difference between men and women in average weight—which just is not so. Even if you found a difference, it would be much smaller than the true difference, and probably not enough to meet the exacting standards of "significance" that will be explained in the next section. This is a situation that we frequently encounter in education. For example, almost all experiments on the improvement of writing ability have been vitiated by the fact that the measure of writing ability was not reliable enough to establish a significant difference. As the record now stands, nothing improves writing ability any better than anything else. This is not credible. Hence we must make every effort to increase the reliability of our weaker measurements if we ever hope to find out that some of our materials and procedures work better than others.

The Significance of a Difference between the Averages of Two Groups

Suppose you have taught two "initially equal" groups in different ways. They do not have to be "initially equal" in everything, such as number of siblings, but there must be no significant difference at the start in their means or standard deviations on any abilities or characteristics that are known to affect the outcome. If there is such a difference, you may eliminate it by transferring a few students from one group to the other. If this is not feasible, you can still carry on the experiment if you do not count the scores of the few students who tipped the scale at the start.

Suppose the average score of Group A on the final test is 60; that of Group B is 50. This difference of 10 points in favor of Group A would be enough to settle the average bet, but you notice that the spread of scores around these averages is quite large; hence you wonder whether this difference could have been a fluke (attributable to the wobble in your measure). You can find out whether this difference is "significant"—meaning real, not a chance difference, unlikely to be reversed if you tried it again—in five steps.

1. Find the difference between the two averages. As we have already indicated, 60−50=10 (the difference). In previous explanations we took this step for granted, but people wrote to us asking, "How do I find the difference between the two averages?" Subtract one from the other.

2. Find the standard deviation of each group by the shortcut Jenkins formula explained above. To keep this explanation simple, let us give each group a standard deviation that will make subsequent computations easy. Let us say that the standard deviation of Group A is 18; of group B, 12.

3. Find the "standard error" of each average: the standard deviation divided by the square root of the number of students. Again to keep things simple, let us assume that there were 36 students in each group. The square root of 36 is 6. (If the number does not have an obvious square root, like 42, any math teacher will lend you a table of squares and square roots of numbers from 1 to 1,000.) Here 18 divided by 6 is 3, the standard error of the first average, and 12 divided by 6 is 2, the standard error of the second average. The chances are 2 out of 3 that the average found on this occasion lies within one standard error of the "true" average. The "true" average is a theoretical concept; if you could get it, it would be the average on an infinite number of parallel tests of the same ability under the same conditions without learning anything or forgetting anything. This is impossible, but one can estimate how far the obtained average is likely to vary from it through chance alone.

4. Find the standard error of the difference between the two averages. Think of this difference as a rope tied between two stakes, which are the two averages. If there is wobble in each stake, there is bound to be more wobble in the rope than in either stake, but not exactly the

sum of the two. Square each standard error, add the two squares, and take the square root of the sum. The two standard errors were 3 and 2; their squares are 9 and 4; the sum of these is 13; and the square root of 13 (look it up!) is 3.6. This is the standard error of the difference between the two averages, which was 10 points. This means that the chances are 2 out of 3 that this difference lies within 3.6 points of the "true" difference (if you repeated the experiment *ad infinitum*).

Let us restate this step to clarify it. The standard error of a difference between two measures is the square root of this sum:

(1) the square of the standard error of measure A, plus

(2) the square of the standard error of measure B.

Those who have had a course in elementary statistics may want to add, "Provided these two measures are not correlated." If they are, the formula gets more complicated. But we shall not worry about this because the averages of two different groups on the final test are certainly not correlated.

5. Divide the difference (10 points) by the standard error of this difference (3.6 points) to see how many times larger the difference was than its standard error. In this case 10 divided by 3.6 equals 2.8; hence this difference was 2.8 times as large as its standard error. This number is usually judged against just three levels of "significance":

a. *Not significant* if the difference is less than twice its standard error.

b. *Significant at the .05 level* if the difference is between 2 and 2.6 times as large as its standard error. (Often marked by one asterisk.)

c. *Significant at the .01 level* if the difference is more than 2.6 times as large as its standard error. (Often marked by two asterisks.)

These significant levels indicate the chances in 100 that the difference could have been a fluke: .05 means less than five chances in a hundred; .01 means less than one chance in a hundred—that a difference this large would be found if there had been no true difference.

In less precise but commonsense terms, think of the standard error of a difference as the amount by which it is likely to fluctuate by pure chance. Being cautious, we want a difference between two averages to be at least twice as large as this before we take it seriously. If it is more than 2.6 times as large as this, we can be quite confident that it is real, since there is less than one chance in a hundred that a difference as large as this would turn up by pure chance.

"Significant" does not necessarily mean "important"; it means only "non-chance." If you are testing whole states and have 100,000 cases in each, a difference of a tenth of a grade-point might be significant, but it would have no perceptible social consequences. On the other hand, the difference between passing and failing, while highly important to most students, is usually so small and unreliable that it could hardly ever meet the exacting standards of significance.

This is only one method of computing the significance of differences between averages and other measures. There are many other methods, but most of them are too complicated for teachers to carry out without the assistance of a director of research. This one may be regarded as the "classic" method and the easiest to compute and understand. It also illustrates the basic idea underlying all other methods of computing significance: how far the difference exceeds the fluctuations that may reasonably be attributed to chance; hence the chances in a hundred that a difference this large would be found if there were no true difference.

Perhaps a word should be said about the significance of differences between test scores for individual students. The best general advice is to forget about it. The standard error of individual scores is usually so large that all one can say with confidence is that the top quarter of the class did better than the bottom quarter.

The standard error of individual test scores is:

    0 when the score is zero or perfect;

    1 when it is 1 or 2 points from zero or perfect;

    2 when it is 3 to 7 points from zero or perfect;

    3 when it is 8 to 15 points from zero or perfect.

The standard error of individual test scores beyond these points is:

    3 on tests of up to 47 items;

    4 on tests of 48-89 items;

    5 on tests of 90-109 items;

    6 on tests of 110-129 items;

    7 on tests of 130-150 items.

As before, this means that the chances are 2 out of 3 that the obtained score lies within this many raw-score points of the "true" score. But if you want to find out whether two scores, each having a standard error of 3 points, are significantly different, the quantity you have to use is much larger than 3. It is the standard error of the difference between the two scores, not the standard error of either score. This is computed as in the case of group averages: square each standard error, add the two squares, and take the square root of the sum. Three squared is nine; two nines are eighteen; and the square root of eighteen is about 4.25. Then the difference between these two individual scores is significant only if it is at least twice this amount: namely, 8.5 points. It is significant at the .01 level only if it is more than 2.6 times this amount: namely, 11 points. Not many scores in the usual distribution of scores on a classroom test of 40 to 50 items are that far apart.

Hence it is really out of the question to prove anything in education with single, individual measures. The only hope lies in repeated measurements: either the same measure applied to quite large groups (preferably more than a single class) or more measures of the same sort applied to the same individual at intervals throughout the year until the cumulative total reaches a respectable reliability.

Even so, we cannot shrink from setting cutting points on important measures in order to place them on an understandable common scale. Suppose we decide that a score of 40 (in a test of 50 items) is to be the lower limit for the top group. Someone may point out that the standard error of a score at this point is 3; hence students with scores of 37-39 have at least two chances in three of deserving a top grade. Do we drop the cutting point to 37 to be on the safe side? If we did, students with scores of 34-36 would have an equal right to be included—and so on down to the bottom of the distribution. This same possibility will exist wherever one draws lines across any distribution of test scores.

About all one can say to a student who stands just below a borderline is this: "True, if you had another chance, your score might easily jump three points and put you in the next higher bracket—but it could just as easily jump downward as upward. Meanwhile, this is the score you made on this occasion. It is the best evidence we have of your present status with respect to this objective. On the next test your luck may change, and you may get a score higher than your true ability warrants. Such chances balance out in the course of the year. Since we have to draw the line somewhere between scaled scores of 4 and 5, this time you get a four. We recognize that one component of this score is ability and another is just plain luck. Better luck next time!"

Scaled Scores

Since this yearbook takes a firm stand against course grades as the only measures that enter a student's record and advocates instead a profile of achievement with respect to the major objectives of each field, it may come as a shock when we translate most of our measures in the Junior High School Record of the concluding chapter into scaled scores of just five numbers—1, 2, 3, 4, 5—with an occasional second digit that refers to a tenth of the standard deviation. These numbers look suspiciously like grades, and many colleges use them for that purpose. When they compute rank in class, high schools also have to translate their letter-grades into numbers like these. How do these scaled scores differ from ordinary course grades?

In the first place, note that there is no single number representing overall achievement in each field but a great many numbers representing final status and sometimes growth with respect to each major objective. We promised a profile, and the profile is there. To be sure, in the last section of our projected record there are spaces for weighted averages of the best predictive achievement measures in each field, and these may be used as a substitute for single grades in each field. If they are so used, it will be with good reason, and the effect will be what we intend. These summary predictions were included for the benefit of hard-pressed counselors, assistant principals, and department heads at the next higher level who, in a very short time, have to schedule hundreds of these students into classes appropriate to their stage of development in each field, their interests, and their aptitudes.

If these busy people had to look at dozens of numbers for each student and guess which numbers, with what weights, in what combinations would best indicate the section of English 10 that he should enter (and so on for each other field), their task would be impossible and they would make disastrous mistakes. We hope to simplify their task and reduce errors by following the records of our students in senior high for at least one year before we attempt these "predictions." Then they will be based on actual regression equations that will show which of our achievement measures in combination best indicate the level of the student in each field and his prospects of success. Out of the dozens of measures recorded in a field like English, it could happen that just four are closely related to achievement in grade 10, and one of these should have a weight of 3, two a weight of 2, and one a weight of 1. This is the sort of prediction we hope to make in each field, and it will be used only to get students into appropriate and congenial classes and sections.

The teachers of these classes will have time to make greater use of the full profile, which shows all aspects of previous achievement in the same field and not merely those aspects that happen to be predictive. They can assume mastery of certain areas and not repeat them; they can be forewarned of certain deficiencies and try to correct them; and they can build on the strengths and interests thus far developed.

A second difference between these scaled scores and ordinary course grades is that these scores are not "given" by individual teachers on God knows what bases; they are "found" by cooperative action of students, teaching teams, and departments. They are not unchecked judgments; they are findings based on tests, performance tasks, records, essays and other products rated anonymously by different judges, interest inventories, attitude scales, sociometric ratings, and the whole panoply of evaluative techniques and procedures illustrated in the foregoing chapters. When these measures are taken, the teachers know as little as the students about how they will turn out, and they have no power to influence the outcome by arbitrary fiat. Hence they are as elated as the students when they turn out well—and as downcast when they turn out badly. The whole process is controlled by an Evaluation Committee that annually reviews the measurement program of each department. Nothing gets into the record unless it has been approved by someone with responsibility for measurement, unless it is related to a major objective of instruction, and unless it represents the judgment of more than a single individual. The results are regarded as information that is of interest and value to the student, his parents, his teachers, his adviser, and his guidance counselor. They are like the laboratory findings that help a doctor to diagnose a case. He does not scold a patient for running a fever, but he shows concern for dangerous symptoms and delight in any signs of improvement.

A third difference between these scaled scores and ordinary course grades is that they are precisely defined and mean the same thing to everyone in the school district. They are based on the standard deviation of the total district population in the grade tested, sometimes with separate norms for boys and girls. A scaled score of 1 is two standard deviations below the mean; 2, one standard deviation below; 3, the mean; 4, one standard deviation above; and 5, two standard deviations above the mean. In rare instances with highly reliable tests, scores of 0 or 6 may be given to exceptional students who are three standard deviations below or above the district mean, but for all ordinary purposes the five divisions of this scale are enough. When a test is sufficiently reliable to justify it, a second digit may be added to these scores to refer to a tenth of the standard deviation. Thus 31 indicates that the score is a tenth of a standard deviation above the mean; 36 indicates that the score is closer to 4 than to 3. Second digits are most often used for cumulative totals for the year across several tests or other measures of a given objective. Without the second digit, 1 is understood to take in everything from 0 to 14; 2, everything from 15 to 24; 3, everything from 25 to 34; 4, everything from 35 to 44; and 5, everything from 45 to 6. In other words, a single digit takes in half a standard deviation below that point in the distribution and half a standard deviation above, but scores of 1 and 5 also include everything that is more than two standard deviations from the mean. Only about 2 percent of the population stands beyond each of these points.

How about tests and other measures that are suitable only for selected groups (either high or low) and cannot be given to the total district population? The position of such groups in the grade population of the district is plotted on the basis of relevant tests of aptitudes and basic skills that are taken by all. Then one can predict what the mean of the selected population on the special test ought to be in terms of district norms and what proportion of the various scaled scores should be expected. For example, in a test on a novel that no other section could read, the mean of the top section in English might be set at a scaled score of 48 on the basis of the verbal aptitude and reading ability of these students; the range might extend from 40 to 57; and half the students in this group might be expected to make scores between 44 and 53. These scores would indicate their probable standing in relation to the total grade population of the district in literary competence. They would also be informed of their standing within this selected group, but this would not enter the record in any way that would jeopardize their rank in class. The official score would be the one that was equated to district norms.

In rating essays and other products, we have had to alter slightly the proportions assigned the various scaled scores because the exact proportions called for by the standard deviation are hard to remember and manipulate. Our aim has been to make the midpoint of the 1 and 5 brackets as close as possible to two standard deviations from the mean. Since 2.27 percent lie beyond each of these points, we also have to take in 2.27 behind them to make the midpoint fall where we want it, and this rounds to 5 percent to be placed in the highest and lowest brackets. If we then put the next 20 percent into brackets 2 and 4, the midpoints of these intervals lies just 1.04 standard deviations from the mean, which is close enough for all practical purposes. That leaves 50 percent of the papers or other products for the middle bracket, which gets a scaled score of 3. Our raters first sort their material into three groups: top quarter, middle half, and bottom quarter. Then they set aside a fifth of the high group as the very high and a fifth of the low group as the very low. One may quarrel with these dividing lines if one is looking at where they ought to fall along the base of the normal curve, but one can have no serious quarrel with them if one considers where the midpoints (medians) stand. At worst they are one percent off.

In less precise measures we use the symbol H for the top quarter, M for the middle half, and L for the bottom quarter; and if the quartiles are unknown, H means outstanding, M means acceptable, and L means deficient. It is unlikely that these imprecise measures will enter into any of our numerical calculations, but if they do, they will be given scaled scores of 4, 3, and 2 so that they will have less weight than measures with the full range of scaled scores.

If anyone still regrets that we have settled on a score scale with the traditional five intervals in order to convey meaning to those who must use the large numbers of measures that we provide, let him reflect that without some such common scale any one envelope sent home by Junior's adviser might include numerical scores like the following: French 164, Writing 118, Literature 65, Mathematics 42, History 35, Science 21, and Library 9. What would Dad make of these scores? Which are high and which are low? Are any dangerously low? It would be impossible to keep in mind separate standards for all the diverse measures that we report. They must be reduced to some common score scale, and one based on the standard deviation has the most precisely defined and widely understood meaning.

There have been many attempts to set standards on some other basis than relative position in large groups, but the only field in which they have succeeded is typing. Until someone invents more objective standards that will work in other fields, we had better interpret our measures in terms that have a solid mathematical basis and can still be understood by everyone from parents to college admissions officers. The only serious objection to the use of relative standings for interpretation is that superior classes may get the same proportions of the various scores as ordinary classes, but we have already explained how this can be avoided. If the base is the total grade population of the district and special groups are positioned in this distribution by way of aptitude scores, all such groups will get the range and level of scores that they deserve.

The ASCD 1967 Yearbook
Committee and Contributors

Fred T. Wilhelms, *Chairman and Editor*
Associate Secretary, National Association of Secondary-School Principals, NEA, Washington, D.C.

Paul M. Allen
Professor of Education, College of Education, University of Arizona, Tucson, Arizona

Walcott H. Beatty
Professor of Psychology, San Francisco State College, San Francisco, California

Clifford F. S. Bebell
Professor of Education, College of Education, Southern Colorado State College, Pueblo, Colorado

Rodney A. Clark
Professor of Education, School of Education, San Francisco State College, San Francisco, California

Elizabeth L. Dalton
Associate Professor of Education, University of Chattanooga, Chattanooga, Tennessee

Paul B. Diederich
Center for Psychological Studies, Educational Testing Service, Princeton, New Jersey

Jack R. Frymier
Associate Professor of Education, School of Education, The Ohio State University, Columbus, Ohio

Phil C. Lange
Professor of Education, Teachers College, Columbia University, New York, New York

Elizabeth Langhans
Associate Professor of Education, Adelphi Suffolk College of Adelphi University, Oakdale, New York

Dorris May Lee
Professor of Education, School of Education, Portland State College, Portland, Oregon

Frances R. Link
Coordinator of Secondary Education, School District of Cheltenham Township, Elkins Park, Philadelphia, Pennsylvania

Jean V. Marani
Curriculum Director, Public Schools, Sarasota, Florida

Charles New
Curriculum Director, Public Schools, Sweeny, Texas

ASCD Board of Directors

As of November 1, 1966

Executive Committee, 1966-67

President, Arthur W. Combs, Professor of Education, University of Florida, Gainesville.

President-Elect, J. Harlan Shores, Professor of Education, University of Illinois, Urbana.

Vice-President, Galen Saylor, Chairman, Department of Secondary Education, Teachers College, University of Nebraska, Lincoln.

Vernon E. Anderson, Dean and Professor, College of Education, University of Maryland, College Park.

Dorris May Lee, Professor of Education, Portland State College, Portland, Oregon.

Sybil K. Richardson, Professor of Education, San Fernando Valley State College, Northridge, California.

Rodney Tillman, Assistant Superintendent in Charge of Elementary Education, Minneapolis Public Schools, Minneapolis, Minnesota.

Members Elected at Large

Herbert I. Bruning, Pub. Schs., Shawnee Mission, Kan. (1968); Mrs. Evelyn F. Carlson, Bd. of Ed., Chicago, Ill. (1970); Arthur W. Combs, Univ. of Fla., Gainesville (1967); Muriel Crosby, Pub. Schs., Wilmington, Del. (1967); Delmo Della-Dora, U.S. AID-Mogadiscio (1970); Mrs. Minnie H. Fields, St. Dept. of Ed., Tallahassee, Fla. (1969); Ned A. Flanders, Univ of Mich., Ann Arbor (1969); Robert S. Fox, Univ. of Mich., Ann Arbor (1967); Richard A. Gibboney, St. Comr. of Ed., Montpelier, Vt. (1968); Anne Gustafson, Pub. Schs., Rockford, Ill. (1967); Mrs. Elizabeth Z. Howard, Univ. of Rochester, Rochester, N.Y. (1968); Mrs. Inabell Kirby, Pub. Schs., Decatur, Ill. (1967); Victor B. Lawhead, Ball St. Tchrs. Col., Muncie, Ind. (1968); Alvin D. Loving, Sr., Univ. of Mich., Ann Arbor (1970); Helen K. Mackintosh, Alexandria, Va. (1969); Karl Openshaw, The Ohio St. Univ., Columbus (1969); Ole Sand, Cntr. for the Study of Instr., Washington, D.C. (1970); Lola Toler, Pub. Schs., Tulsa, Okla. (1968); Kenneth D. Wann, Teachers College, Columbia Univ., New York, N.Y. (1970); Hugh B. Wood, Univ. of Ore., Eugene (1969).

State Representatives to the Board

Alabama—Robert C. Hatch, Alabama State Col., Montgomery; Otto Holloway, Auburn Univ., Auburn; John T. Lovell, Auburn Univ., Auburn. *Arizona*—James J. Jelinek, Ariz. State Univ., Tempe; John C. White, Pub. Schs., Mesa; Herbert Wilson, Univ. of Ariz., Tucson. *Arkansas*—Wallace C. Floyd, Pub. Schs., Ft. Smith; Hattie Ann Kelso, Pub. Schs., North Little Rock. *California*—Richard L. Foster, Pub. Schs., Danville; Barbara Hartsig, Calif. State Col., Fullerton; Mary H. Mitchell, Pub. Schs., Palm Springs; Norman H. Naas, Pub. Schs., Concord; Mary S. Reed, Pub. Schs., El Segundo; Joe D. Severns, Co. Schs., Los Angeles. *Colorado*—William Liddle, Pub. Schs., Colo. Springs; Doris Molbert, Univ. of Denver, Denver; Rolland Waters, Pub. Schs., Englewood. *Dakota (North* and *South)*—A. P. Sonstegard, Pub. Schs., Watertown, S. Dakota. *Delaware*—Donald L. Farrar, Pub. Schs., Wilmington; Melville F. Warren, Pub. Schs., Dover. *District of Columbia*—Mrs. LuVerne C. Walker, Pub. Schs., Wash., D. C. *Florida*—E. L. Bowers, Escambia Co. Schs., Pensacola; Joseph W. Crenshaw, St. Dept. of Ed., Tallahassee; John McIntyre, Dade Co. Schs., Miami; Rodney E. Nowakowski, Dade Co. Schs., Perrine; Nelle Wright, Tallahassee. *Georgia*—Alice W. Arden, Pub. Schs., Savannah; Mrs. Edith E. Grimsley, Bibb Co. Schs., Macon; John Lounsbury, Ga. St. Col. for Women, Milledgeville; Tom Sills, West Ga. Col., Carrollton. *Hawaii*—Ernest J. Cherry, St. Dept. of Ed., Honolulu; Robert W. Laird, Church Col. of Hawaii, Laie. *Idaho*—Doyle Lowder, Minidoka Co. Schs., Rupert; Parker Richards, Pub. Schs., Pocatello. *Illinois*—Inez E. Bishop, Glenview; Lillian Davies, Ill. St. Univ., Normal; Earl M. Dieken, Pub. Schs., Glen Ellyn; Mary C. Lacy, Bd. of Ed., Chicago; Theodore R. Storlie, Pub. Schs., Flossmoor; Eugene T. Swierczewski, Pub. Schs., Medinah. *Indiana*—Mrs. Mary Castle, Pub. Schs., Indianapolis; Harriet Darrow, Ind. St. Univ., Terre Haute; Frank Hunter, Pub. Schs., Indianapolis; Herbert J. Reese, Pub. Schs., Columbus. *Iowa*—Ernest Barker, Pub. Schs., Waterloo; Mildred Middleton, Pub. Schs., Cedar Rapids; Mrs. Mable Root, Pub. Schs., Des Moines. *Kansas*—Mrs. Perva Hughes, Kansas St. Col., Pittsburg; Jeanne M. Kuhn, Ft. Hays Kansas St. Col., Hays; Melvin L. Winters, Pub. Schs., Kansas City. *Kentucky*—Margaret Clayton, Pub. Schs., Louisville; Alice C. Harned, Bullitt Co. Schs., Sheperdsville; Joe Wise, Fayette Co. Schs., Lexington. *Louisiana*—John D. Greene, East Baton Rouge Parish Sch. Bd., Baton Rouge; Gaither McConnell, Tulane Univ., New Orleans; Malcolm Rosenberg, Pub. Schs., New Orleans; Beverly L. White, St. James Parish Sch. Bd., Lutcher. *Maryland*—G. Alfred Helwig, Baltimore Co. Bd. of Ed., Towson; Norman J. Moore, Cecil Co. Bd. of Ed., Elkton; Mrs. Mildred Sowers, St. Bd. of Ed., Baltimore; Fred G. Usilton, Caroline Co. Bd. of Ed., Denton. *Michigan*—Barbara R. Bird, Pub. Schs., Grand Rapids; Charles Blackman, Mich. St. Univ., East Lansing; Wendell Hough, Wayne St. Univ., Detroit; Dorothy McCuskey, Western Mich. Univ., Kalamazoo; William C. Miller, Pub. Schs., Detroit; Phil Robinson, Pub. Schs., River Rouge. *Minnesota*—Eugene L. Bristol, Pub. Schs., Excelsior; S. A. Christian, Pub. Schs., Rochester; A. E. Edstrom, Pub. Schs., Hopkins. *Missouri*—J. E. Morris, Pub. Schs., Ferguson; W. J. Underwood, Pub. Schs., Lee's Summit; Homer Willis, Pub. Schs., Louisiana. *Montana*—A. G.

Erikson, Pub. Schs., Helena; James L. Weir, Pub. Schs., Helena. *Nebraska—*
Hollie Bethel, Univ. of Omaha, Omaha; Maria Laas, Pub. Schs., Omaha.
Nevada—Monty Boland, Pub. Schs., Henderson; John R. Gamble, St. Dept.
of Ed., Carson City. *New Jersey*—Robert S. Fleming, St. Dept. of Ed.,
Trenton; Marion W. Fox, Atlantic City; Laurence Hopp, R.E.A.P., Somerset;
Malcolm Katz, Pub. Schs., Ridgewood; Robert Ward, St. Dept. of Ed.,
Trenton. *New Mexico*—F. Elena DeVaney, Pub. Schs., Carlsbad; James
C. Porterfield, Pub. Schs., Gallup. *New York*—Mrs. Lillian T. Brooks,
Bd. of Ed., Rochester; Robert Harnack, St. Univ. Col., Buffalo; Milton Michener,
Pub. Schs., Valley Stream; John Owens, Pub. Schs., Roslyn; O. Ward Satterlee,
St. Univ. Col., Potsdam; Mrs. Mildred Whittaker, Pub. Schs., Lancaster.
North Carolina—Robert Hanes, Pub. Schs., Charlotte; Annie Lee Jones, Univ.
of North Carolina, Chapel Hill; Mrs. Virginia Waller, Pub. Schs., Henderson;
Helen Wells, Buncombe Co. Schs., Asheville. *Ohio*—Roy Bacon, Heidelberg Col.,
Tiffin; Howard Brown, Pub. Schs., Springfield; Lloyd W. Dull, Pub. Schs.,
Akron; Mrs. Audrey Norris, Univ. of Cincinnati, Cincinnati; Lorrene Ort,
Bowling Green St. Univ., Bowling Green. *Oklahoma*—Hugh Bish, Pub. Schs.,
Lawton; Gene D. Sheperd, Pub. Schs., Oklahoma City. *Oregon*—Alma I. Bing-
ham, Portland St. Col., Portland; Dealous L. Cox, Pub. Schs., Medford; George
Henderson, Pub. Schs., Lebanon; Lloyd F. Millhollen, Jr., Pub. Schs., Eugene.
Pennsylvania—Richard DeRemer, Univ. of Pittsburgh, Pittsburgh; Gerald M.
Newton, Pub. Schs., Beaver; Margaret McFeaters, Pittsburgh; J. Ernest Har-
rison, Baldwin-Whitehall Schs., Pittsburgh; Elwood L. Prestwood, Merion Schs.,
Ardmore. *Puerto Rico*—Mrs. Awilda Aponte de Saldana, Univ. of Puerto Rico,
Rio Piedras; Ana D. Soto, Univ. of Puerto Rico, Rio Piedras. *South Carolina—*
Nancy Jane Day, Bd. of Ed., Columbia; Ray Miley, Pub. Schs., Greenville.
Tennessee—Emily Beebe, Pub. Schs., Memphis; Arthur C. Rauscher, Jr., Pub.
Schs., Memphis; G. H. Waters, Pub. Schs., Nashville. *Texas*—Joe A. Airola,
Spring Branch Pub. Schs., Houston; Herman Benthul, Pub. Schs., Dallas; Witt
Blair, North Texas St. Univ., Denton; Mrs. Bernice Railsback, Pub. Schs.,
Levelland; Margaret Wasson, Highland Park Schs., Dallas. *Utah*—Raynold B.
Hansen, Pub. Schs., Duchesne; James O. Morton, Univ. of Utah, Salt Lake City.
Virginia—Virginia Benson, Pub. Schs., Falls Church; Evelyn L. Berry, Pub.
Schs., Petersburg; Julian B. Dunn, Pub. Schs., Williamsburg; John F. Leahy,
Univ. of Virginia, Charlottesville. *Washington*—Mrs. Ellen Herminghaus, Pierce
Co. Schs., Tacoma; Clifton A. Hussey, Co. Schs., Spokane; Arthur Lind, Pub.
Schs., Richland; Florence Orvik, Spokane. *West Virginia*—Lucille Heflebower,
Jefferson Co. Schs., Charles Town; M. Louise Shimp, Berkeley Co. Schs., Mar-
tinsburg. *Wisconsin*—Richard Carleton, Pub. Schs., Stoughton; Glen Eye, Univ.
of Wis., Madison; Edna R. Palecek, Pub. Schs., Kaukauna; Doris G. Phipps,
Pub. Schs., Sheboygan. *Wyoming*—Dorothy Gibbs, Pub. Schs., Sheridan; Clar-
ence L. Ward, Pub. Schs., Torrington. *New England* (Connecticut, Maine, Mas-
sachusetts, New Hampshire, Rhode Island, Vermont)—John Economopolous,
N.H. Dept. of Ed., Concord; Raymond Houghton, Rhode Island Col., Providence; L. Gertrude Lawrence, Pub. Schs., Wethersfield, Conn.; Ruth E. Mayo,
Stoneham, Mass.; Sidney P. Rollins, Rhode Island Col., Providence.

ASCD Headquarters Staff , 1967

Executive Secretary: Leslee J. Bishop

Associate Secretary; Editor, ASCD Publications: Robert R. Leeper

Associate Secretaries: Robert J. Alfonso, Louise M. Berman,
Richard V. Brown

Administrative Assistant: Virginia Berthy

Staff Assistants:

Sarah Arlington
Susan G. Atkinson
Carolyn O. Cottrell
Ruth P. Ely
Ruby J. Funkhouser
Marie K. Haut
Lois Howell
Teola T. Jones

Suzanne Kannan
Mary Ann Lurch
Sharon McCormick
Frances Mindel
Gloria Richardson
Phyllis Stockman
Kathleen Vail

ASCD Publications

(The NEA stock number appears in parentheses after each title.)

Yearbooks

Balance in the Curriculum (610-17274)	$4.00
Evaluation as Feedback and Guide (610-17700)	$6.50
Fostering Mental Health in Our Schools (610-17256)	$3.00
Guidance in the Curriculum (610-17266)	$3.75
Individualizing Instruction (610-17264)	$4.00
Leadership for Improving Instruction (610-17454)	$3.75
Learning and Mental Health in the School (610-17674)	$5.00
Learning and the Teacher (610-17270)	$3.75
Life Skills in School and Society (610-17786)	$5.50
New Insights and the Curriculum (610-17548)	$5.00
Perceiving, Behaving, Becoming: A New Focus for Education (610-17278)	$4.50
Research for Curriculum Improvement (610-17268)	$4.00
Role of Supervisor and Curriculum Director (610-17624)	$4.50
To Nurture Humaneness: Commitment for the '70's (610-17810)	$5.75
Youth Education: Problems, Perspectives, Promises (610-17746)	$5.50

Booklets

Better Than Rating (611-17298)	$1.25
The Changing Curriculum: Mathematics (611-17724)	$2.00
The Changing Curriculum: Modern Foreign Languages (611-17764)	$2.00
The Changing Curriculum: Science (611-17704)	$1.50
Changing Supervision for Changing Times (611-17802)	$2.00
Children's Social Learning (611-17326)	$1.75
Cooperative International Education (611-17344)	$1.50
Criteria for Theories of Instruction (611-17756)	$2.00
Curriculum Change: Direction and Process (611-17698)	$2.00
Curriculum Decisions ⟷ Social Realities (611-17770)	$2.75
A Curriculum for Children (611-17790)	$2.75
Curriculum Materials 1970 (611-17882)	$2.00
Discipline for Today's Children and Youth (611-17314)	$1.00
Early Childhood Education Today (611-17766)	$2.00
Educating the Children of the Poor (611-17762)	$2.00
Elementary School Mathematics: A Guide to Current Research (611-17752)	$2.75
Elementary School Science: A Guide to Current Research (611-17726)	$2.25
Elementary School Social Studies: A Guide to Current Research (611-17384)	$2.75
The Elementary School We Need (611-17636)	$1.25

Ethnic Modification of the Curriculum (611-17832)	$1.00
Freeing Capacity To Learn (611-17322)	$1.00
Guidelines for Elementary Social Studies (611-17738)	$1.50
The High School We Need (611-17312)	$ .50
Human Variability and Learning (611-17332)	$1.50
The Humanities and the Curriculum (611-17708)	$2.00
Humanizing Education: The Person in the Process (611-17722)	$2.25
Humanizing the Secondary School (611-17780)	$2.75
Hunters Point Redeveloped (611-17348)	$2.00
Improving Educational Assessment & An Inventory of Measures of Affective Behavior (611-17804)	$3.00
Improving Language Arts Instruction Through Research (611-17560)	$2.75
Influences in Curriculum Change (611-17730)	$2.25
Intellectual Development: Another Look (611-17618)	$1.75
The International Dimension of Education (611-17816)	$2.25
The Junior High School We Need (611-17338)	$1.00
The Junior High School We Saw (611-17604)	$1.50
Language and Meaning (611-17696)	$2.75
Learning More About Learning (611-17310)	$1.00
Linguistics and the Classroom Teacher (611-17720)	$2.75
A Man for Tomorrow's World (611-17838)	$2.25
New Curriculum Developments (611-17664)	$1.75
New Dimensions in Learning (611-17336)	$1.50
The New Elementary School (611-17734)	$2.50
Nurturing Individual Potential (611-17606)	$1.50
Personalized Supervision (611-17680)	$1.75
Strategy for Curriculum Change (611-17666)	$1.25
Student Unrest: Threat or Promise? (611-17818)	$2.75
Supervision in Action (611-17346)	$1.25
Supervision: Emerging Profession (611-17796)	$5.00
Supervision: Perspectives and Propositions (611-17732)	$2.00
The Supervisor: Agent for Change in Teaching (611-17702)	$3.25
The Supervisor: New Demands, New Dimensions (611-17782)	$2.50
The Supervisor's Role in Negotiation (611-17798)	$ .75
Theories of Instruction (611-17668)	$2.00
Toward Professional Maturity (611-17740)	$1.50
The Unstudied Curriculum: Its Impact on Children (611-17820)	$2.75
What Are the Sources of the Curriculum? (611-17522)	$1.50
Child Growth Chart (618-17442)	$ .25

Discounts on quantity orders of same title to single address: 2-9 copies, 10%; 10 or more copies, 20%. All orders must be prepaid except for those on official purchase order forms. Shipping and handling charges will be added to billed orders. **The NEA stock number of each publication must be listed when ordering.**

Subscription to **Educational Leadership**—$6.50 a year. ASCD Membership dues: regular (subscription and yearbook)—$20.00 a year; Comprehensive (includes subscription and yearbook plus other publications issued during period of the membership)—$30.00 a year.

Order from: **Association for Supervision and Curriculum Development, NEA**
1201 Sixteenth Street, N.W.   Washington, D.C. 20036